Industrious Children

Industrious Children

Work and Childhood in the Nordic Countries 1850-1990

Edited by Ning de Coninck-Smith, Bengt Sandin
and Ellen Schrumpf

Odense University Press 1997

Industrious Children is published with the generous support of
Joint Committee of the Nordic Research Councils for the Humanities

© The Authors and Odense University Press 1997
Printed in Denmark by Narayana Press, Gylling
Cover illustration: Avisgutten [The newspaper boy] painted by Christian Krogh, Oslo 1914.
Cover design: Klaus Bjergager, DesignCo

ISBN 87-7838-269-6

Odense University Press
Campusvej 55
DK-5230 Odense M

Tlf. + 45 66 15 79 99
Fax + 45 66 15 81 26
E-mail: Press@forlag.ou.dk
Internet location: http://www.ou.dk/press

Contents

Introduction 7

Bengt Sandin
" In the Large Factory Town"
Child Labour Legislation, Child Labour
and School Compulsion 17

Ellen Schrumpf
From full-time to part-time:
Working children in Norway from the
nineteenth to the twentieth century 47

Pirjo Markkola
"God wouldn't send a child into the
world without a crust of bread"
Child labour as part of working-class
family economy in Finland 1890-1920 79

Mats Sjöberg
Working Rural Children
Herding, child labour and childhood
in the Swedish Rural Environment
1850-1950 106

Ning de Coninck-Smith
The struggle for the child's time –
at all times
School and children's work in town
and country in Denmark from 1900
to the 1960s 129

Ólöf Gardarsdóttir
Working children in
Urban Iceland 1930-1990.
Ideology of Work, Work – Schools and
Gender Relations in Modern Iceland 160

Anne Solberg
Seeing Children's Work 186

Contributors 210

Introduction

In the spring 1996 a group of children aged 10-12 years turned up at the Committee on Labour Market Affairs, a subcommittee of the Danish Folketing (i.e. parliament). These children came to protest against a new EU directive that was to raise the minimum age for newspaper delivery work from 10 to 13 years. Roughly 3,200 children were expected to loose their jobs as delivers of mainly advertisements and weekly newspapers on that score. The members of the Committee were highly sympathetic with regard to the children's indignation, but, eventually, they had to send them back home with the message that the Danish Folketing had no authority whatsoever to change this decision.[1]

The new rules applied from 1 August 1996 – but in many places the children have continued to do their work. However, now an intermediary has entered the stage, in fact, either parents or older siblings. Officially, they run the newspaper route, while it is really the children and younger siblings, who are delivering the newspapers after school. The children's economic activities have by that become illegal and invisible.

The history behind this EU directive can be understood in two ways. First, this directive was merely another offshoot in the debate about schoolchildren's paid work, which, throughout the unemployment-plagued 80s, had been going on between representatives of the trade union movement, the educational authorities and the political parties in Denmark. There had been a sharp division of opinions. On one side stood those who believed children and youth prevented unemployed adults from getting jobs, and that working took too much time away from schooling. Furthermore, it gave cause for concern that children and youth easily earned an excess of spending money. On the other side were those who believed children and youth should be respected as workers and, accordingly, ensured the same working conditions as adults. While the first group talked about restrictions and a higher minimum age for paid work, the last group favoured information campaigns and a demand that children and youth should eventually join a trade union. Seen in this light, the history behind the EU directive clearly illustrates those subtle ambiguities attaching to the relationship between children and work, and these ambiguities are again rooted in the ideas of the 20th century about the good childhood. Consequently, in the 20th century work is not a natural element of the current ideas concerning what makes a good childhood. Unlike for adults, work does not ennoble children. Childhood ought to be filled with play and learning in both formal and informal settings. Second, history shows us that directives and legislation are one thing – the world of realities is something else entirely, and it is complex and difficult to grasp. Here legislation is confronted with children's wish to be allowed to work, with the parents' support for the children's wishes and with the commercial interests in children and youth as a workforce. Similarly, one cannot disregard that many families even in the Western world still need the children's income and daily help, and the children are consequently working more because they must than because they enjoy it.

Third, the history of the newspaper boys and girls in the 1990s also contains a tale about an old child occupation, which perhaps now is changing its status among children. From being an acceptable occupation, which every millionaire is said to have had once, and serving as an opening to get the youngest children into the labour market – it is now a job left for the socially most vulnerable children and youths. Ever more immigrants are taking over the newspaper routes: Children and also youths or adults. The likely reason for this is that delivering newspapers and advertisements in the aftenoon is one of those children's jobs in which the hourly rate is the lowest and the work involved the hardest. And so it does not attract Danish children over 13 years, who may readily find another easier job with better pay.

This contradictory view of children's work is not a uniquely Danish phenomenon. This debate has been an attendant feature all over the world whenever childhood has changed. The debate is not conducted in the same even tones everywhere, however, which is because of different social and cultural conditions.

If one considers the Nordic countries alone, it is obvious that this debate is dominated by negative connotations in Denmark, Norway and also Sweden and Finland. Iceland is different however. The rather late modernization of the Icelandic economy, combined with a commercial structure dominated by its seasonal fishing industry, has meant that child labour has continued to be a socially acknowledged need. Even to the extent that the school calendar is still adjusted according to the commercial demands for the children's workforce. Despite the public debate children have continued working and one of the main objectives of this book is to reveal the many tasks Nordic children have done for approximately the last 150 years. As a kind of backdrop for the work life lived by children, we find throughout this book the public debate about child labour. The aim of this book is therefore to reveal and understand children's work within a broad perspective of social and cultural history.

Another objective of our studies has been to further a history of childhood in more general terms. Based on the differences in the historical development of child labour in the Nordic countries, we have wanted to develop both the theoretical and the methodological debates in the field of childhood history. Thus the papers in this anthology are not alike, but based on different approaches to the subject. Right from the political and legal history dealing with factory and school legislation, via the social and cultural history behind the importance of work in children's daily lives – to the exploration of children's work today.

Also, some authors have chosen to describe children's work during a limited period, while others prefer to sketch the long lines. Thus each contribution to this book highlights children's work in all its diversity, and the changes influencing its structure and macroeconomics are emphasized. Accordingly, it becomes obvious that, from the mid-1800s until today, the history of child labour is, not least, a history of the adult world's reluctance to accept children as social and cultural agents.

Industrious children

If the disagreements about child labour and childhood are considered in the light of history, then another dimension is added to the complex and ambiguous attitudes towards children's work, in fact, a dimension of ignorance. We are even talking about several levels of ignorance.

First, a basic empirical ignorance. Historical research has been highly focused on industrial child labour in the 1800s. The reasons it arose and disappeared have been thoroughly investigated, and many explanations have been presented, ranging from technological changes, legislation against child labour, obligatory schooling to demography, family economy and strategy.[2] The extent and nature of industrial child labour should be understood as resulting from a combination of these factors. The emphasis placed on the various factors has differed in the ongoing scholarly debate. Some have emphasized one or more related conditions, while others have stressed the importance of f.ex. technological or economic changes. Furthermore, comparative studies of the history of industrial child labour have focused attention on how culturally diversified views of the child and its development have affected children's involvement in factory work.[3] Finally, some scholars have pointed out the relevance of comparing the development in industrial child labour with the other kinds of work children have done, f.ex. in agriculture.[4] In the 20th century the major focus on child labour has been on children's work in the third world. Only a few studies have dealt with conditions in the industrialized Western world.[5]

It should be noted, however, that this empirical ignorance was not only caused by the priorities of the scholarly world as such, but also because the source material available for the history of child labour was scarce. The conflict primarily concerned industrial child labour, which left many traces in the archives. In contrast, all the other and much more common kinds of child labour, for example in agriculture or for local shopkeepers, have not received the same degree of attention. Consequently, they are so much harder to document in the sources.

Thus children's work has traditionally been linked to industrial work, which has both overshadowed all the other occupations filled by children, and also those lines of unpaid work that children have had. As Mats Sjöberg argues in his description of children's agricultural work in Sweden from 1850 to 1950, an emphasis on paid work means that the crucial role children played on family farms is easily ignored. Something that has often been ignored is that the children's outstanding qualification was that they had time when the adults did not, and the children's "help" was an absolute precondition for a flexible distribution of the family's total working strength. Another ancient child occupation, which is not acknowledged as such either, is minding other children for family or friends with or without pay. And this although it was many girls' foremost occupation. For example, this is still the case in Iceland, as Olof Gardarsdottir shows in her article. During the last few years there has even been an increase in the extent of this, since more and more mothers have entered the labour market – although the number of institutions has not kept pace with this trend. Like the minding of children, there are the many domestic chores or "duties" done by children. They stack and collect firewood, carry water, take out the refuse and help do the laundry.[6] Finally, there are those children's lines of work literally existing in the cracks of the adult world. For instance, in Anne Solberg's article about children's work in Norway in the 1970s and 1980s, we meet boys earning good money by selling cod tongues, a special Norwegian delicacy – and we meet boys collecting returnable bottles and children going from door to door selling potted plants. Around the turn of the century their historical counterparts were children who raised skittles and sold paper flowers or jumping jacks at Christmas time.

These examples of ignored occupations of children show the need for a more fundamental discussion about the work concept in relation to the children's life experiences; they do, however, also reflect a general insensitivity towards the significance of gender – and of age – in the work done by children. The small and the big children did not necessarily do the same tasks – neither did boys and girls. Minding children was by tradition girls' work, whereas the messengers and factory workers mostly were boys. Still, if no girls were available then the boys had to look after the younger siblings, and in areas dominated by the textile industry – such as the Finnish workers' town Tammerfors, which is the focus of Pirjo Markkola's article – it was the girls who did the factory work. Whereas the boys had to take whatever jobs they could get.

Second, there exists a certain ignorance about the history of children's work, which, popularly speaking, is caused by cultural blindness. This is to be understood in the sense that the Western way of regarding the child in the 20th century has strongly coloured the research done into the history of children's work. The stipulation that, in principle, work is no part of childhood has in fact had several consequences for which questions were selected for further investigation. Consequently, the scholars have been preoccupied with discontinuity rather than continuity, appearance and disappearance rather than change, and by that ignoring the changes in structure as well as content affecting children's work.

Foremost among these structural changes is the question of the reorganization of the children's time and of the socially and culturally conditioned struggles during the 19th and 20th centuries, before the school turned into an established institution in all children's lives. Thus the school established the agenda of how children should spend their time – and where they ought to be during the daytime. Educational legislation has played a central role towards this end. Clearly, in Bengt Sandin's article about the school debate in the Swedish Rigsdag (parliament) in the 1850s and 1860s, the discussion about children's work not only reflected the attitudes towards children's work as such, but it was also about the plight of street children and the need to ensure that the school became the proper place for children to stay as an alternative to the family. The debate was basically dealing with the moral and cultural content of childhood.

As mentioned before, legislation is something other than the socially and culturally conditioned tasks of daily life. In Ellen Schrumpf's article about the changes in children's paid work in the late 1800s, educational legislation is studied in relation to the actually lived lives of children. Her conclusion turns out to be that the paid children's work, as at the beginning of WW1, changed from a full-time job into a part-time job, primarily done after schoolhours.

When children's work is analyzed on a basis of everyday life, it offers an opportunity to discuss the actual significance of legislation in relation to the changes in children's work. These everyday accounts shift older notions about the school's authoritarianism and the disappearance of this work. Instead it seems that child labour and school work have coexisted for a long time. But it also draws a picture of vast differences between town and countryside. As Ning de Coninck-Smith explains in her analysis of the development of child labour in Denmark between 1900 and 1960, the struggle for the children's time first emerged in the towns during the decades around the turn of the century. But it was not before the 1950s that childhood in town and countryside seemed to come closer to each other.

These conclusions lead on to a discussion of the macroeconomic development of child labour. It runs as a leitmotif throughout this book that before the emergence, during the 1920s and 1930s, of a modern social welfare institution under the State and a more stable labour market capable of offering unemployment benefits, the children's assistance and income were absolute preconditions if poor families were to cope during poverty, diseases, harsh winters and periodic unemployment among the adults. Furthermore, there existed a broad popular tradition that regarded children's work as a natural aspect of a proper upbringing. Also, the demand for child workers seems to have been conditioned by a conglomeration of factors that varied with time and place. From the emergence of the family farm in the late 1800s in Sweden, via the explosive growth in retail trade in the 1880s' and 1890's Danish urban culture to labour shortages, national interests and the opportunity to make good money on peat production in Denmark during the Second World War, and in the 1980s and 1990s there was also the women's massive influx on the labour market in Iceland. Partly, the discussion about the macroeconomic development of children's labour is also the fact that certain occupations were specially created for children, or they developed themselves into being for children. The first category includes milk delivery boys in Copenhagen and milk girls in Stockholm who, from the 1870s until WW1, helped milk drivers supply the urban population with milk. The second category includes the shepherding children – mostly boys – who during the 1700s took over the guarding of farm animals from the elderly.

The other side of this development shows the occupations prohibited for children under 14 or 15 years of age – to protect their health or morals. This applied particularly to factory and mining work, which had largely disappeared at the beginning of the First World War. Legislative efforts were also made in agriculture – to prevent children from tending potentially dangerous machines. How much that really helped reduce agricultural child labour is an open question however. In addition, children's night shift work was prohibited and also work that, according to the adults, gave children too much spending money. Eventually, the multitude of jobs children had done following in the footsteps of adults were limited, and a specific labour market for children began to take shape. Specific in the sense that what was in demand here was the commodity time at the times of day when the adults had no time – typically in the afternoon or early hours of the evening. And unlike in former times, where children to a greater extent were paid according to the job they did, then the pay on this new labour market for children was first of all decided by age.

Child labour in the service of training

On one side, from the school's point of view child labour ought to be weeded out – on the other side, there was an awareness of the fact that it might also be used for training purposes. Olof Gardarsdottir, in her article about children's work in Iceland between 1930 and 1990, therefore shows how the pedagogical theory of work school, which was of German origin, was institutionalized in summer work camps and school gardens for Icelandic schoolchildren. In an economy that was highly influenced by seasonal work, the children were, as mentioned, an important reserve labour force, and the Icelandic school system was therefore organized in accordance with this need. During bad times when it was difficult to find enough work for the children, the camps were called upon to provide it.

Another place, where work quite legally entered the services of pedagogy, is at the first philanthropic youth centres, also called work rooms, such as we find in Tammerfors around the turn of the century and described by Pirjo Markkola. A third – but often largely overlooked place – where children's work has been a legitimate part of children's daily lives, was in the orphanages. Just as in the youth centres, the idea was that by having to work the children would be trained into becoming hardworking, diligent and thrifty citizens. Although the actual work disappeared from the youth centres around the turn of the century, it remained, however, at the orphanages well into the 20th century. For pedagogical as well as economical reasons.[7]

Children's work between the cultures of work and child

Among historians of child labour there is a general tendency to describe this history as a historical period where children were presented as the victims of adults' ignorance, whether they were profiteering capitalists or irresponsible parents, who had failed to understand that it was better for their children to attend school. This negates children's right to play a socially active role throughout history.[8] Also, the children's contributions are often toned down in family-strategic analyses of the history of home economics.[9] If it is dealt with at all, then it is mostly on the level of a quantitative analysis.[10] By contrast, the memories of the old child workers present a more detailed picture of the efforts they had to exert to earn their weekly wages. Pirjo Markkola's description of child labour in Tammerfors in the decades around the turn of the century is one example. Perfectly in line with the milk delivery boys in Copenhagen, who, during the great milk boy strike in 1899, had to be highly creative to secure their weekly income. They collected bottles and scrap iron, which they later sold. The strikes of the milk delivery boys and the work culture, of which the milk boys were a part, are described in Ning de Coninck-Smith's article. The use of bibliographic materials in other contributions to this book – for instance, the one by Ellen Schrumpf about Norwegian industrial child labour in the late 1800s – have made it possible to sketch a picture of children as agents operating on the labour market in cooperation with and in opposition to the adults. What emerges here is children's work seen not only as a part of children's cultural history, but also as a part of the history of working-class culture.

Cultural blindness and empirical ignorance

The cultural blindness, which we noted in relation to the history of child labour, may, as mentioned, come about because the modern view of the child achieves its predominance behind the scholars' backs, so to speak. But this cultural blindness can also be explained by the empirical ignorance, which is based on the scarce sources and on the ambiguous attitude towards children's work found among the adults. On one hand, legislation has increasingly made children's work illegal, while, on the other hand, there both is a popular tradition for children's work and also a social-economic dependence based upon it. These inherent contradictions have led children and adults to invent several strategies to circumvent the law. The Danish newspaper boys and girls are merely the latest example of this trend, but, as Ning de Coninck-Smith points out in her contribution, around the First World War the milk boys in Copenhagen had to literally make themselves invisible and dress as adults – after schoolchildren were prohibited from being milk boys. These inherent contradictions have also resulted in an unwillingness to perceive children as workers in their own right. Adults do not see children's economic and social activities; they prefer to look the other way, which was obvious in Denmark during the Second World War when the children formed an important reserve labourforce in the peat production. But the unwillingness to perceive children as economic agents is alive and well today. The sociologist Anne Solberg's journey into the land of children's work, from the fishing settlements in northern Norway to suburban Oslo, is thus a sincere description of the difficult art of taking contemporary children's work seriously.

It is this culturally conditioned empirical ignorance we have tried to remedy. Consequently, we have – as far as possible – endeavoured to describe children as social and cultural actors with the same status as adults – and we have attempted to describe children's work in all its diversity. From industrial to agricultural, from recorded to unrecorded, from paid to unpaid work. The articles depict children at home, on the street and in small or large enterprises, just as they make it obvious that children's work was different for boys and girls.

However, this perspective does not only include a series of different occupations for children, we have also worked with a time frame reaching all the way up to the present. Thus, unlike studies focusing solely on industrial child labour, and by that on its rise and later disappearance, we have viewed the history of children's work in the context of a history of continuity and change. New occupations emerge, old forms perish and new groups of children emerge.

Furthermore, we have wanted to highlight how children's work and its transformations have entered a socially and culturally conditioned construction of the modern childhood in which age limits become the key indicators.[11] Here both educational as well as labour market legislation, along with police regulations about children's movements in public places, have joined hands.

Seen in this light, it is possible to say that the history of child labour is just as much about the children as it is about the adults – and about the variety of interests they have had in the children's workforce and general well-being. From parents and employers to schoolteachers, physicians and politicians. Not to mention the educational experts, who – while traditional child labour became illegal – realized the pedagogical and socializing merits of work.

Through these choices we believe we have added a series of new perspectives to the history of child labour, which we hope may offer nuances to be taken into consideration in any future debate and legislation on the work done by children and youths.

Notes

1 Material in the archives of the Folketing Committee on Labour Market Affairs (Folketing Library and Archives).
2 See the research survey in Bolin-Hort (1989) and Schrumpf (1993).
3 See Cunningham and Viazzo (1996).
4 For example, Cunningham (1990) and Sjöberg (1996).
5 Sutherland (1990) and Tucker (1994).
6 See Sutherland (1990) and Solberg (1994).
7 See Rahikainen (1995).
8 See Schrumpf (1993).
9 See f.ex., Economic and Social History in the Netherlands. Vol. 6, 1994, about "Family Strategies and Changing Labour Relations." As far as children's work is mentioned, it refers only to children in the Third World.
10 See Horrell and Humphries (1995) and the contributions in Cunningham and Viazzo (1996).
11 See further in James and Prout (1989).

References

Bolin-Hort, Per, (1989): *Work, family and the state. Child labour and the organization of production in the British cotton industry, 1780 – 1920.* Lund.
Cunningham, Hugh, (1990): The employment and unemployment of children in England, 1680-c.1851. *Past and present*, 126: 115-150.
Cunningham, Hugh and Pier Paolo Viazzo (ed.), (1996): *Child labour in historical perspective 1800-1985. Case studies from Europe, Japan and Colombia.* Unicef, International Child Development Center, Florence Italy.
Horrell, Sara & Jane Humphries, (1995): "The exploitation of little children": child labour and the family economy in the industrial revolution." in *Explorations in economic history* 32 (4): 485-516.

James, Alison & Allan Prout, eds., (1989): *Constructing and reconstructing childhood: contemporary issues in the sociological study of childhood*. London.

Rahikainen, Marjatta, (1995): "The fading of compulsory labour: the displacement of work by hobbies by the reformatory schools of twentieth-century Finland." in *Scandinavian economic history review*, 43 (2): 251-262.

Schrumpf, Ellen, (1993): "Synet på industrielt barnearbeid – et oppgjør med elendighetshistorien." [Examining children's industrial labour – rebelling against the history of misery] in *Norsk historisk tidsskrift* 72 (2): 207-220.

Sjöberg, Mats, (1996): *Att säkra framtidens skördar. Barndom, skola och arbete i agrar miljö: Bolstad pastorat 1860 – 1920* [Ensuring the harvest of the future. Childhood, school and work in the agricultural setting: Bolstad parish, 1860 – 1920]. Linköping.

Solberg, Anne, (1994): *Negotiating childhood: empirical investigations and textual representations of children's work and everyday life*. Stockholm, NORDPLAN.

Sutherland, Neil, (1990): ""We always had something to do": the paid and unpaid work of Anglophone children between the 1920s and the 1960s." in *Labour/Le travail* 25 (Spring): 105-141.

The Netherlands Economic History Archives, (1994): "Family strategies and changing labour relations." in *Economic and social history in the Netherlands*, 6.

Tucker, Barbara M., (1994): "Agricultural workers in World War II: the reserve army of children, black Americans, and Jamaicans." in *Agricultural history*, 68 (1, Winter): 54-73.

Bengt Sandin
"In the Large Factory Towns"
Child Labour Legislation, Child Labour and School Compulsion

Introduction

The circumstances in which children grow up today are totally unlike in the nineteenth century as is our understanding of the nature of childhood. Today's children spend much longer in school. They consequently spend less time on the streets, and their first experience of work comes increasingly late in life. During the nineteenth century, school assumed duties that had previously been the responsibility of the family. The development of school was affected by the need for child labour. It was also influenced by a concern for the morals of the working-class family; the way the working class rears their children has always been a problem for those in power in society. There are indications of a deliberate aspiration to get children into school and out of what were considered harmful settings – the lower class home and the streets.[1] Towards the mid -19th century children's work was looked upon as a threat to the children's souls as well as to the well-being of their bodies. Naturally, these opinions also meant a change in the value system. It became increasingly unchildlike in the eyes of the educated opinion for children to work for wages. A child was in essence a schoolchild.[2]

This paper deals with a period in Sweden when the discussion about children included concern for the way – and where – they ought to spend their formative years. Thus, it addresses the issue of how childhood was restated. How the nature of urban childhoods was perceived in the Parliamentary debates about child labour and what role child labour seems to have played in the life of urban children are central issues in this text. The overall problem addresses the issue of how and why the proper childhood was redefined during the latter part of the 19th century. First, I shall examine the background of the 1881 Ordinance on Child Labour in Industry. The aim is to present a political and institutional context that will allow us to understand the authorities' interest in legislative regulation of child labour. Second, I will touch on the development of schools in urban environments and how they can be related to the reconceptualization of the child. The present state of research on child labour is so contradictory on some points that more research is called for. Therefore, I shall begin by looking at the legislation and previous research in Sweden about child labour.

The state of research

From the mid-nineteenth century, child labour became an issue for debate in the Swedish Parliament and among the bourgeoisie. After having discussed the question of minors' labour for a few sessions, the Parliament eventually managed to agree to set up a committee to deliberate on legislation. The resulting Minority Ordinance of 1881 prohibited children under twelve from working in factories, while children between twelve and fourteen had their working day restricted to six hours. Children employed by factories, craftsmen, and other tradesmen were obliged to have instruction in school at times directed by the School Council.[3] According to earlier research, it was largely a humanitarian attitude towards children that brought an end to child labour. The legislation meant that child labour, which was never very widespread to begin with, could cease completely.[4]

Legislation on child labour has attracted renewed attention. Lars Olsson, in his study, *Då barn var lönsamma* (When Children Were Profitable), questioned the prevailing views about the relationship between legislation and the end of child labour. He argued that the growth of factory manufacturing during the first half of the nineteenth century caused a greater use of child workers. Division of labour in the factories meant that children could do simple, monotonous jobs requiring no skills. Later, when the factory owners sought to increase and control production, they mechanized some parts of the work, so that there was neither need nor use for the children. They were replaced by machines. Children were no longer employed in these child-intensive businesses, even before the Ordinance of 1881 could have had any effect on the extent of child labour. Olsson therefore challenged the view that the humanitarian and idealistic ambitions of factory owners and representatives of the authorities can explain the abolition of child labour. He also points out that the legislation made exception for the sectors where children were still employed.[5] Olsson argues his case convincingly about the decline of child labour in the businesses he had studied. The background for the legislation itself, however, is not discussed in any detail. There is therefore reason to present previous research in somewhat greater detail.

Hjalmar Sellberg, in his dissertation on *Staten och arbetarskyddet 1850-1919* (The State and Industrial Welfare 1850-1919) discussed child labour legislation under the heading "The Conservative-Liberal Phase". The initiative for legislation on safety was taken, according to Sellberg, by both Conservatives and Liberals. It was largely motivated by humanitarian concerns – without "subsidiary political motives".[6] There was, however, a certain fear of discontented Socialist agitation: Sellberg refers to the fact that the Child Labour Committee brought up the risk of such an agitation in connection with the presentation of the Belgian legislation. The proposed legislation in Sweden was mostly the work of the clergy and the farmers. In addition, some initiatives were taken by groups of entrepreneurs. No social groups in the debate stood out as particular advocates for or against this legislation. The clergy and teachers may have had certain professional interests making them more enthusiastic than others. Sellberg points out that the clergy had an interest in closing loopholes in the school legislation, but he does not develop this line of thought. What was characteristic of the period, according to Sellberg, was the lack of outright conflicts between interests and ideologies.[7]

Barbro Hedvall has devoted greater attention to child labour legislation and the Parliamentary debate, but she also fails to see any pattern in the positions taken for and against legislation. In her view the advocates and opponents of legislation to protect minor workers cannot be clearly divided by the type of argument they used, their social and economic status, or their political outlook.[8]

Hedvall also shows how factory owners argued on both sides of the debate, but that "the proportion of representatives of the authorities, including clergy and teachers, was greatest among the advocates of legislation." By contrast, most of the employers were opposed to it. Hedvall concludes that it is difficult to see definite patterns in the attitudes for or against legislation, but the "economic and professional interests" in a broad sense were decisive for most of the employers – also for clergymen, teachers, and doctors.[9]

What Hedvall demonstrates more clearly than Sellberg is that the issue of industrial welfare had two components. One concerned the problem of the working environment, while the other concerned children's knowledge and school attendance.[10] Hedvall classifies the arguments for legislation into three groups: humanitarian concerns, the need for preventive social measures, and the example of foreign countries. Humanitarian views find expression in the concern for the children's physical well-being; children were to be protected from the short-sighted interests of both parents and employers by means of state intervention. Moreover, the children's spiritual – intellectual – development was to be guaranteed.[11] The clergy discovered the intellectual deficiencies of the children during confirmation classes and demanded that the State acted to maintain children's education, especially their Christian knowledge. A crucial argument, according to Hedvall, was that knowledge was valuable in itself, and she concludes that "it was in the interest of society as a whole to have knowledgeable, enlightened citizens. The employers had greater use for educated workers who could be entrusted with more difficult tasks."[12] The State was to provide good elementary education and by that assert the long-term interests of society.

The humanitarian arguments were both expressed by representatives of patriarchal conservatism, who valued the interests of society higher than private interests, and among representatives of classical liberal ideas, who attached importance to "general education and the notion that enlightenment was an important condition for society's progress".[13] Hedvall claims that influences stemming from Continental and English legislation were significant for the Swedish legislation. There was also a pronounced social-conservative impulse for preventive action. It was the responsibility of the State to ensure that workers' conditions did not grow so harsh that their discontent might express itself in violent outbursts. Hedvall, however, does not attach as much importance to foreign examples as Sellberg.[14] The critics put the emphasis on the expected negative consequences for industry and for the families' ability to provide for their children when parents were deprived of the extra income from child labour. Many were opposed to State intervention, believing that the law was unnecessary.[15]

Hedvall and Sellberg both start with the assumption that child labour was on the increase during this period. On this point they share the perception expressed by some people who were active in the debate. It was maintained that child labour was increasing and that legislation was necessary to halt this trend. The reality was different, however. In the trades studied by Lars Olsson, it was found that child labour was decreasing from 1860 for the entire group of children under fourteen. For the 10-12 age group child labour was relatively insignificant in scope already in the 1860s. This development is explained by changes in the production process.[16] Humanitarian ideas and a positive view of learning are thus not enough to explain the abolition of child labour. This shakes the foundation of previous research into the decline of child labour.[17] After Olsson's dissertation, Eva Österberg and Rolf Nygren have had cause to discuss child labour and legislation. Both seek in different ways to assert the importance of ideas for the ending of child labour and the passing of legislation. Eva Österberg, in her review of Lars Olsson's book, expresses the view that fluctuations in the extent of child labour caused by the economic cycles, the manpower supply and the general development of ideas, with changes in technology, explain the changes in child labour – and therefore also why it ceased.[18] This explanation has been rejected by Lars Olsson in a reply where he points out that changes in the economic cycle and variations in manpower supply cannot be seen as alternative explanations of the structural change.[19]

Rolf Nygren puts great emphasis on the humanitarian views of children and child labour as an explanation for the change in legislation. In this respect he concurs with previous research and avoids taking a stance vis-à-vis Lars Olsson's results. His article is characterized by a highly positive view of the legislation as an expression of the authorities' desire to protect the children and guarantee their right to an education. The State acted to save the children both from parents and employers, and, based on the humanitarian outlook, influenced the scope of child labour.

Ironically, Olsson's explanation of the end of child labour, although inspired by historical materialism, means that the former idealistically oriented view of the background for the legislation holds firm. For if child labour was already declining before legislation, how can the legislation be explained if not by reference to humanitarian ideas? Why introduce a law that was unnecessary? Research until now has explained that humanitarian ideas were the fundamental reason for the passing of this law, quite irrespective of whether the law ended child labour or not.

The problem

As the state of research is today, only one explanation for the child labour legislation of 1881 has been presented. Humanitarian beliefs united philanthropists from different camps to pass laws to protect children. Legislation was intended to safeguard the physical well-being and intellectual development of the children. However, the different components of the research findings do not cohere very well. There is a fundamental discrepancy between Olsson's results and the explanation for this child labour legislation as a consequence of humanitarian ideas. The passing of the law now seems incomprehensible, at least if one doubts the value of ideas as the central explanatory factor behind political decisions.

There are several possible explanations for the present topic that have not been considered by previous research. Let us therefore again attempt to sketch a conceivable explanation for the child labour legislation – one that can also account for the fact that child labour in child-intensive industries was discontinued early as a stage in the development of the production process.

Research into the child labour legislation can be used as a starting point for demarcating the problem area – both regarding facts and theories. The school question played an important role in the debate, according to both Sellberg and Hedvall. Despite this, neither of them discusses the development of school in the light of child labour legislation. They have even less considered the latter in the light of the former. There is therefore good reason to look more closely at the connection between the development of the school and the child labour legislation. It may then be appropriate to begin by presenting the way in which the school question was defined in connection with the debate about child labour, as for both the contents and the matter of school forms. Next, I shall present the relevant details in the development of the school system.

There is also a theoretical reason for choosing a perspective different from that expressed in the earlier studies. Sellberg and Hedvall consistently present the debate about child labour from the viewpoints of the individuals or the professional groups involved – it is always a question of the doctor, the teacher, the employer or the public official. There is no discussion of what these concepts might mean when translated into terms of class or politics. Apparently, the consequence of this individual-oriented approach is an unproblematic view of knowledge, which is mechanically coupled to vaguely defined societal needs and knowledge requirements. But what sort of knowledge mattered? The child labour debate was not about children in general – it was about working-class children. In that way it was an expression of power relations. The right and opportunity to influence the life and existence of another social class were a given part of the political system. One must then ask why working-class children were not supposed to work. Another important question is: What institutions administered and expressed the socially determined demands and opinions about the labour of working-class children? Who pursued the issue of the abolition of child labour, and why?

Another problem is how reality is perceived. Was child labour on the increase, as Hjalmar Sellberg and Barbro Hedvall seem to think, or was it declining, as Lars Olsson shows? Sellberg and Hedvall accept the picture of reality as portrayed in the contemporary debate. How could people then believe that child labour was increasing if it really was decreasing? Let us begin by following the debate about child labour.

"A certain measure of knowledge"

We can begin by noting that questions concerning the teaching of children did not form a discrete educational issue but also affected legislation in other areas. From the early nineteenth century at least, the education of children had been an important sphere of responsibility for poor relief. It was not until the passing of a law in 1842 that school was clearly defined as a distinct sphere, but cooperation with poor relief was still to remain of central importance for the school system.[20] In addition, legislation concerning crafts and industry had long considered the instruction of the working children. Master craftsmen were responsible for the moral development of their employees. It was the duty of employers to ensure that their subordinates had a reasonable knowledge of the catechism.[21] The Factory and Craft Ordinance of 1846 decreed that no one under twelve could be taken on as an apprentice, factory worker or craft worker. Minors, who fell short of the minimum requirements specified by the Elementary School Code, were to be given instruction at times decided by the employer.[22] In 1850 the Handicraft and Industry Association in Göteborg took the initiative for legislation to protect minor workers. They expressed a will, as also expressed later by the County Administration and the City Council, to prohibit night work for minors, to limit working hours, and to demand proof of knowledge and age[23]. It appears to have been mainly tradesmen on the City Council and the Factory Association who argued in favour of these demands, while the representatives of the cotton industry opposed them. The former claimed that children's knowledge must be maintained until the age of confirmation, and above all that children without the required minimum knowledge should not be employed[24]. When the Government in 1852 prohibited night work for children under twelve, no action was taken about the level of children's knowledge.[25]

Demands for certificates of education, however, were rising during the Parliaments of the four estates in 1856-1858 and 1859-1860. Dean Rundgren from Norrköping proposed a motion to change the conditions for employment in factories. Children were to have reached the age of twelve and have a certificate to show that they had acquired a minimum of elementary school learning, "at least reading and religious knowledge." In the Parliament of 1856-1858 Rundgren's proposal was supported only by the clergy, despite favourable treatment in the committee. During the following Parliaments, 1859-1860 and 1862-1863, support diminished further, and the motion had no direct consequence for later legislation. Rundgren's argumentation may nevertheless be of interest in this context.[26]

He began with the Factory and Craft Ordinance of 1846 and the prohibition of night work in 1852. According to the former, it was the duty of factory owners and others to monitor the minor employees' "piety, orderliness, and good conduct." Children without proper knowledge were to be made to attend Sunday schools or other places of learning intended for factory and craft workers. The prohibition of night work also meant that children under twelve could not be employed. Rundgren thought that the existing legislation was obviously insufficient, chiefly because it was poorly enforced. He declared that although it was impossible, even in an industrialized society, to prohibit the employment of children under twelve, it was difficult to ensure that those minors who lacked Christian knowledge were given sufficient instruction. The extent to which the law was followed came to depend on "the employer's perception of his duty to those who are left in his care."[27]

Rundgren was therefore of the opinion that legislation should not content itself with stating an age limit of twelve. The law should also state the other criterion for determining maturity, namely that "the children shall have attained a certain degree of knowledge, a certain intellectual development."[28] He also looked at the international scene for support. He took his examples from England and France, where children had to have certificates to show that they had attended or were attending school. In Prussia, according to Rundgren, the law required documented proof of literacy or three years' school attendance if the factory did not have its own school.[29]

Industrial development in Sweden made similar regulations necessary. To begin with, it was not so easy to catch up on neglected education after the age of twelve; moreover, 12-year-olds who had attended school needed continued instruction if they were to retain their knowledge. The law must be clear on these points, said Rundgren,[30] who urged that

> "as a condition for starting employment there should be prescribed a certain measure of knowledge of religious truths, which can be inspected so that the state may be sure that the young citizen is not totally ignorant in this respect. A certain knowledge at the age of twelve can, if it is forgotten, easily be relearned."[31]

A modicum of knowledge was to be required before children were allowed to work. Since the Elementary School Code had certain minimum requirements for the knowledge of school leavers, these should be prescribed as the level of basic knowledge required for starting to work. Thus, school legislation would be coordinated with labour legislation. In this way there would be less conflict between work and school in factory towns. Children's education would not be neglected if people knew that it was a necessary condition for getting a job.[32]

> "A strong helping hand would thereby be given to the school's present weak authority over parents. The conflict between work and school ... would be diminished. ... The employer who needs young labour would also be given an interest in the work of the school, and children would come to understand that not only physical but also intellectual development is necessary to enter the ranks of the employed."[33]

At the following Parliament of 1859-1860, Rundgren again brought up the relationship between work and school. He emphasized the danger of families choosing "to sacrifice their children's education for immediate gain; the employer has no less a temptation to ignore the spiritual well-being of someone else's child with an eye only to his own temporal interests."[34] Society must also consider the growth of spiritual forces, so the minimum requirement of elementary school must be coordinated with laws for safety at work. Rundgren and Dean Sondén of Jönköping (who supported Rundgren in both Parliaments) were not interested in schools run by the factories themselves. The quality of teaching could not be inspected so easily, and the employer could evade fines simply by referring to his factory's school, despite its educational standards. Above all, argued Sondén, employers could not be expected to make work subsidiary to school at their factories, and it would scarcely be possible to increase the knowledge of children who were working at the same time. "For a factory owner can rarely allow the children enough time for attending school."[35] Nor could he be expected to have sufficient control over a school. Despite this, Sondén claimed that he knew employers who favoured the proposal, since it would make the work of the factory school easier.[36]

Rundgren argued his case eloquently. He claimed that it ought to be a joy and a security for employers to see their work being carried out by thinking people. Based on this truly enlightened rhetoric, Rundgren pleaded for legislation that did not even demand all the minimum standards of the Elementary School Code. It was enough if children met the requirements of "reading and religious knowledge".[37]

At the Parliament of 1856-1858 another motion was proposed, according to which working hours for children in factories should be limited. Children under fifteen were to work no more than eight hours a day. Both this and Rundgren's motion were supported by the General Appeal and Economy Committee. In Parliament the motion was supported only by the clergy, while the motion to limit working hours was supported by all the estates except the bourgeoisie. Rundgren's motion was supported by the clergy with no debate in 1856-1858 and 1859-1860, but it was rejected there in 1862-1863. The other estates in Parliament gave Rundgren's motion a chilly reception on all these occasions.

The peasantry rejected Rundgren's motion without debate at the two last Parliaments. At the first, however, there was some debate. It was asserted that it was unreasonable to fine an employer who took a child into his factory out of mercy, and there was a risk that demands for certificates of education would also arise in the countryside. Barbro Hedvall sees the negative attitude of the peasants as due to the risk that the proposal would in the long term "affect the peasant farmers as employers." At the same time, however, the demand for shorter working hours for children in factories was accepted by the peasantry.[38]

The bourgeoisie rejected the proposal to reduce working hours in 1859-1860. Only one speaker favoured the motion. The criticism of Rundgren's motion on certificates of education was not so compact. Although some entrepreneurs, such as Waern and Murén, dismissed it as a coercive measure, others favoured it, including Ekman, a mill owner, and Swartz, a factory owner from Norrköping. The latter was a zealous advocate of certificates of education in the bourgeoisie in the 1850s.[39]

In short, the demand for certificates of education received scant support in Parliament during the period in question. Support from the committees also declined after the Parliament of 1856-1858, probably as a result of the changed composition of the committees. A Parliamentary letter to the government in 1857 concerning a restriction of working hours for minors did not mention certificates of education. This letter was referred to the Board of Trade, who asked for opinions from factory associations in Stockholm, Göteborg, Karlshamn, Gävle, and Nyköping. Their reaction was mostly unfavourable. They could conceivably accept general legislation, not laws directed against certain trades only. On the other hand, the Factory Association in Göteborg also expressed a view – fully compatible with the attitude they had expressed previously – that protective legislation was above all "required out of concern for the children's education and instruction."[40] A reduction in working hours was intended to give children time for schooling and must therefore encompass all trades.[41]

The Board of Trade declared in its pronouncement to the Government that a change of current legislation was scarcely called for. If the time was ripe for a more detailed investigation of the matter, a committee of experts should be established, "on which doctors, primary school teachers and factory owners should preferably be represented".[42] No committee was set up, and the estates' letter together with legislation on freedom of trade did not result in any changes in children's working hours or required knowledge.[3]

"In respect of children employed in factories"

The issue came up once more in the reformed bicameral Parliament of 1870, where a parish clerk named Jöns Rundbäck (Farmers' Party) proposed a motion about children's factory work in the Lower House. The plight of factory children was painted in vivid colours and with critical pungency. Working hours were too long, he declared, and the teaching given to children was really limited. The existing legislation was insufficient. At the age of twelve a child was not sufficiently developed to endure factory work. Nor could children's upbringing and education be considered complete. Rundbäck demanded that the working hours for children between twelve and sixteen should not exceed ten hours per day.[44] The committee considered the motion favourably, and a majority of those who spoke in the House favoured a regulation of working hours. The Mayor of Jönköping, however, was highly critical. Objections were also expressed by the former proposer of motions on the issue, Dean Rundgren of Norrköping. His view was that the crucial problem was rather that the age of employment was too low, and that a certain degree of knowledge should be required before employment. Other suggestions, such as a limit of twelve working hours, were made, and the earlier Parliamentary letter was brought up again. The result was that Rundbäck's proposal was again referred to committee consideration, after which Parliament had no time to deal with the matter.[45]

Jöns Rundbäck returned to the next Parliament with new ideas about the issue. He now attached greater importance to the educational question. Rundbäck suggested that working hours in the factories be limited to ten hours a day for children and young people between twelve and eighteen. For craft work a restriction of working hours was not as essential, since the sanitary conditions were generally better there than in the factories. The minimum elementary school knowledge and an age of at least twelve were to be the absolute minimum requirements for employment in shops and factories or apprenticeship to craftsmen. Yet another important addition was made: children were to have the opportunity to have "necessary" teaching for about an hour every weekday and the chance to attend Sunday school.[46]

Some amendments were suggested when the proposal was examined by a committee. It was not the working hours that were a problem, but the sanitary conditions of the younger workers. Moreover, conditions were not the same in every branch of industry. Legislation should therefore apply primarily to factories where the sanitary conditions were worst. Those specially mentioned were the textile industry – spinning and weaving mills – along with cigar, paper and match factories. The demands for a minimum of knowledge needed particular attention "in respect of children employed in factories." Factory work had a detrimental effect on children's ability to assimilate instruction. The problem was greatest for children with the least knowledge when they began work in production. The committee therefore felt that it was justified in demanding as a minimum elementary school knowledge of child factory workers. Unlike the regulation of working hours, the knowledge requirement was to apply to all factories without exception, but it was not to apply to children employed in shops and craft work. Shop workers, according to the committee, were bound to gain more knowledge than what was required by the decreed minimum, while children working in crafts did not work so intensively as to prevent general schooling. Simultaneously, the committee rejected the demand for daily instruction of child workers, since this was considered to impair the children's chances of finding work[47]. The Lower House passed the motion by acclamation.[48]

Rundbäck's motion met a different fate in the Upper House. The committee, considering the motion and the proposal from the temporary committee in the Lower House, reached quite different conclusions. There was a detailed account of the treatment of the matter in the Lower House, and there was an admission of the general importance of the problem for the State. At the same time, it was asserted that the country was not suffering any great problems owing to "insufficient statutory regulations" – industrial activity was far too limited for this. Statistical calculations now showed that the number of young people in factories was increasing. There was therefore good reason to intervene in time against "the evil", while the problem was still limited in scope. The experience of other countries, however, scarcely gave any unambiguous indicators of the most suitable approach. The point of departure for legislation was not only the work environment but also the need for sufficient education. Regulation could be justified because of

> "the more or less harmful effect of factory work on young people, who have not yet attained that stage of development where they have the necessary resistance to the harmful influence of factory work on the health, ... (as well

as) the need for the requisite time to be granted to them to acquire the degree of knowledge intended by our normal elementary school instruction."[49]

Foreign legislation provided guidance in the latter respect. It had been shown that working hours should be limited to a different extent for each age group. The committee was therefore negatively disposed towards the decision of the Lower House in favour of restrictions on working hours only for children working in particularly insanitary industries. Something had to be done about health hazards in factories, but the need for schooling justified the restriction of working hours by legislation affecting "factories in general or in greater conformity with the motion as proposed."[50] The time young people spent in insanitary places had to be limited, and effective supervision had to be established. The committee agreed with the Lower House regarding the need for legislation. The complicated nature of the matter, however, meant that a committee of inquiry should be set up. This was also the core of the proposal submitted to the Upper House, but with the recommendation that the motion as presented in the Lower House should be rejected.[51]

The debate in the Upper House was short. The proposed committee to inquire into the need for a reduction in working hours was rejected. Rundbäck's motion was thus defeated by the opposition of the Upper House. The debate gives little information about the reason for this negative attitude. Evidently, the regulation of working hours and the proposed control system were delicate issues. The favourable statement of the committee had been accompanied by a dissenting opinion to the effect that relations between the classes, one of the knottiest problems of this period, risked being undermined by a law that could not be supervised or enforced. It was necessary to avoid reducing further the confidence in their masters and employers felt by the servant class, in particular "the generally less peaceable factory workers in the larger towns."[52]

In both houses the education question had a central place in the discussion about what was the core problem of child labour. It was also obvious that the regulation of working hours for children was now viewed not only as a health issue, but was in equal measure concerned with the possibilities of educating children. In addition, the question could be presented as a need for general legislation for all factories, because the demand for knowledge did in fact apply to more children than those working in insanitary conditions. The significance of the education question is also shown by the fact that the discussion referred primarily to "young people" – including minors up to the age of eighteen.

"In the large factory towns"

A motion about child labour was proposed in the Upper House in 1875 by F. F. Carlson, the Minister of Ecclesiastical Affairs (whose portfolio included educational affairs). At the same time the question was put forward in the Lower House by A. W. Staaff.[53] Both motions mentioned the consequences of labour for the children's health and the need for a more rigorous examination of children's knowledge on their entry into working life. Different arguments were emphasized. Staaff described conditions in the cities. Pupils often left school without the prescribed degree of knowledge, "which should now be unconditionally required of every member of society." The causes were the poverty of the population and the need for "quick gain", and also the attraction of the many jobs as a way of allowing children to contribute to the support of the household. According to Staaff, it was admittedly true that the Freedom of Trade Ordinance of 1864 made employers responsible for ensuring that children were receiving schooling, but "how shall this come about when the children are put to work from early morning until evening?" He wondered if it was possible to expect the "strength and inclination" for study after a hard day's work. For all those children who lacked the necessary skills in reading and writing, "for which daily exercise is required," an occasional hour's teaching on Sundays was of little help. The situation was "of a pernicious and profoundly far-reaching nature for the population of the large towns and cities, and of no little significance for the future of our native country."[54]

The importance of the matter demanded as comprehensive and effective regulations as possible, and "also changes with regard to working hours." It was not enough to append to previous legislation a provision for certificates of the minimum elementary school education. Parliament should request the Government to restrict working hours and to prohibit the employment in shops, crafts and factories of children without the necessary knowledge.[55]

In his motion in the Upper House, F. F. Carlson referred to foreign legislation – the foremost models were coming from Denmark and England – and to conditions in the large factory towns. He also referred to the Law of 1864, pointing out its weaknesses. There were no regulations about the length of the working day or sanitary conditions, and "it is left to employers to decide the days and hours when factory children can enjoy schooling."[56] Further regulations were called for. In view of the increased number of young workers, he felt that conditions "in the large factory towns appear both to show the necessity for guarantees for the enforcement of the existing law and to call for new legislation."[57]

F. F. Carlson supported his argument by referring to reports from the school authorities in Stockholm, Norrköping and Malmö. The Elementary School Inspector in Stockholm had presented material to show the great number of children under twelve who had left school during the period 1872-1874 to work

Figure 1. The dubious consequences of child labour. Errandboys taking a break to smoke in Stockholm around 1920. (Photo. The City Museum of Stockholm)

in factories and craft workshops. In addition, he was able to present details of working hours for those pupils who attended continuation schools and catechetical (catechism/catechizing) schools. The school board in Göteborg deplored the children's long working hours and the consequences for their "health", "languishing strength" and "spiritual development." The elementary school board in Göteborg had already appealed to the government for a change in the 1864 Freedom of Trade Ordinance regarding the stipulations about the education of factory children. The school board in Malmö had also expressed a desire that the 1864 legislation should be coordinated with the regulations of the Elementary School Code,

> "and that irrespective of age, no children may be employed in factories other than those who after attending the minimum teaching have received a leaving certificate from the school. For it has been found that a great multitude of children, as soon as they reach the age of twelve, disappear from the elementary schools not only in the towns but also in the surrounding localities, although they have often failed to acquire even primary school knowledge." [58]

In Norrköping the School Council had tried to reach an agreement with employers to allow children to attend continuation school on Wednesday afternoons. The efforts of the School Council had been unsuccessful.[59]

F. F. Carlson concluded that the consequences of this development were so obvious that they scarcely required any comment. "Physical weakness and the seeds of lifelong illness must be thus incurred, and no less a threat is the vulgarity which otherwise results when the door to education is closed." It was necessary to promulgate "regulations concerning the length of the working day, concerning daily teaching for the children, concerning the sanitary conditions in the factory and the supervision which the State should exercise in this respect." In conclusion, F. F. Carlson appealed to the government to draw up a statute regulating the use of young people in factory work.[60]

The motions were passed on for consideration by committees. The chairs of the two committees were occupied by F. F. Carlson and A. W. Staaff. Barbro Hedvall points out that it appears as if there was some consultation between the two committee chairmen, since their two motions concluded in an almost identical wording.[61] It is moreover obvious that the Lower House committee had been influenced by the arguments put forward in the Upper House by F. F. Carlson, since there was a consideration of foreign legislation, and an illustration of the argument with reference to conditions in Swedish towns. The temporary committee of the Lower House emphasized the duty of State and Local Government to work for an increase in educational standards. It was a fundamental demand that no child should lack that "little measure" of knowledge encompassed in the minimum requirements of the elementary school. It was claimed that current legislation was often ignored. Not only were children under twelve employed, but their continued teaching was also highly unsatisfactory. The children's long working hours made proper teaching impossible.

> "That no small number of the urban population thus grows up without acquiring other than in a highly imperfect manner the most essential general knowledge is an experience which finds support from the observations which the clergy have been forced to make when preparing young people for communion. It is also not infrequently evident that many children of both sexes have not had any instruction, or at least only very incomplete instruction, for several years, occasionally not since the age of nine or ten."[62]

The Lower House Committee therefore found it desirable to introduce a regulation about the degree of a child's knowledge on employment, and, so that knowledge would not remain at this low minimum, "there is also a great need for a restriction of working hours, adjusted to suit the different ages." The physical well-being of the children now had to be given greater consideration than before. In addition, the State was to introduce effective supervision to ensure that the regulations were observed.[63]

In the Upper House committee the education problem was further underlined. Industry had developed vigorously and the number of minors employed had doubled in the preceding ten years. Since working hours were not restricted, the provisions of the 1864 Freedom of Trade Ordinance, to the effect that children should regularly attend Sunday school, did not have the intended effect.

> "It is in the nature of things that a previously deficient education cannot be successfully made complete; not even what has previously been learned can be maintained, and the consequence is that a significant part of the population is growing up in a serious state of vulgarity. "[64]

The school boards in the factory towns had not been able to cope with the child labour problem with the aid of current legislation. The factory owners had not been able to meet the demands of the school boards, not even in isolated cases, because of the risk of losing competitiveness against other, less scrupulous employers. It was therefore necessary that

> "no children should be allowed, at least not without the authorization of the relevant school board, to be employed as shop assistants or factory or craft workers, unless they have been duly certified to have learnt the minimum requirements prescribed by the Elementary School Code. A foundation would thereby be laid, upon which could be built, with some hope of success, a continued education limited to a small number of hours per day. It is further considered necessary that there be rules to determine how many hours a day a minor may be kept at factory work.... This would be a way to remedy not only the complaints that have been heard, that monotonous and strenuous work with long periods between breaks hampers or disturbs physical development, but it would also provide an opportunity to obtain tuition during a certain part of the day."[65]

The problem of industrial welfare thus had different components. The demand for certificates of education meant a more specific coordination with the Elementary School Code's minimum knowledge requirements. Changes in working hours were advocated primarily with reference to the need for education, but largely also for health reasons. Regarding the need for education, the Upper House motion did for the first time make a clear distinction between children aged 12-14 and young people aged 14-18. In addition, the committees proposed that legislation should apply to all factories and craft occupations. This stance was also influenced by the more general problem of school and education, although in the debate it was mostly the conditions of factory children that were emphasized.

According to Barbro Hedvall, Parliament handled the motion like a skilful pilot negotiating potential shoals. There was, for example, no discussion of any concrete proposals that might provoke objections from the various interested parties. The formulation of a statute was left to the government and a committee of inquiry. The success of these tactics naturally depended on the positive attitude of the Government. F. F. Carlson's place in the Government guaranteed this.[66] It was probably also important that the legislation was expected to apply to all spheres of business. It was stated in the committee proposal that in other countries this had meant a breakthrough in gaining the approval of employers. This suggestion thus disarmed the criticism that had greeted the proposals in the 1850s, 1860s, and 1870s, to the effect that they would have negative consequences for some factories and businesses. The only concrete suggestion in the motions and committee resolutions was the stance adopted on the issue of schooling, the demand for certificates of education and continued teaching. It was this that justified the age distinction, as well. All other questions were left to a committee of inquiry. A proposal to probe further into the matter was passed by acclamation in both Houses.[67] The debate, however, was not without interest.

In the Upper House, industrialists questioned the need for a reduction in working hours, while rural interests were doubtful about the examination of children's knowledge. Rev. Rundgren from Norrköping was also against a reduction in working hours, but in favour of a more comprehensive examination of knowledge. Those who supported the motion included educationalists, clergymen, doctors, a few farmers and a few public officials, the publicists S. A. Hedin and Lars Johan Hierta, Granlund the coach-builder, Wedberg the wholesaler, and the two Göteborg businessmen Aron Philipsson and Peter Hammerberg.[68]

The Elementary School Inspectors' data of the number of children who left school prematurely was questioned by Berg, a cotton manufacturer. As far as he knew, no children under twelve were employed in the factories. He therefore doubted whether the children under twelve who left school actually got work in the factories and craft workshops. If this happened it was because they lied about their age. He also thought that the working hours were incorrectly reported and that the work was generally light. In his opinion, the factory owners themselves should be allowed to decide when children should go to school, for example in the way he himself had handled the problem. Berg, however, did not propose any motion. He only declared that he wished to contribute some information on the matter. F. F. Carlson observed that no other motions had been proposed and that there was no reason to doubt the reports of the Stockholm Elementary School Inspector. The house passed the motion as proposed.[69]

The debate in the Lower House was more extensive. An estate owner named Ehrenborg, for example, criticized the way the committee had been given such freedom to draw up a proposal. The concrete views on the need for education were severely criticized. Compulsory schooling was impossible to carry out, and in any case the factories were a far better moral and physical environment than the workers' homes. This was guaranteed by the owners' magnanimity and concern for the children. It was appropriate, however, to restrict working hours so that children could attend school, but this could be achieved by amending the legislation already in effect.[70]

Ehrenborg's speech received a reply from A. W. Staaff, the proposer of the motion. He refuted the criticism of the formal procedure and went on to discuss the core of Ehrenborg's argument – that certificates of education were unnecessary. Experience from the elementary school pupils of the capital, and from those children who had gone out to work, had convinced him that it was absolutely essential not only to reduce working hours but also, if knowledge was to be maintained, to demand certificates of education.

> "We should also see to it that it should no longer be possible for children to leave school so early that they know nearly nothing. My original intention was not so much to speak of a specific measure of minimum knowledge, which could be expected, since some knowledge, however slight, ought to exist." [71]

The committee, however, had already decided that it was most suitable to express the expected degree of knowledge in terms of the minimum elementary school requirements. Staaff claimed that these requirements should not be any deterrent. If children started attending school at the age of eight, seven, or even six,

> "then by the age of twelve, thirteen, or at the latest fourteen they should have managed to get through the work required. ... Now it is obvious that every demand must be qualified, ... there is always some elasticity in this minimum. To take Christian knowledge, for instance, or even reading, it is clear that it is only at a more advanced age that they can show any real insight in the former or true skill in the latter; but at the age mentioned they ought to be at least reasonably well acquainted with and trained in these subjects. I do not think that this is asking too much."[72]

He also challenged the view that legislation had become too strict, adding: "I would further emphasize that something must unconditionally be done." The House was not to have exaggerated fears about the implementation of the law. His Majesty's Government was free to establish the conditions and "grant exemptions where particularly pressing circumstances may dictate."[73] The House approved the motion that the matter should be further investigated.[74]

There is no need to follow the debate further. To be sure, some time was to pass before the law came into force. A committee of inquiry first examined the matter and reported its opinion, after which the Royal Ordinance was approved. This prohibited child labour in factories for children under twelve. It also restricted working hours for children aged 12-14, for whom it required organized school attendance. Evidently, the school question, here as in the parliamentary debate, had a guiding influence on the classification of children's age groups. It was declared that children under fifteen, whether working in factories or in crafts and other trades, were obliged to "avail themselves of teaching" at times decided by the School Council, after consultation with the employers. The demand for education thus applied not only to child factory workers but also to all children in towns.

Practically nothing new was said about the issue after the parliamentary decision to set up a committee of inquiry, although the differences between the committee's proposal and the wording of the final statute are rather interesting. The daily extent of teaching, for example, was not regulated by the ordinance, although the committee had suggested that the children should be taught for two hours a day. [75] Nor did the ordinance heed the committee's suggestions for proper measures to supervise and enforce the statute.

The crucial question can now be asked: Why did the issue of child labour achieve a breakthrough in Parliament, a breakthrough that actually led to legislation? My intention here is not to identify the actors in the affair, but rather to try to show the social forces channelled into the public debate.

"The school's present weak authority over parents"

We can begin by observing that the expected knowledge appears to have been relatively modest. Nothing more than the minimum elementary school requirements was even hinted at. Knowledge of the catechism was what was demanded. Even when the rhetoric spoke of the need for educated, enlightened workers, the arguments boiled down to demands for the most basic and rudimentary requirements of the Elementary School Code. The conclusions drawn by previous historians about the need for educated workers thus seem to find little support, not only in the Elementary School Code of 1842 but also in the debates of the 1870s. The demands for knowledge did not envisage any development of school education, aspiring only to attain the lowest expected school standards. When the question first came to the fore, the problem was formulated as a need to strengthen the weak authority of the school over children and parents. The same can also be illustrated with arguments used in later debates, as should be clear from what has been said above. The pattern is well known from earlier years. The debate about elementary school education and the Elementary School Code itself exemplifies legislation, which was ultimately a critical questioning of families' ability to look after their children in a satisfactory way.[76]

At the same time, however, the Elementary School Code did not provide a particularly powerful weapon for the authorities to use against "contumacious" parents. Compulsory school attendance was formulated as the extent of knowledge the children were obliged to be taught; no particular ages were stated between which children were expected to attend school. It was expected that the minimum knowledge would be acquired before children attended church confirmation classes. The parliamentary debate shows that this weakly formulated rule brought problems when the authorities sought to impress the importance of school attendance upon working-class parents and children. The lack of clear age limits in the Elementary School Code made it difficult to demand school attendance up to the age of twelve.

Obviously, the representatives of the countryside argued most vehemently against any legislation that would link the employment of children with certificates of elementary school knowledge. It is even more evident that the advocates of legislation took their examples from urban settings. When Parliament finally decided to set up a committee of inquiry, it was with reference to conditions in Stockholm, Göteborg, Malmö and Norrköping, since these had been presented to the Minister of Ecclesiastical Affairs in special pleas from the respective school authorities. A. W. Staaff was not only the rector of one of Stockholm's inner-city parishes but also a member of the School Board. Jöns Rundbäck's arguments in Parliament may also be seen against an urban background. Although he represented the Farmers' Party and a rural constituency, this was on the outskirts of the city of Göteborg. The constituency included the Gamlestaden textile mill and a timber-yard. C. H. Rundgren similarly represented not merely the clergy's interest in general education but also the School Council in Norrköping, of which he was the chairman. The same applies to Swartz, the industrialist from Norrköping, who also had a seat and a vote on the School Council. Dean Sondén of Jönköping probably had a similar position.

Among those in favour of legislation we may also note representatives of finance and industry from Göteborg, as well as a group of Members of Parliament from Stockholm that included the bank director A. O. Wallenberg and L. J. Hierta. The list could be made longer and more detailed, but it will suffice here to observe that the regulation of minors' working hours was manifestly supported by urban representatives.

In addition, this support coincides in part with the support from public officials pointed out by Hedvall. The officials were often based in urban settings, and it may be suspected that the political life of the towns was the decisive factor, probably combined with a critical and conservative attitude to industrialism. This point corresponds with the fact that child labour and its relationship to the minimum school standards were sometimes expressly defined as an urban problem, and, even more specifically, as a problem for the large factory towns. This correspondence has its corollary in the fact that the demand for certificates of education was vigorously opposed by rural interests. Anyway, it is perfectly clear from the analysis of the parliamentary debates that the political discussion was more and more about the interests of school and the cities.[77]

Among the bourgeoisie the problem of the cities had been emphasized early in the debate. Swartz expressed the opinion that children usually had sufficient knowledge at the age of twelve or when they left school, but

> "in a city like Norrköping it happens not infrequently that people from the countryside move in with their children, with the very motive of harvesting an income through them, because the children have already reached or will soon reach the age when they can be put to work."[78]

If children went to school for a shorter time up to the age of twelve, their lack of basic skills meant that teaching was completely wasted. The lacuna could scarcely be filled after the children had left school. No extra tuition could be allowed by the employer, and the working-class children hardly ever attended any catechetical examinations.[79]

Other speakers in favour of regulating working hours pointed out the generally poor control the urban schools had over attendance. It should perhaps be underlined that all the industrialists, who spoke in the debate, declared that they did not employ children under twelve, referring to the Factory Ordinance. They also claimed that the education provided by the factory schools ably met the expected standards. This was questioned by several speakers, who said that the teaching in the factory schools was unsatisfactory owing to the children's exhaustion. Those who spoke against regulation maintained that the factory at least offered the children an environment that was better than what they had at home.[80]

Let us leave the debate in Parliament and ask a new question. Can it be that child labour and the low level of school attendance were a problem for urban authorities? To answer this question in detail would require a thorough analysis of the development of schooling in Swedish towns and cities. No conclusive answer can be given here, but it should be possible to clarify some lines of development.

Schooling in the cities[81]

Clearly, the urban school authorities had aspirations and demands for the school far exceeding the code that applied to the nation. In this respect there are distinct parallels to development before the passing of the Elementary School Code in 1842, when there was a fundamental difference in the scope and nature of the school system in the towns and in the countryside. After 1842 the capital Stockholm and the cities of Göteborg, Norrköping and Malmö issued local codes according to which school attendance was to be compulsory from the age of six or seven up to twelve. Steps were also taken to provide organized primary school teaching before proper elementary school began. School could not build on the teaching of reading in the home, as the national code had decreed; this must also be taught in school. The authorities also took steps to provide essential instruction for children who had left school. Sunday schools and continuation schools were arranged for working children. A Royal Circular of 22 April 1864 also decreed that the school councils were responsible for ensuring that children who had left school maintained their knowledge. This circular from the Department of Ecclesiastical Affairs must be seen in connection with the parliamentary debates of 1862-1863 and the regulations concerning education, which were introduced then and renewed in the Freedom of Trade Ordinance of 1864.

The authorities' demands and expectations of schooling bore the stamp of an extremely negative view of conditions in working-class families. On the one hand, they condemned working-class "indolence" and "lack of discipline", while, on the other hand, they felt compassion for the harsh conditions prevailing in working-class homes. In both cases the same conclusion was drawn: children had to be separated from the injurious environments of home and street and the unsuitable environments of work and factories. School was the instrument to achieve this objective. It was symptomatic that the elementary school board in Stockholm in 1860 did not consider it necessary to specify the minimum educational standards in the same way as in the national code, since it was thought that no one could fail to learn so little while the pupils were obliged to attend school. In the light of Staaff's complaint some fifteen years later about schoolchildren's defective knowledge, this attitude appears a trifle optimistic.

The consequences of poor education were of the utmost political importance. The elementary school board in Göteborg formulated its goals in 1865 as follows:

> "The constantly increasing immigration from the countryside, ... of which the majority comprises poor labourers, should not fail to call upon every effort on the part of society to counter the perils which would otherwise

derive from this source. What is required to forestall the threat of a proletariat from this quarter is, first and foremost, that the elementary schools take in the growing children from the families in question in order to communicate to them good and honest knowledge, obedience to law and justice, love of God and one's neighbour."[82]

Still, this was easier said than done. The children's attendance was highly irregular. It varied according to the need for the children's help in the home and according to their chances on the labour market. This is why the schooling of girls and boys differ. The girls started schooling later than the boys because they were helping with the scores at home, while they stayed longer in the schools because of their poor luck on the urban labour market when aged under 15. The boys on the other hand did not help at home and came to school from the age of seven but ended their schooling quite early between the age of 10 to 12, since they could obviously find work on the market from that age.

From the point of view of the authorities it was even more serious, because the children left school without consent from the teachers when either they or

Figure 2. Springtime 1926. Schoolboys damming floodwater after school in a park in Stockholm. (Photo. The City Museum of Stockholm)

their parents considered it suitable. The children who started work did not really worry about retaining their knowledge by attending continuation school. This then created a gap between the end of schooling and the beginning of confirmation classes. When the student appeared for these classes, all their knowledge of scripture was lost. The clergymen felt and expressed their grief over having to begin from the beginning again to instill Christian values in the children. A new circular about the registration of children in continuation schools was issued on 15 October 1869.

The difficulties are underlined by the fact that the authorities did not exactly know how many children there were in the towns. Registration was imperfect and mobility high. For Stockholm the establishment in the early 1880s of the roteman system (with a person responsible for each ward) meant a more effective registration of schoolchildren, who could by that be more efficiently supervised and controlled.

The school authorities exerted themselves to make the children come to school. Towns such as Norrköping, etc. were divided into districts with inspectors responsible for supervising the children's school attendance. Teachers were entitled to fetch the children from their homes, and parents and children were warned of divine wrath and secular punishment before the class or the school board. Children received corporal punishment for failure to attend school. The establishment of reformatories made it possible occasionally to remove children from unsuitable homes. In this way the development of school in the towns in the period 1847-1875 meant a massive institutional and educational process of change. The internal work was consolidated by the establishment of a functioning school administration and a decidedly hierarchical organization, which was largely created to simplify supervision of school attendance. Simultaneously, the authorities grappled with the difficulties of creating effective sanctions at a local level without much support of national legislation. The school administration and particularly their school inspector became important opinion-makers both locally and internationally on issues about the plight of children in lower class families, on the streets and at work. They had, no doubt, their own professional axe to grind.

In spite of this, in all the cities mentioned it is possible to illustrate that there were difficulties in making employers respect the laws and give the older children the opportunity to attend classes. In Norrköping and Göteborg meetings were held with employers to discuss the problem, but with no result. In Malmö the legislation of 1864 was published several times in the newspapers, urging employers not to take on minors and to respect the needs of the school. According to a Norrköping textile manufacturer, it was impossible to let children between twelve and fourteen attend classes without causing grave production problems; no children under twelve were employed. The school boards also began to collaborate with the police to ensure that children of school age did not roam the streets, sell newspapers and pamphlets, or commit thefts of various kinds. New local ordinances on street order and the regulations of children's whereabouts in the streets were issued, and children caught in cities such as Malmö, Gothenburg and Stockholm, for example, were recorded in the "detectives' register of minors receiving punishment or warnings" for thefts of coal, clothes and food. Punishment consisted of a caution or a flogging, sometimes in the presence of parents summoned to witness it.

These measures were only partially successful. And it is in this context we begin to understand why the city schools of Sweden started to create a national issue about the child labour question. The administrations had grown in competence and size, but they were only partially successful. For example, we can observe that although the number of older children registered in the schools between 1852 and 1870 was increasing, most of the children had already left school at the age of ten or eleven. Moreover, at the beginning of the 1870s more children were leaving school at an earlier age than before. The statistics show that the number of children in school in the age group from 12 to 14, out of the total number of children in that age group in Stockholm, was decreasing. Fewer children than before in these troublesome age groups came to the schools. In other words, the boys must have been on the streets or in different forms of employment. This development must be understood in relation to the concerns created by immigration to the towns, which were emerging then. It was difficult for the authorities to prevent children from leaving school once they attained the minimum level of knowledge, and – perhaps to an even greater extent – to get the children, who had recently arrived, to come to school. Thus there was an increase, not in the number of children working in factories, but in the number outside school. Child labour and street activities were not confined to industrial work but were compromised by many different activities, from minding children to hawking things in the streets. And the latter activity has surely been a source of worry. The number of street children recorded by the police gives us a perspective on the absent schoolboy. The registration was done under the premises of the 1864 Criminal Law making all individuals under the age of 14 exempt from legal action, only to be punished – i.e. warned and whipped by the local police officers. The ledgers for Stockholm, which are of interest here, started in 1864 and continue until 1910 and record a great variety of offences against public order – street hawking, petty theft, loitering, window breaking, etc. In these we find a tremendous increase of boys aged 11-15 detected and punished for various street crimes. Thus, the all-powerful professional school administrations in the cities could not actually force the children off the streets, and their inability to do so was displayed daily by the presence of all the street children. The combination of these two factors: a) the development of powerful school administrations and b) the increase in the number of children beyond the control of the educational system, i.e. on the streets, thus creates the social basis for the debates in the Swedish Parliament. Still, we must look for a connection at the central level to get the wider context. It was all a matter of the need for a new national school legislation.

School, towns and state – a perspective

Let us now return to the introductory questions. Although a detailed analysis of the development of school in urban settings remains to be made, it can already be stated that the national legislation can be explained with reference to conditions in Stockholm, Göteborg, Malmö and Norrköping. Social development meant that the weaknesses in the school system were manifest there. It was not possible to socialize children via school in the desired manner. Children were not kept off the streets, and it was doubtful whether the negative influence from the families could be countered. The interval between leaving school and confirmation was felt to be a problem. That the school authorities were negotiating with employers bears witness to the belief that part of the solution was to be found in a restriction – or a regulation – of the demand for child labour (especially children aged 12-14).

At the same time there was a development in State regulation and supervision of conditions in the municipalities. For the elementary school this meant the appointment of school inspectors and the development of a subsidy system. This control went hand in hand with the development of the local school administration. The cities dealt with here were made into separate, consolidated school districts at an early date – with local appointed school inspectors. At the beginning of the 1870s, the inspectors in the cities were of great significance. Moreover, the state system of inspectors and subsidies meant that a close link was established between the urban school boards and the authority in charge, the Ministry of Ecclesiastical Affairs. The evidence for this comes from the reports and correspondence about the minors' question, of which there was a steady traffic between this ministry and the urban school boards. This is an example of a general feature of the way the new State power ruled and brought the autonomous local government along with it.[83]

It was therefore no coincidence that it was the head of the ministry responsible for school affairs, F. F. Carlson, who proposed a motion that was actually within the sphere of responsibility of the Ministry of Public Administration. The proposal strove to regulate a question of crucial importance for the urban school system, namely: between what ages must children attend school, and how shall education be organized for children who leave school early? The impact of the education question – on the debate, on the committee inquiries, and on the wording of the ordinance itself – makes it legitimate to ask whether the idea of legislation on industrial welfare was not a disguise for school legislation and an expression of a new national ambition to include all children in the national project of compulsory education. The Minority Ordinance was, it seems, an attempt to prepare the way for a renewal of the school law? This was issued in 1882, one year after the Minority Ordinance, and meant that school attendance was compulsory between the ages of seven and twelve, and children were obliged to have teaching up to the age of fourteen. An ordinance concerning State subsidies to continuation schools had been issued in 1877 – by the very same Minister F. F. Carlson.

The explanation for child labour legislation must be sought in the social development of the towns and in the establishment of influential school boards. It was not, at least at this point, a question of any development of a humanitarian ideology, but rather a problem of social conflicts in towns and an administrative solution to problems of forming a modern childhood. The conflicts were about where was best for children to spend their years of growth. The choice was between the home, the street, work or school. The answer in respect to children was not naturally given, but the answer of the politically important circles could only be one – the school. By that paving the way for a new type of world in which normal childhood was associated with schooling – and all breaches from these rules were deviant. [84]

Notes

1 Sandin 1986.
2 Zelitzer 1985, Cunningham 1991, Sandin 1992.
3 Svensk Författningssamling (SFS) 1881:64.
4 Sellberg 1950; Hedvall 1978, Gårdlund 1942; Fogelberg 1973.
5 Olsson 1980, chap. 8-11.
6 Sellberg 1950, pp. 66-67
7 Ibid p. 21-24, 66-68.
8 Hedvall 1978, p. 219. Sellberg 1950 p. 21-24, 66-68.
9 Ibid.
10 Ibid.
11 Ibid. pp. 213-220.
12 Ibid. pp. 213-214 Quote p. 214.
13 Ibid.
14 Ibid. pp. 215-216
15 Ibid. p. 216.
16 Olsson 1980, pp. 105-145.
17 Ibid.
18 Österberg 1982; Olsson 1983, Nygren. 1982, pp. 197 – 236.
19 Olsson 1983.
20 Sandin 1986, chap. 5 och 6.
21 Ibid. pp. 144-153.

22 SFS 1846:3.9
23 Civildepartements Konseljakter 22.5.1852, Nr 3.
24 Hedvall 1978, pp. 132-134.
25 Ibid. p. 134-137.
26 For a general presentation of this issue see Hedvall 1978, pp. 138-140.
27 Prästeståndets protokoll 1856-1858, pp. 341-342.
28 Ibid.
29 Ibid.
30 Ibid.
31 Ibid. p. 343.
32 Ibid.
33 Ibid.
34 Prästeståndets protokoll 1859-1860 I, pp. 313-314.
35 Ibid. p. 316, pp. 313-316.
36 Ibid. p. 315.
37 Ibid. p. 315.
38 Hedvall 1978, pp. 138-148, quote p. 147.
39 Ibid. pp. 144-148; Borgarståndets protokoll 1859-60 III, p. 612 ff.
40 Ibid. p. 149.
41 Ibid.
42 Ibid.
43 Ibid.
44 Motioner Andra kammaren (Motions to the Lower House) 1870, no. 88.
45 Andra kammarens protokoll 1870:3, pp. 307-309.
46 Motioner Andra kammaren (Motions to the Lower House) 1871, no. 68.
47 Bihang till Riksdagens protokoll 1871 saml 2., adf 2., band 14., häft no. 25.
48 Andra kammarens protokoll 1871.
49 Bihang till Riksdagens protokoll 1871, saml 2., afd 1., band 7., häft no. 8, quote p. 5.
50 Ibid.
51 Ibid. p. 7.
52 Ibid. p. 7. Första kammaren protokoll 1871;4, p. 467 -469.
53 Motioner Första kammaren (Motions to the Upper House) 1875, no. 19 (FF Carlson) Motioner Andra kammaren (Motions to the Lower House) 1875, no. 126 (A W Staaff.)
54 Motioner Andra kammaren (Motions to the Lower House) 1875, no. 126, p. 23.
55 Ibid.
56 Motioner Första kammaren (Motions to the Upper House) 1875, no. 19 p. 25.
57 Ibid. p. 28.
58 Ibid. p. 29.
59 Ibid.
60 Ibid. p. 30.
61 Hedvall 1978, p. 158-159.
62 Bihang till Riksdagens protokoll 1875, 8 saml., 2 band., 14 häft. no. 21, quote pp. 2-3.
63 Ibid.
64 Bihang till Riksdagens protokoll 1875, 8 saml., 2 afd., 1 band., 4 häft. no. 4, p. 4.
65 Ibid.
66 Hedvall 1978 pp. 160-165.
67 Ibid. see footnote p. 165.
68 Hedvall 1978, pp. 158-165.
69 Första kammaren protokoll 1875:III 36, pp. 3-5.
70 Andra kammaren protokoll 1875:39:IV, pp. 5-9, quote p. 8.
71 Ibid. pp. 9 -19 quote p. 10.
72 Ibid.

73 Ibid. pp. 11.
74 Ibid. pp. 18-19.
75 Hedvall 1978, pp. 164-190.
76 Sandin 1986, chap. 6.
77 Hedvall 1978, pp. 146-169.
78 Borgarståndets protokoll 1859-1860 III, p. 612.
79 Ibid. pp. 612-614.
80 Ibid. Första kammarens protokoll 1875:111:36 p. 2-4. Andra kammarens protokoll 1875 IV, p. 5-9.
81 The presentation of the development of the urban school system is condensed from a not yet published study on the urban school system in Sweden and based on unpublished school council and school board minutes and documents from the period 1847-1880, from the Stockholm Board of Education, the school board and council in the Stockholm parishes of Katarina and Klara, and the school boards and councils in Malmö, Norrköping and Göteborg. (These records are kept in the city archives of these cities). In addition, the published annual reports and the statistics they contain are used, as well as material from the parliamentary records and unpublished demographic records from the census 1870 and 1880 for Stockholm, Norrköping, Gothenburg and Malmö from the archive of Statistiska Centralbyrån in Stockholm.
82 *Berättelse* rörande Göteborgs stads folkskoleväsende 1865-1866, p. 19.
83 Norrlid 1983.
84 Sandin 1992.

References

Andra kammaren protokoll 1875 IV., 1875:39:IV., 1870:3., 1871:1.
Berättelse rörande Göteborgs stads folkskoleväsende 1865. Göteborg 1866.
Bihang till Riksdagens protokoll *1871* saml 2., adf 2., band 14., häft no. 25. *1871*, saml 2., afd 1., band 7., häft no. 8. *1875*, 8 saml., 2 afd., 1 band., 4 häft. no 4. *1875*, 8 saml., 2 band., 14 häft. no 21.
Borgarståndets protokoll 1859 – 1860:III.
Civildepartementets Konseljakter 22.5.1852 Nr 3. Riksarkivet Stockholm.
Cunningham, Hugh, (1991): *The Children of the Poor: Representations of Childhood since the Seventeenth Century*, Oxford.
Fogelberg, T., (1973):"Den minderåriga arbetskraften inom glasindustrin" In *Kronobergsboken*.
Första kammarens protokoll 1871. 1875:III:36.
Gårdlund, Torsten, (1942): Industrialismens samhälle.
Hedvall, Barbro, (1978)· "Debatten om barnarbete i industri och hantverk 1850-1883" in *Ideologi och socialpolitik i 1800-talets Sverige*, ed. Hammarlund Ingrid. Uppsala.
Motioner Andra kammaren 1870 no. 88, 1871 no. 68, 1875 no. 126, 1875 no. 19.
Norrlid, Ingemar, (1983): *Demokrati, skatterättvisa och kommunal demokrati*. Lund.
Nygren, Rolf, (1982): "Barnarbete och arbetsavtalets frihet. En studie kring vår första samlade lagstiftning om skydd av minderårig arbetskraft i inudstriellt yrke." in *Kontroll och kontrollerade. Formell och informell kontroll i ett historiskt perspektiv*. Utg. S. Åkerman, Umeå. Olsson, Lars (1984): "Barns arbete och arbetets barn" in : Aronsson/ Cederblad/Dahl/Olsson/Sandin, *Barn i tid och rum*. Malmö.

Olsson, Lars, (1980): *Då barn var lönsamma.*
Olsson, Lars, (1983): "Den empiristiska eller den materialistiska historieuppfattningen som utgångspunkt för att förstå samhällsförändring", (Svensk) Historisk Tidskrift 2.
Prästeståndets protokoll 1856 – 1858, 1829 – 1860.
Sandin, Bengt, (1986): Hemmet, Gatan, Fabriken eller Skolan. Arkiv.
Sandin, Bengt, (1992): *The Creation of the Normal Child. Working Papers on Children and Childhood.* Department of Child Studies. Univ of Linköping, Linköping. Sweden.
Sellberg, Hjalmar, (1950): *Staten och arbetarskyddet 1850 – 1919.* Uppsala.
Svensk Författningsamling 1846:39. 1881:64.
Zelitzer, Vivianne, (1987): *Pricing the Prizeless Child: The Changing Social Value of Children,* New York.
Österberg, Eva, (1982): "Barnarbetet i Sverige" (Svensk) Historisk Tidskrift 1982:1.

Ellen Schrumpf

From full-time to part-time: working children in Norway from the nineteenth to the twentieth century

Norwegian childhood politicized

As the nineteenth century gave way to the twentieth, Norway was in the midst of a sweeping modernisation. Characteristic signs of modernisation were specialisation, division of labour, rationalization in society and in the work place, new social classes, individualism and the breaking away from nature, kin and one's destiny. Massive reforms were put into effect to build a modern Norway – with much of this reform zeal directed at the child and childhood. One example comes from the Central Office of Statistics, which was set up in 1875 with a brief to produce an overall view of the country's development and structure, as a basis for the planning of tomorrow's society. The first major task given to its Secretary was to discover the extent of child labour and to prepare legislation on this issue. Jacob Neumann Mohn's enquiry was the forerunner of the first labour law – the Factory Inspection Act of 1892. The most important features of this were that children under 12 years of age were forbidden to work in industrial undertakings and that work done by children and teenagers of between 12 and 18 years was to be regulated.[1]

The child and its childhood were also at the centre of major reforms in education. The Education Act of 1889 extended the duration of schooling and also the number of subjects in the elementary school curriculum. More school meant less work in a child's life. Furthermore, the laws were based on the principle of a common school for town and countryside.[2] *All* children were to be included, and the school was to be a mechanism for ironing out differences between the urban and rural communities and between social groups. Universality was also a core principle.[3] And the school was seen as an important element in nation building.

The principles of a school that town and country had in common, and of universality, presupposed that the State would look after the interests of the aberrant child. Therefore, in 1900 Norway became the first country in the world to set up an official child welfare agency. The law on the 'treatment of neglected children' was a trail-blazing one. Whenever the family, parents or guardians failed a child, the public authorities would step in and assume the responsibility.[4]

These are but a few of the many examples illustrating the great efforts made by the Norwegian authorities for children – at the turn of the 'children's century'.[5] The State became actively engaged in the development of a new childhood. The school and the public authorities took responsibility for and control of the child's upbringing at the expense of the family and the work place. Then as now it was universally accepted as a fundamental truth that the child was the father of the man and the mother of the woman, and that the child of today carried within it tomorrow's future. In a modern society it was important that the child's upbringing and development should be under official control. There were, however, differences of opinion about how childhood should be shaped. Consequently, it became politicized.

Childhood in Norway was undergoing a process of change, central to which was the changeover from work to school. That changeover is the theme of this chapter. Till then, work had been the most important socializing factor in a child's life. Through the social and cultural impact of the processes of work, the child was formed in terms of gender, age and social class. Now the school took over the role of the work place in shaping and socializing the child.

Children were a flexible labour force and took part in a wide range of paid and unpaid work inside and outside the home. Here we shall look first at children's *paid work*, starting with two statistical inquiries into the Norwegian children's participation in the work place. One was the already mentioned study of children's work carried out by Jacob Neumann Mohn in the years 1875-77.[6] The other was an inquiry into paid work among school children in Kristiania (Oslo) in 1912.[7] These provide the basis of the picture of children's paid work to be presented here: the kind of work undertaken by children, what they earned and how the work was organized. In addition, they provide the starting point for a discussion of the significance children's work had for the family, the society and for the child's development. Finally, the two inquiries will be brought together to highlight some of the important changes in children's work in the period 1875-1912.

Paid work was however only a small part of the work carried out by children inside and outside the household. Two actual accounts of childhood will give us an insight into the range, flexibility and totality of the tasks undertaken by children. They will tell us what the work meant to the child itself, and how it was remembered and retold in later life. Through their reminiscences the children assume the role they had in real life, and the one they have in this account of the experience of childhood. They were both participants and subjects and made an active contribution to their own development and to that of their families and local communities[8]. The child partly shaped him- or herself – and partly was shaped by others. Here we are dealing with Hans and Torleif, two boys who grew up in different parts of Norway – one before, the other after the turn of the century. Hans was born in 1865 in the rural community of Ulefoss. Torleif was born in the town of Porsgrunn in 1910.[9] The story of their childhood will both widen our perspective and help tie the statistics, representing the many thousands of anonymous children, to the experiences of two children's lives. They will help create a reality out of history and show just how the everyday life of a child and its upbringing in the family and in society worked out. But let us first look at the general picture.[10]

The child, work and school at the end of the nineteenth century

When The Department of the Interior gave Jacob Neumann Mohn the task of preparing a bill on 'the employment of children and young people for regular work outside the home,' he set to work with all the thoroughness and dedication expected of a senior public official at that time. By training Mohn was a lawyer. It was, however, through his work as a statistician he had gained a thorough understanding of the economic and social conditions in Norway. As he said himself, 'it was a matter of urgency that a carefully prepared and accurate account be drawn up of the extent and nature of the work currently carried out by the youth of our country.'[11] He also compiled a comprehensive account of other countries' laws on the subject. Furthermore, he made a thorough study of Norwegian schooling and surveyed the ways in which school and work had an impact on the child's life. In addition, he personally visited Norwegian factories to collect information on children's contact with and tasks in the work place. He visited one of the Danish factory inspectors to discover the impact of legislation in that country, and also referred to a large amount of written material, collected from the school directors in the towns, and from industrialists around the country, about the nature of the schooling and work experience of Norwegian children. Both the 1875 Census and the factory statistics from the 1870s were used. Thus, a perfectly solid piece of work accompanied the legislative proposal of 1878. It provided a good insight into the work carried out by Norwegian children.

Children's work in town and country

The main conclusion of Jacob Neumann Mohn's enquiry was that in the second half of the nineteenth century it was common practice for Norwegian children to work, and that they worked wherever there were opportunities for doing so. Consequently, children were to be found in a vast range of occupations. There were many similarities but also vast differences in what they did, both in the towns and in the countryside.

In 1875 over 13,000 children, aged 13–14 years, were registered in the rural districts as being in paid work outside the home. Jacob Neumann Mohn was well aware that his information was incomplete and that the totals in both censuses and the factory statistics were too low. He was, therefore, unable to say what percentage of all children were in paid work. It is not, however, the totals that are the most important. What Mohn's table gives us is the extent to which children were distributed across a wide range of different tasks and the differences between the sexes.

Children's work in Norway's rural districts, 1875

Occupation	Boys	Girls	Total
Servant	2767 (32%)	5533 (68%)	8300 (100%)
Shepherd, goatherd	1634 (68%)	756 (32%)	2390 (100%)
Milkmaid	–	98 (100%)	98 (100%)
Other work in agriculture, forestry, fishing	205 (91%)	19 (9%)	224 (100%)
Factory, mine	770 (74%)	268 (36%)	1038 (100%)
Handicraft	149 (96%)	6 (4%)	155 (100%)
Manufacturing matches	71 (51%)	67 (49%)	138 (100%)
Seamstress	–	21 (100%)	21 (100%)
Domestic crafts	30 (58%)	21 (42%)	51 (100%)
Building site	40 (100%)	–	49 (100%)
Trade	20 (91%)	2 (9%)	22 (100%)
Rafting	19 (100%)	–	19 (100%)
Seaman	46 (100%)	–	46 (100%)
Transport	44 (88%)	6 (22%)	50 (100%)
Running errands	222 (90%)	22 (10%)	244 (100%)
Railways, roads	19 (100%)	–	19 (100%)
Day labour	104 (61%)	56 (39%)	160 (100%)
Provision of food, drink, lodging	2 (50%)	2 (50%)	4 (100%)
	6151 (47%)	6877 (53%)	13028 (100%)

Source: Mohn (1878) Table – Appendix 1.

Surprisingly, Mohn found that in the rural districts more girls than boys were in paid work. The table shows that girls and boys had many activities in common: both went into service, worked in factories or herded animals. Some jobs were, however, clearly sex-specific. The running of errands was typically a boy's job – virtually no girls did it. Furthermore, only boys went to sea and worked on building sites, railways, roads and with timber rafting. On the other hand, we find only girl seamstresses and milkmaids working in the dairy. This suggests that both girls and boys followed in their parents' footsteps from childhood as to sexual division in the work place. As far as the rural districts were concerned, it seems that women took charge of the local and home-based work, while the men were occupied with activities further afield. Another significant feature is the tremendous variety of jobs undertaken by children. Children could make themselves useful and were to be found in just about every field of work: in the mines, in land and sea transport, in forestry, in the dried cod and fish processing industries, in craft and domestic industry, on building sites, on the docks, in cafes and inns.

Child workers were to be found as young as five or six years. Around 400, or 3 per cent of the more than 13,000 children, were under 10 years of age. Many of the very young were occupied in the home with outwork from the match factories. There, small boys and girls could be found, assembling and sticking matchboxes together.

Mohn had to admit that it was more difficult to establish the extent of children's work in the towns. The census returns were unreliable – so it was impossible to produce the same statistics as he had in the rural districts. But children's work was just as widespread and the range of tasks just as many. On one hand, many tasks were the same as in the countryside. Town children went into service, minded young children, herded animals, took part in potato picking, worked on farms and in gardens. In the coastal towns children were involved in the fisheries, and helped with the washing and drying of cod. On the other hand, factory work was more widespread among town children, and, in general, the towns could offer a wider range of work opportunities. Delivering messages was typically a child's occupation in the towns; also, delivering papers, taking food to the workplace, carrying goods to and from the markets and quays, delivering beer. They were active in retailing in the market and on the streets. Children were paid to sweep streets, tend lights, chop wood and stack timber, bricks, etc. on the building sites. Children were often to be found loading ice, laying paving stones and acting as bricklayers' mates. They were in dance halls, restaurants and other places of recreation. They even worked as travelling acrobats, tightrope walkers and bareback riders. This part of Mohn's inquiry does not distinguish between male and female work, but one must reckon that, as in the countryside, the children's work in the towns was similarly sex specific – with the girls' work to a greater extent linked to the home.

The broad spectrum of work opportunities for children in town and country shows that their entry into the labour market was open and provided many opportunities for different types of work. It also suggests that children were an accepted element on the work place. In commenting on the participation of children, Mohn remarked:

> The above shows that child labour has penetrated, to a greater or lesser extent, most fields of activity in this country.[12]

The variety of tasks undertaken by children also suggests that they were flexible and that *flexibility* was one of their advantages in the labour market. In the early years of industrialisation, output took place unevenly with a greater seasonal element than later. Moreover, adult workers were less committed to their work. Edvard Bull, the Norwegian social historian, argued that not tying one down to a particular work place was part of that independent streak, which was such a feature of unskilled day labourers in nineteenth century Norway. [13] Workers moved from one work place to another. The flexibility inherent in child labour helped to even out the irregularities in the working year, so that one did not end with a backlog. Children helped eliminate the bottlenecks in the production process. They went in and out of different jobs, taking work where they were needed. Work also suited the needs of the family and the household. The rhythm of children's work was decided by the family cycle and the possibilities offered by the labour market.[14] These constant changes broke down the boundary between life inside and outside the home. This flexibility and the loose links with the world of work are partly why it was so difficult to make a record of children's work. A statistical account of such a complex matter was *no* easy task.

The Department of the Interior had also given Jacob Neumann Mohn the task of highlighting the *unfortunate* aspects of child labour. He did not find many. Like his contemporaries he had no objection in principle to children working. Children's work was accepted as a good thing. It kept children occupied and contributed positively to their upbringing. In only a few areas was it felt necessary to regulate and/or forbid child labour: principally in factories, mining, crafts and herding. It was argued that much of the work in these areas damaged children's health. In both factories and workshops children were exposed to noise and accidents. Poorly clad shepherds and goatherds suffered from colds and lung ailments, when they were looking after animals during late, chilly autumn evenings. Apart from their health, children needed moral protection. Children's morals and their moral conduct were at stake when they worked in bars and other places of entertainment, or when, on a tour, they took part in public performances. Worries about health and morals were also in keeping with contemporary line of thought. A campaign on diet and hygiene was carried out across the country and, within a few years, the debate on morals and moral conduct was to become *the* major cultural conflict in Norway.[15] Health, hygiene and morality were important components in the creation of a modern Norway. Children were in the centre of this. They were especially in need of protection.

Children in the factories

When children worked in factories both their health and their morals were at risk. Not only were the premises dirty and polluted, the human environment also exposed the children to dangerous elements. Karl Marx, in writing of the unfortunate influences children working in industry were exposed to, had this to say:

> The crude language they heard from their tenderest years, the indecent and shameless behaviour, which unknowing and lost they grew up with, makes them lawless, depraved and slovenly for the rest of their lives.[16]

Daily contacts with a 'coarse and brutal' working class produced measures to control and protect the coming generation exposed to industrialization. Also, in Norway children's work in factories was the subject of special attention. In 1875 the country had little modern industry. Of a total of 45,000 industrial workers about 3,000 were children, i.e. around 7 per cent. Nevertheless, from 1870 the number of children working in industry had risen by 60 per cent. Mohn's inquiry was therefore conducted at a time when the extent of child labour was on the increase and seemed destined to reach a considerable size. This caused alarm in some quarters and was one reason the inquiry was set up. That children would put paid work before schooling, was also a cause for concern. Mohn discovered that, compared with other countries, there were a relatively large number of children in the Norwegian industry.

> Our factories, compared to those of other countries, appear to employ many, and in several important branches, very many children. (…) They are to be found more or less established in all of the most important kinds of industrial activity.[17]

Given that there was insufficient registration, Mohn found the following distribution of children working in factories. They were found in both the 'old' and the 'new' industries.

Children as a percentage of the workforce in several branches of Norwegian industry in 1875

Industry	Total workforce	Children as a % of the workforce	Boys	Girls
Tobacco	613	43	508	105
Matches	422	33	246	176
Glass	143	18	139	4
Spinning/weaving	301	8	154	147
Sawmill	793	6-7	793	–

Source: Mohn 1878, Table – Appendix 3.

Factories were primarily the workplaces for boys. In all branches of industry more boys than girls were found.

Some industries stood out as having an especially large number of children employed. For instance, in 1875, every other worker in the tobacco industry was a child – with five times as many boys as girls. The balance between the sexes was more even in the matchmaking industry, where around one third of the workers were children. The share of children in the glass industry, was also high, and here there were virtually no girls. The total *number* of children was at its highest in the saw and planing mills, but the *proportion* was lower. And there were no girls in the sawmills.

At this time the saw and lumber industries were the country's most important industrial enterprises. The sawmill industry had a long history, reaching back to the sixteenth century. There was a long tradition of child labour in the industry.[18] One might argue that children were part of the old labour force and that the children working in industry, as registered by Mohn in the 1870s, were no new phenomenon. Rather it was the continuation of an old industrial tradition. This was prolonged in the newly 'industrialized' old enterprises and carried into the new.[19] A general explanation as to why some activities were open to many children, while others were open to boys but not to girls, is unlikely to be

Sawmills had more children under 15 years of age than any other Norwegian industry. This photo from Sellebekk Sawmill in Østfold (1898) shows young male workers in the front row and in the upper left corner. (Arbeiderbevægelsens arkiv og bibliotek, Oslo)

forthcoming. The explanations will be specific to particular industries and particular localities, based upon methods of production, technology and local work cultures, employment opportunities in each locality and the local traditions as to the upbringing of children. Methods of recruitment are also important. Often particular jobs were passed from one generation to the next. Boys and girls came into a factory next to their mother and father – as Mohn also observed.

> When one looks at the individual factory or the individual workplace, one usually finds that the workers employed there obtained employment for their children at the same enterprise or in the same place.[20]

A persistent feature of industrial work for children was that they were found everywhere. They worked in rope walks, in fish fertilizer factories, in spinning mills, brick works, breweries, the canning industry, nail making factories – to mention but a few of their activities. Most children working in factories were over 10 years of age. Six per cent were under 10. There was some division of labour by age and this had to do, among other factors, with the fact that some tasks demanded a certain amount of physical strength. Therefore, the somewhat older children were found in the factories. The youngest children were mostly at home, doing unpaid work. This applied also to girls. While the socialization of boys often took place in the company of their fathers in paid work, the girls learned their adult roles from their mothers in the household or in paid domestic service. The household was an important work place for many children and as both paid and unpaid workers, children played an important role in the family economy.

Children in the factories: hours of work, school and pay

Whether working at home or outside it, the child's job was to assist the adults. Children and adults worked as a team, each depended upon the other. A child's hours of work were therefore fixed. They had just as long a workday as the adults.

> The adults' activities are based upon the help they receive from the young so they cannot allow them more control over their time (...). In general, the children's' work day is as fixed as that of the adults.[21]

Mohn found that in the 1870s the working day for children employed in factories in the countryside was between 10 and 11 hours. In the towns it was shorter, around 10 hours. If the children in the towns went to school every day, then they went to the factory either in the morning or the afternoon. They then worked 5-6 hours in every 24. In the countryside children went to school only every other day. Most children went to school two days a week and to the factory for four. Some had three days at school and three days in the factory. At several glassworks children worked every day and went to school in the evening. Some work was seasonal, for instance, at the saw mills. In the winter ice on the river hindered production and brought the mills to a standstill for various lengths of time. Thus, boys at the sawmills went to school in the winter and worked during the summer. When the mills were operating, they had to exploit all their resources to the utmost: the working day lasted 12 hours and a shift system operated. The children also worked shifts – including the night shift. At the Ulefoss Sawmill this was arranged as follows:

> The shift ran from 12 noon to 12 midnight – with the next from 12 midnight to 12 noon. It might happen, when there were two boys of the same age each doing a different shift, they had to be escorted to work, especially when it was dark. Usually, the mother took the one who began work at midnight and brought the other home.[22]

There were also many alternative arrangements. The allocation of time to school or work depended upon the nature of the work and whether the child was in a rural or an urban school. In general, a child's day was organised so that its time out of school was filled with work.

> Day after day a full day's work was done so that any time outside school hours was completely filled.[23]

The length of time filled by work and school was different for children in the town and in the countryside. Mohn found it to be as follows.

Total number of hours spent annually in school and at the factory – in the towns and country districts

	School	*Work*
Rural child	400	2000
Urban child	750	1750

Source: Mohn 1878, pp. 16-18

If children attended school for the prescribed number of hours, then the child who worked at a factory in the town spent almost twice as much time at school as his country cousin. Moreover, children in the countryside spent five times as much time in the factory as in the school, while children in the town spent only slightly more than twice as much. The country child was thus to a greater extent a worker, and his urban counterpart, a scholar. On the other hand, both groups of children spent a long time every year in the factory. It was their main sphere of activity. Mohn, in any case remarked that in reality *all* children spent more time at work and less at school, because more often than not the latter was neglected in favour of the former. There were also similarities and differences in the life of the urban and rural child. One significant difference was that in the towns, children both attended school and went to work simultaneously throughout the year – unlike in the countryside where work and schooling was decided by the seasons. Children worked in the summer and went to school in the winter. Nevertheless, work and school were adjusted to fit the lives of all children. That many children played truant suggests that work often took precedence to schooling. Other reasons for missing school might be that the pupils lacked clothes and shoes, or it was a long way to school, or the parents were not concerned about their children's education at school. It might also be an expression of protest on the parents' part against the religious and ideological indoctrination to which the children were exposed at school.[24]

Children had just as long a working day as adults, but a shorter working year. Nor did they carry out the same work. For children had smaller physical frames, less strength and experience. So the work was adjusted to suit the child:

> As to the work to which the young are put in the factories, there is, in general, a natural limit, which is decided by their being less strong and having had less practise. The heavier work and the immediate control of the machines are not their concern. In the main, their job is, partly, to carry out lighter labour jobs for the adults and, partly, to perform various simple secondary operations, which, as a rule, still bear such a relationship to the main activity that they determine its success.[25]

Factory children were treated – and regarded – both as workers and as children. The fact that they worked a long day together with adults – and without any special protection under the law – shaped them as adults. Their more sporadic connections with the work place, their shorter work year, and that they were assigned special tasks, shaped them as children. In the factories the children were not responsible for the actual output. They assisted the adults. Yet they were an essential part of the production chain. They had to carry out their work at the right time and in the correct tempo so the productive process moved as it should. For example, at the sawmills the boys had to carry timber to the saw by the chute or carry finished beams and planks into the yard. There they tagged and stacked them. They swept the place, cleared away and chopped the scrap timber. They helped the sawmaster. They were an essential part of the production process – and thus they earned a position in the work place that was both meaningful and responsible. This was the foundation for the mutual respect adults and children had for each other – and for the children's sense of themselves as both useful and necessary. This sense of their worth of self was reinforced by the fact that children earned good wages for the work they did. Mohn discovered that the average income of a child working in a factory was high. In fact, he thought it was extraordinarily so, in relation to what the children did, and that employers found it unrenumerative.

> At least in this country, as well as elsewhere, one not infrequently hears or reads the comments of employers, to the effect that child labour is, in essence, of little value to them. Children are frequently taken on at the request of their parents, who want them to make themselves useful. This is especially so when their fathers work in the same place.[26]

It is difficult to judge the relationship between what children contributed by their labour and what they earned. But children could earn 160 kroner annually, and, if they worked every day, as much as 400 kroner. An adult worker earned around 800 kroner annually. In other words, a child working in a factory could earn up to half an adult wage. Such pay was more or less the same in both the countryside and in the town. There is no mention of differences in the wages paid to boys and girls. The implication of this is that at the end of a week in the factory, both girls and boys took home a relatively full wage packet, which might cover a considerable part of a family's expenditures. We can imagine several situations like this one:

> I got 0.75 kroner a day. When the season ended and my account was settled, I had 60 kroner. The manager scarcely trusted me to go home with the money. I was almost in tears. In the end I got the money. When I got home, I said to my dad: 'Now we'll go and buy some cotton cloth to make trousers and a jacket for me'. That came to 7-8 kroner. "The rest you can have to pay off some of our debt at the shop." I thought that would mean we would be creditworthy again, and that turned out to be the case.[27]

The good wages earned by children show that it was not a child's wage they received, in the sense that it was based on their age. The children were paid as workers. True, they were not fully mature workers. That is why they were not paid as much. But the work they did and the money they earned related to the tasks they undertook[28]. Children were paid according to their contribution. We have seen that when the boy, we have cited above, came home from the sawmill with his first pay packet, his contribution had a significant impact on his family's economic well-being. However, it is also possible that it had a social and cultural impact as well. It meant something for the child's position in the community and in the family. It had an influence on child-adult relationships. Pay said something about the child as a child – and as a worker. It shaped a child's identity and self image.

To sum up, we can suggest that Jacob Neumann Mohn's inquiry into child labour in Norway in the 1870s sprang from a time and a culture in which work was a way of life. To most people life meant work – and work gave both meaning and content to one's existence. Work was economically necessary, but it was also a norm and a *mentalité* that embraced all; women and men, children, adults, the elderly.[29] A family's economy and livelihood were based on work. In cooperating around this purpose, its members became a social and cultural entity. Through work children were given practical skills, they acquired social roles and were shaped culturally. What they learned was mostly through practical work and less from school, although the actual balance between the two

From full-time to part-time

depended on whether one grew up in the town or in the country, and whether one was a boy or a girl. Their entire upbringing was based on the kin group and under the family's control. A whole way of life was transmitted from one generation to the next. This transfer – through work and with the child as the central link – was at the heart of family formation, and the development of society as well.[30]

Schoolchildren in Kristiania, 1912: work and school

A generation later, in 1912, a large questionnaire-based inquiry was carried out among Kristiania's schoolchildren, to find out the extent to which they took part in paid work.[31] This initiative was taken by the Kristiania School Board. Class teachers were responsible for collecting the information from their pupils. Therefore, educational authorities and the teachers had a central role in this inquiry. The results showed that children continued to do paid work, with one in five schoolchildren in Kristiania engaged in it: one in three boys and one in ten girls[32]. Although children worked, they also attended school each day. Work was adjusted to their schooling. The majority went to school in the morning and worked in the afternoon. Three out of four working boys were errand boys – one-half of the girls were in service. Only 2 per cent of the children worked in factories. Otherwise, we find children working in cinemas, theatres, cafés and restaurants, in shops, and with veterinarians.[33]

On average the children worked between three and five hours a day, with the boys doing slightly more than four hours, the girls around three. The boys had the better wages: 2.40 kroner a week or 120 kroner a year. The girls earned about half as much. The difference was greater than the difference in the working hours would indicate. The work of girls was not valued as much as that of boys. This was part of the general sexual division of renumeration levels – of which children's work was but a part. Within this, the girls' roles and tasks were regarded as less significant than those of the boys.[34] Boys were closer to the heart of the money economy and to the support of their families, both in the long and short term. Most girls were in service. This had become a job for females and was one of the poorest-paid occupations – for adults and for children.

There was a big difference between the pay of children and adults. For example, in 1914 an adult pottery worker earned 800 kroner annually and a skilled craftsman about double that amount.[35] In other words, while a well-paid boy in 1875 *could* earn as much as around one-half of an adult worker's pay, the gap between the two had widened considerably by 1912. By then adult workers earned often many times as much as well-paid elementary school children in the towns. The main reason for this was that the total hours the children spent working had been drastically reduced by 1912. At that date children were part time workers. Their *hourly rate* was however relatively high, and the less hours they worked the higher it was. Thus, a boy who worked less than one hour a day earned almost three times as much per hour (19 øre) than one with a working day of between six and eight hours (7.2 øre). Taken as a whole, however, children working part time in 1912 were able to contribute a significantly smaller sum to the maintenance of their families. To board and lodge a child cost 5.25 kroner a week, according to Kristiania's Local Health Insurance Board.[36] The average pay of a boy was 2.40 kroner, which would barely cover half of this expenditure. Children working part-time were far from able to support themselves. This applied especially to girls. Thus, the children's pay meant far less for both the family and the child than it had a few decades earlier, when they were well able to support themselves on the wages they earned.

Even in 1912 some children did paid work at a very young age. Almost 300 children were seven years or younger when they began their working lives. Some of the elementary school pupils said they had been as young as three years of age. But the older the children were the more work they did, adjusting it to their schoolwork. Although school took up much more of a child's day than it had some decades earlier, there is no evidence to suggest any conflict between work and school. Teachers, when asked if they felt that paid work meant that school work was neglected, somewhat surprisingly replied that it did not seem to affect attendance or cause any significant problems. Less attention might be paid to homework and if the combination of schoolwork and paid work was too long, then this reduced the child's time for rest and play. But the teachers stressed that work was good for children. They became accustomed to orderliness, obedience and punctuality. Children learned to use their time to the best advantage, to make the most of it. Work kept children off the streets and helped to keep them in check. In fact, school and work was an ideal combination. Children learned both abstract and practical skills and adjusted to the demands of society with good morals and an effective use of their time. The inquiry had to admit that the children who worked were often the best pupils in the class.

> A short period of work each day must be regarded as a good thing, especially for children aged 11-12 years and above. Children get accustomed to orderliness and obedience and they gain routine in how to use their time. Besides, work keeps them out of mischief on the streets. Many schoolmasters and schoolmistresses say that children who work are often the most diligent and the brightest of their pupils. (...) It is worth noting that the

abovementioned Danish inquiry of 1908 was not able to show that gainful employment had any unfortunate impact on teaching. The inquiry asked if a pupil belonged to the brightest, middle or weakest third of the class. That no result was forthcoming from this was explained by the State Office of Statistics as due to the fact that employers preferred to take on children who were the best equipped, mentally and physically. This was, as indicated above, what was found by this inquiry.[37]

In the 1870s it was the schools that had warned of the unfortunate impact of work on a child's schooling.[38] In 1912 teachers had to acknowledge that children who worked were among the schools' best equipped, both mentally and physically, and that work in no way adversely affected a child's health, at least not the boys. Boys who worked were less likely to be ill than those who did not. However, for girls the reverse was the case. That was not because of work itself but its nature and where it took place, often it was indoors.

> On the other hand, the state of health of the girls who work is much worse than it is among those who do not. (…) That the situation is so much worse for girls is more likely due to the indirect results of the work than to the work itself, and especially the fact that working girls are more often required to remain indoors.[39]

While boys ran about in the fresh air as delivery and messenger boys, the girls' health was weakened in badly ventilated houses and often through heavy physical work. Common to boys and girls, however, was exposure to *moral* dangers at work. Certain moral limits were not to be transgressed. Girls should not work for men living alone. It was also not proper that either girls or boys model for artists, work for hotdog sellers at night, or work in the entertainment business. If these limits were observed, however, work could actually strengthen a child's moral sense.

The best pupils, mentally and physically, in the school class were working. Neither socially nor economically were all Kristiania's child workers badly off. Kristiania was divided along social lines into a better-off West End and a working-class East End. The child workers were almost equally divided between schools in the two areas. If anything, children attending schools in the centre and west of the town were more likely to have jobs than those from the east side. This distribution was also reflected in the social classes to which the working children belonged. In families where the main breadwinner was self-employed, one in five boys had paid work. Approximately the same proportion did so where the main breadwinner was a factory worker. In the families of senior public servants, however, only one in ten boys was in paid work.[40] This suggests that it was cultural influences, in the form of *mentalité* and childrearing principles – rather than purely economic considerations – that were at the root of many families' desire that their children should, or should not, work. In other families, however, economic necessity might be more pressing. This was, for example, the case where single women were the family's main breadwinner. Usually, they worked in badly paid women's jobs such as sewing, laundering and cleaning. That one in three children in such families had paid work was probably the result of economic need.

Children in work from 1875-1912: continuity and change

By placing the two inquiries together, we can compare their findings. The comparison must be carried out with care for the two inquiries are very different from each other. This applies to both the children who were the subject of the inquiries and the way the inquiries were carried out. In quantitative terms both are flawed and not at all comparable. But the qualitative elements give us an insight into contemporary views on children's work and its significance for society for the family and the child's upbringing. It is then based on this qualitative material that a comparison will be made and a summing up attempted.

The picture is one of *work* as an important feature of childhood. This was the case throughout the period 1875-1912. At the beginning of the period, work itself was the way a child entered adulthood. Children assisted adults. They worked side by side. Often children occupied an essential place in the production process. In addition, they were flexible, with flexibility as their supreme advantage – from a work point of view. Through their place in the labour force they were integrated into society and family, both socially and culturally. Through work they became useful and significant.

Throughout the period children tackled a wide range of jobs. They were everywhere that work was to be found and they were paid for the work they did. As full-time workers they were paid well, especially the boys. At the beginning of the period children could more than support themselves through the wages they contributed to the family economy. Later a reduction in the number of hours they worked meant their pay and contribution to the family fell sharply.

Recruitment was wide-ranging. This appears clearly from the 1912 inquiry. It was not just children from the poorest families who had paid work, but also children from the families of senior public officials and the self-employed. Money was not always the reason why parents wanted their children to work. Rather an important explanation lay in the fact that work was the norm. It accorded with the principles of childrearing.

Changes in children's work had above all to do with changes in hours of work. The length of the working day fell. While it was common in the 1870s for this to last 10 hours, by 1912 merely a small proportion of children's work lasted for such a long day.[41] There was less room for work in a child's life, more for school and organized, or unorganized, leisure time. Yet there continued to be many children in the towns, and probably even more in the countryside, who still had paid work in 1912. Children's work continued to be socially acceptable. But it now took second position in a child's life.

Child labour also changed its character. Whereas Jacob Neumann Mohn had found an enormous number of children in factories in the 1870s, very few remained there in 1912.[42] By that date children working full-time and children working in industry were virtually a thing of the past. Essentially, children were now part-time workers as domestic servants or employed in the service sector generally. The work was child-specific, organized outside the family and cut off from the world of adult labour. It did not provide children with a training for future work. The school was now the most important agent of socialization for the child, at least in the towns. It filled a child's day: 'Since then (1870s – my note) schooling has increased dramatically. So to work 14 hours in 24, as then, would simply not be possible, was how document No. 36 summed up the matter.[43] While in the 1870s it had been the school authorities who had taken the initiative to ensure that child labour was regulated and adjusted to the needs of the school, by 1912 teachers were happily able to say that the school had now taken first priority in a child's life. The working child had become the schoolchild.

These two inquiries have described the character of children's work, its organization and its place in the life of the child, the family and society at large. They have also shown the changes that occurred. So far, our story has been about the many and about child labour seen from the outside. By writing down the reminiscences of individual workers it is, however, possible to link our quantitatively based story to a qualitative assessment, a view from the inside – as expressed by two boys who lived through it. What place did work have in their lives? What meaning did it have for those who actually experienced it? The children are called Hans and Torleif. Based on their accounts we shall reconstruct and compare two children's lives. But we shall also widen the perspective. Our analysis of the childhood of Hans and Torleif will enable us to construct two models: one of the child in the traditional society, the other in the modern. Thus, their stories will deepen our understanding of their lives and contribute to a greater understanding of the development of the modern child.

Two accounts of childhood

Hans Olsen Solvold was born in 1865 in Holla, Telemark country. He grew up in a family attached to the Ulefoss Sawmill towards the end of the last century, his father being a master sawyer. His mother was from Kviteseid and had worked on a mountain farm before she married and moved to the sawmill. The family lived on a cotter's holding, belonging to the home farm at Ulefoss. There were six children of which five grew up in reasonable comfort. They lived in a house that was standard for that time at Ulefoss. There were a living room and a kitchen. The children lay two or three in a bed, a homemade affair filled with straw and wood shavings. Fleas were thriving in beds like this. The everyday fare included flat-bread, homebaked rye bread, porridge, herring and potatoes. They kept a pig, which was killed in the autumn. So on Sundays and feast days they had meat or fried pork. Their clothes were made of linen or homespun cloth. Hans's mother made his clothes. They had leather shoes in the winter, but in summer they went barefoot.

The livelihood of the family was quite adequate, it was said. It was many-sided too, with the whole family contributing. Hans began to work at an early age. He was flexible and stepped in where he was needed. At first he worked at home with his mother. He watched the cows, worked on the arable land and chopped wood. He was seven years old when he began to go to school. At eight and a half he began work with his father – a master sawyer – at the sawmill. He was a boy-helper. He worked 12 hours a day earning about 60 øre. With this he could buy either a kilo of pork, half a kilo of butter, 10 kilos of potatoes or six loaves.[44] It would seem that Hans could more than satisfy his own nutritional requirements. The sawmill was in operation during the summer half of the year. It ceased production in the winter, at which time Hans went to the work's school. The school was a small, red-timbered building situated among the houses of the workers and the work's buildings. The school was open every other day from 9.00 am to 3.30 pm with a one-hour break in the middle of the day. This private work's school was a good one. Hans recalled that the teachers were strict, but clever. He learned to read and write and do arithmetic. He studied a bit of religion, some geography and some history. But he had no practical subjects. When they were introduced, following the 1889 Education Act, they were for a long time taught outside the normal school hours. The subject gymnastics was not introduced until 1910.[45] Practical things were learned outside the school. School was a place for book learning only. At 14 Hans was confirmed. That was the end of his schooling and he began to work fulltime at the sawmill like the other adult workers. He lived at home until his marriage in 1893. He was then 28. His parents managed his money until he was 20 years of age. After that he paid for his own upkeep.

Torleif Albretsen was born in 1910, a generation and a half later, in the town of Porsgrunn also in Telemark country. His father was a jack of all trades and changing jobs often. He worked in a bicycle factory, trained to become a baker and ended as a stevedore for Norsk Hydro. His mother stayed at home. She and her husband had six children, two of whom died of tuberculosis. The family occupied a small house on the east side of Porsgrunn. It contained a kitchen, living room and bedroom downstairs and two small rooms in the loft. The living room was only used on special occasions. Electricity was installed, but water and the lavatory were outside. They had a pig and hens in the back garden. There was also an outhouse. Torleif's father fished and sold a little of what he caught. His mother was clever at everything she did, said Torleif. She made the boys' suits. They had enough to be able to share with others, if the need arose. A parish nurse lived nearby and she would generally come with an empty container on the days she knew they had freshly made soup.

For seven years Torleif went to the elementary school on Porsgrunn's east side. It was a custom-built general school in large new buildings of a modern design. When he was between 10 and 12 years of age, Torleif began to use his leisure time to deliver newspapers, along with his brother. He earned 25 kroner a month. He kept five kroner and gave his mother the rest to save. It was to be used to buy his clothes. One thing he had learned. If he were going to buy anything he would pay cash. Finished with elementary school, many of Torleif's friends went on to secondary school. He did not. He said he was dyslexic. He wanted to go to sea, but his mother was against it. Instead, aged 15, he began work at the in porcelain factory Porsgrunn. He was employed as a painter and did straw patterns. He earned good money as an apprentice painter: 40 øre an hour. That was half of what a fully trained man received. Some of his wages went to pay for his keep at home, the rest he kept himself, for visits to the cinema and other places of entertainment. He lived at home until he was married, aged 27.

This is a brief account of the childhood of two boys and children, as they remembered and later retold it. Their accounts fitted well in the picture painted by the statistical inquiries into childhood. Like the children in the statistics, Hans and Torleif *both* went to school *and* to work. Furthermore, both contributed to a livelihood made up of many different jobs. At first they contributed through unpaid work in the home. There they worked with their mother, lending her a hand as needed. She was responsible for a wide range of household jobs, involving many types of productive and reproductive work. She needed the labour the children could provide. Later they went out to work, their earnings going to support the family's economy.

They had much in common, but there were also important differences. To a large extent these stemmed from the difference between a more traditional childhood based on work and a more modern one based on school. Allowing for the fact that the individual child's life was made up of the present and the past, and that both the traditional and the modern contributed to the process, we call childhood, we shall nevertheless analyse the two experiences based on this one overriding perspective: that their childhood was a product of the tension between the traditional and the modern.

So far as *work* was concerned it stood at the heart of Hans's life as a child and took more of his *time*. Hans belonged to a culture where work was a way of life, and since he was quite small, his day was filled with a variety of jobs. They began with his working at home alongside his mother. Later he went out to do paid work at the sawmill. He also went to the school at the works. School was important but work came first. School was adjusted to his working life, adapted to it. It functioned only on a seasonal basis – and then every second day.

School took up most of Torleif's childhood from the age of seven to fifteen. It operated every day and throughout the year. Torleif also worked, but either before or after school. School came first. As for the time they filled, school and work swapped places in the childhood experiences of Hans and Torleif. While work took the leading role in Hans's life, school did so for Torleif. After seven years of elementary school, Torleif, a working class child, could have continued, but because of his dyslexia he was convinced that he did not have the necessary qualifications for secondary school.

Work then played a different part and had a different meaning for the two boys' childhood. Hans was well trained for his future job and socialised into adult life in the widest possible sense through work. He was employed at a sawmill where the work passed, as an inheritance, from one generation to the next. He worked together with his father. Thus the practicalities of work, its social roles and culture were transferred from father to son. The foundation for continuity and stability in both the family and society lay in the work recruitment and work training.

Torleif's early work experiences were not a part of family-based, practical training. Consequently, Torleif's father had neither control of nor influence upon his son's work training and introduction to adult roles.[46] Training and socialization were to a much greater extent outside the family's control and placed in institutions where adult professionals had a hand in the child's training. These professional educators were above all teachers, but psychologists, doctors and psychiatrists also came to have an important place in a child's life. The child and childhood were subjected to scientific analysis, simultaneously as they were institutionalized. One imagines that with such a development feeling for kin would be weakened, and the family itself would take on a different role and meaning in a child's life.[47]

Nevertheless, Torleif did gain useful work experience as a newspaper boy. He had to learn how to dispose of his time and get used to the rhythm of work.

He had to learn to be punctual and responsible as far as money was concerned. Through his work he was socialized into an urban, industrial society's rhythms, roles and *mentalité*. But this work did not lead to a particular occupation in the future. As a newspaper boy Torleif worked in specifically a child's job, as did the children in the Kristiania inquiry. What is more, he worked in a typical boy's job in towns around the turn of the century. Not until he was 15 did he begin to work in the place that was to be his future, namely the porcelain factory. Torleif's career both at school and at work, reflected the provisions of the new education and factory acts.

So the school was more important to Torleif's upbringing. It also had a different function and meaning in the lives of the two children. At the work's school in Ulefoss, Hans acquired a knowledge of the basics. Practical subjects had no place there. The school and the community were bound together as one. The little school house did not even look very different from the other houses in the sawmill's environs.

The school played quite a different role in the urban society of Porsgrunn. It was both more pervasive and more restrictive. For example, attendance was more strictly controlled. Absence led to parents being called before the school board, and repeated absenteeism was punished with fines.[48] In many ways the Porsgrunn school was a cultural system that drew Torleif away from his roots in the family and neighbourhood.[49] The modern school buildings on Porsgrunn's east side were large, even monumental. One imagines that Torleif and his parents must have felt strange and of little consequence when they walked into the Porsgrunn school grounds.[50]

Torleif spent much of his childhood at school. There he acquired abstract and theoretical knowledge and some practical skills. Through the learning process itself he was shaped as an individual. To learn to read and write lays the foundation of an identity and defines one as an autonomous individual. Torleif was turned inwards focusing on himself. "Children are perforce withdrawn from face-to-face communities," Barbara Finkelstein says about learning from the book.[51] The school also promotes the merits of rationality, individualism and precision. The foundation of the school itself was the idea of enlightenment and a belief in reason. The foundations of individualism were best laid by competition for top marks between the pupils themselves. Torleif failed there because he was dyslexic. The strict demands of the timetable itself promoted punctuality. For Torleif the school bell was a source of authority. That it had a powerful hold on the children was shown by the way they fell into straight lines as soon as they heard its ring.[52] There was no school bell at Ulefoss. Hans and the other children were called in by the teacher.

Torleif was probably less physically tired than Hans, though mentally more so, when he went to bed at night. But the body was also an important instru-

Uleforss Sawmill provided primary education for children in the community. Hans O. Solvold attended this school during the 1870s. (Holla Historielag, Ulefoss)

ment in modern culture. It had to be kept strong, in fighting trim, unflinching and able to reproduce itself.[53] Physical education was introduced into the school as a compulsory subject – an hour a week on Torleif's timetable.[54] The new athletics movement aimed at enrolling working class children in the conquest of the body. *Porsgrund Gymnastics Club* was established in 1880, and by the turn of the century, associations and clubs covered most forms of athletics, gymnastics, skiing, skating, swimming, rowing, wrestling, football and track events[55]. There was no gymnastics at school for Hans. At Ulefoss it was thought unnecessary and was not introduced as a school subject until 1910.[56]

Children's pay also had a different role and a different meaning in the lives of Hans and Torleif. It moulded them differently. The money Hans earned went in full into the family's common purse until he was well into his twenties. Personally he had nothing at his disposal. Indirectly, however, he could take pleasure in the fact that what he earned served to increase the family budget. The traditional family economy based on all pay going into a common purse shaped it into a collectivity. Nevertheless, it also had a significance for Hans's view of himself as someone who was both useful and needed.

As far as Torleif was concerned he kept a part of his pay and used it for pleasure. The rest was laid aside to be used to buy his clothes. When he became an adult he continued to live at home and paid his parents for his upkeep. Consequently, his pay was to a greater extent his own, even though it also eased the family budget somewhat. Nevertheless, his pay had a different orientation to that of the family income economy. It was geared to Torleif's person and contributed to a greater extent to shape him as an individual.

Torleif belonged to a more modern family in which the housewife and children were assigned specific jobs. The mother was to make sure that Torleif and the other children grew up in a healthy, hygienic, natural, private, loving and sheltered environment.[57] It was possible for her to accomplish this because the family was *materially* so much better off than the working class family in Ulefoss. Torleif, as he grew up, had a more varied diet, he was dressed in clothes brought at the shop, and his home was more spacious. But there was a cultural side to this higher material standard. New and increased demands were made on childrearing. In as much as Torleif's father occupied a less central role in the socialization of his children, because his sons did not work beside him, so the mother became the central figure. Mother and child formed the ideological and emotional core of the modern family. Childrearing was to advance an inner harmony and social responsibility.

The working class family embraced new ideals: it should be proud and respectable. One expression of this was that Torleif's family had 'a room for best use'. It symbolized the fact that the family had more than absolutely necessary: a room that was not used every day, but only for special occasions. Another feature underlined by Torleif was that his family did not depend on support from others and had sufficient means to give – out of feelings of common human concern – to others in need. In keeping with this it was also important that the family paid cash for whatever was bought. Torleif's family was then representing of a proud and respectable working class.[58]

It has been argued that the respectable working class family had been transformed into 'bourgeoisie' and, thus, the modern child was a middle class child. Possibly the process of becoming bourgeoisie for the working class family in Porsgrunn could be explained by the fact that it was exposed to an ideological pressure exerted through an all-pervasive campaign covering housekeeping, looking after children, diet, hygiene and education. The campaign was especially directed towards working class women with new behavioural norms and ideals. Its bourgeois message had clear moral overtones.[59] It was disseminated through many channels around and after the turn of the century: through local papers, magazines and other publications – from one woman to another in the many local charitable and philanthropic organizations, within the Labour movement and through the school.[60] Dissemination might also occur in more subtle ways. The working class espoused the bourgeois way of life and behaviour merely by observing it and following suit. The Norwegian social historian, Edvard Bull, suggested that servant girls probably played an important role in transferring domestic ideals from the middle class home to their own homes.[61]

It is unlikely, however, that Torleif's family either directly or passively assumed a middle class stock of values and a middle class culture. Orvar Löfgren argues that the middle class message was received in different ways by the working class and was remodelled to conform with the working class family's own dreams, expectations and practices. Traditional, cultural resources were used and changed to meet a new situation.[62] In such a way new forms of behaviour and new ways of life were expressed differently and given a new meaning by the working class. In Torleif's family it was a matter of living a respectable family life in a pretty, orderly home – with a stay-at-home housewife, a father who worked outside the home and a limited number of children who were healthy, wholesome, clean and went to school. A more instrumental relationship to life replaced a fatalistic one. The parents took the fate of their children into their own hands. They sent them to school. This was not necessarily an expression of a desire for their children's social and economic advancement. It was just as much the parents' wish to ensure a secure future for their children based on visions and desires in the broadest sense. Earlier, they had been at pains to ensure that their children acquired the skills necessary to hold down a specified job. As time passed schooling became a norm and a necessity.

Hans and Torleif had their identities shaped both by work and school. But identity was more than knowing what rules applied and what forms of behaviour were acceptable in different circles. Identity was also a question of becoming skilled in how to behave, and in the body language expected of a child. Through practice and action Hans and Torleif took part in the shaping of childhood within the framework set by the family and society.[63] The frameworks were different, just as the frameworks for children in the two statistical inquiries were different. Thus, Hans and Torleif and the many children in the statistics had different childhoods. To be a worker's child in a rural and traditional industrial society was to have quite a different life from that of a worker's child in a modern, industrialized, urban society. The two accounts of childhood and the two statistical inquiries also contain a time element and tell us something about historical change. Therefore, to grow up after the turn of the century was quite different from the decades before.

Conclusion: the modern child is a child of the school

Hans and Torleif and the thousands of Norwegian children included in the 1875 and 1912 inquiries grew up and lived for most of their lives, though for different lengths of time, in the family, at work outside the household and at school, in a society that went through vast changes in working life, social structures, the household and the family. The child and childhood were at the centre of these processes of change. According to Edvard Bull, it is precisely the relationship between the generations – that is to say the way childhood is organized – that is one of the most central of all historical phenomena.

> The relationship between the generations is one of the most central of all historical phenomena. The development of society – even 'historical development' – cannot happen without a constant transfer of experience and entire patterns of social life from generation to generation. The mechanics of this transfer must be of interest to the historian that is to say the structure of upbringing and the relations between adults and children, old and young.[64]

Here we have told a story of great variety, of similarities and differences, of changes in children's work and of the conditions under which they grew up – within a period around the turn of the century. Work undoubtedly became a smaller part of childhood. Norwegian school children sat at their desks for several additional hours after the turn of the century than they had done before. Normatively the school gained ground too. At the end of the century, the debates over the major legislative activity concerning the regulation of children's work and the extension of schooling, created the conditions upon which new ways of thinking were based. That children should not work but should go to school won acceptance and became one of the basic norms of modern society. In the long term this interest in children and in childhood changed the pattern of thought. It was not that one pattern replaced another. Different and complex patterns existed side by side and simultaneously in the child's life, the family and the community.[65] That is to say, the childhood focused on work and also that focused on school existed side by side within the mental structures.

In modern society the child's life became more separate from that of the adult. The State took charge of the child with progressive legislation and by building its own institutions for children, above all the school. However, the modern child was also an organized child. In organizations designed specifically for children, they were introduced to particular roles and ways of behaviour. Simultaneously, as the child was made public and institutionalized, modern childhood is characterized by a process of *familiarization*, an encircling of the child by the family, and a growing intimacy of family life.[66] This development provided the conditions for the growth of a specific child culture. Here the codes and behaviour patterns of childhood were acquired, the identity of the child – regarding age, sex and social class – was formed. The child learned that he or she was *different* from other children.[67] This applied to gender. Yet age became especially important in the formation of the modern child.[68] Birthdays were the object of great attention and the fact that children at school were separated by age, and that factory legislation focussed on age, defined the child in a new way.

A childhood of schooling was a norm that won strong support. Nevertheless, children continued to work. Often school and work were combined, as with the children in Kristiania in 1912. The child was a *schoolchild and a covert part-time worker*. Children's work has become invisible in our own times and within our own culture.[69] Making something invisible is an expression of cultural prejudice. That occurs also when – in our part of the world – we moralize and condemn the practices of other countries and cultures concerning children's work. The story of child labour in our own industries is similarly handled – with clear moral overtones in the historical literature.[70] In working with the history of childhood we must adjust our sights and become conscious of our prejudices. Children's work must be understood and explained within the cultural and historical context of which it was a part.

Notes

1 Norway was a late starter in this area. Denmark made a similar law in 1873, while Sweden had a law making night work illegal for children and young people as early as 1853.
2 There was a long tradition for different acts for urban and rural schools. There were still two laws in 1889, one for the towns and one for the rural districts. Nevertheless, by then the aim was to make them as similar as possible. The principle of one school for all was upheld more strongly in Norway than in the other Nordic countries, or, for that matter, in European countries generally. See Jordheim 1984, p. 91.
3 On universatility as a principle of Norwegian social policy, see Seip 1984, pp. 185-86.
4 See Stang Dahl 1978.
5 For more on this, see Seip 1984, chapter 10.

6 Mohn 1878.
7 The inquiry was undertaken by a committee appointed by the Kristiania School Board. The committee was also to prepare proposals for changes in the Elementary School Act. Document No.36 1912-1913.
8 Prout and James1990, p. 8.
9 Hans Olsen Solvold was interviewed by Edvard Bull in 1953. The transcript can be found in the Arbeiderminne samlingen (collection of worker reminiscences), Departement of History, University of Trondheim. Torleif Albretsen was interviewed by the author of this chapter. The audiotape can be found in the Labour Movement's Archives in Telemark.
10 Childhood and upbringing were sexually conditioned. It would, therefore, have been desirable if one of the children had been a girl. Unfortunately, only boys appear in the Ulefoss and Porsgrunn material. This was in part because worker reminiscences were only collected from among industrial workers, with the result that girls were excluded.
11 Mohn 1878, p. 3.
12 Mohn 1878, p. 6.
13 Bull 1985, p. 319
14 On the flexibility of child labour and the needs of the family, see, for example, Hareven 1982, p. 213. On the family cycle, economy and work, see Fløystad 1979.
15 See, for example, Avdem and Melby 1985.
16 Marx 1983, p. 116.
17 Mohn 1878, p. 8.
18 See Schrumpf 1997, chapter 3.
19 The extent to which children working in industry was a mark of change or continuity was discussed by contemporaries and subsequently by historians. See, for example, Olsson 1980. Olsson argues that it did in fact represent a break with pre-industrial child labour.
20 Mohn 1878, p. 31.
21 Mohn 1878, p. 14.
22 Isak Lindalen's account of his father Ole Pedersen Lindalen, born 1859.
23 Mohn 1878, p. 15.
24 Dokka 1879, p. 32.
25 Mohn 1878, p. 28.
26 Mohn 1878, p. 31.
27 Cited by Bull 1953, p. 32.
28 On age and task orientated work, see Thompson 1967.
29 On work as a way of life, see Slettan 1989, and on the *mentalité* of work, see Thorsen 1993, p. 22.
30 Bull 1979, p. 35.
31 The answers related to 1. February 1912 and covered 85 per cent of schoolchildren in the city. The Board reckoned that 'the inquiry covered just about all productive employment carried out by schoolchildren in Kristiania'. Document No.36 1912 – 1913, p. 9.
32 More precisely 30 per cent of the boys and 12 per cent of the girls in the elementary schools. All paid work inside or outside the home as per January 1912, or in the course of the last school year, was included.
33 Document No.36 1912 – 1913, p. 29.
34 On the sexual division, see Blom 1994, p. 40.
35 Schrumpf 1996, Chapter 5.
36 Document No.36 1912 – 1913, p. 37.
37 Document No.36 1912 – 1993, pp. 40, 43.
38 Bull 1984, p. 81.
39 Document No.36 1912 – 1913, p. 22.

40 The inquiry is not wholly reliable for other than the working class. This was because a greater number of children from the other classes were educated in state (as opposed to local authority) or private schools. These were not included in the inquiry and totalled around 7,000 children.
41 The figures show that in 1871 around one in three boys and one in four girls worked for 10 hours a day or more. By 1912 the percentages had fallen to 0.07 and 0.17 respectively. Document No.36 1912-1913, p. 52.
42 The figures show that in 1871 some 3.8 per cent of boys and 1.5 per cent of girls in Kristiania's elementary schools, worked in factories. By 1912 the percentages had fallen to 0.42 and 0.08 respectively. Document No.36 1912-1913, p. 52.
43 Document No. 36 1912 – 1913, p. 52.
44 *Historical Statistics* 1968.
45 Ytterbø 1957, pp. 225-226.
46 On this kin-based learning, see, for example, Seccombe 1993, p. 18.
47 One consequence of changes in kin feelings has been described by Edward Shorter thus: 'whereas once people had been able to answer such questions as "who am I" by pointing to those who had gone before and would come after, in the twentieth century they would have other replies.' Shorter 1975, p. 4.
48 Minutes of the Porsgrund School Board 1890 – 1900.
49 On differences in the child's experience of school in urban and rural districts, see Finkelstein 1979.
50 On the significance of school architecture, see Coninck-Smith 1992.
51 Finkelstein 1979, pp. 114-115.
52 The role of the school bell for childhood in the modern period is emphasised by Sutherland 1993, Chapter 10.
53 On the body in middle class culture, see Rudberg 1983, pp. 163-164.
54 Minutes of the Porsgrund School Board 1890 – 1900.
55 Tønnessen 1957, p. 501.
56 Ytterbø 1957, pp. 225-226.
57 An important advocate of this new view of the family, the child and childrearing was the Swedish Social Democrat, Ellen Key. She influenced Social Democrats, popular communicators and educationalists throughout Scandinavia. See Ambjørnsen 1981, pp. 43-44 and Gordon 1985. She argued that the new way of bringing up children strengthened women's role and enhanced a woman's sphere of influence.
58 On respectability and the working class family, see Seecombe 1993, p. 206.
59 See for example Avdem and Melby 1985.
60 Anna Darvin argues that the school's most important aim was to convey the middle class view of the family to working class children and so create a new generation of parents, especially mothers, Darvin 1982, p. 643.
61 Bull 1985.
62 Löfgren 1982. In the same way Liv Emma Thorsen argues that the cultural identity of young girls of farming stock was strengthened rather than weakened when meeting that of the middle class. See Thorsen 1993, p. 83.
63 See James and Prout 1990, p. 8.
64 Bull 1970, p. 35.
65 On the procedural character and separability of *mentalités,* see Thorsen 1993, p. 20.
66 Qvortrup 1990, p. 48.
67 On similarities and differences in the forming of the child in gender terms in early modern times, see Sandmo 1995.
68 See Chudacoff 1989.
71 See Anne Solberg's chapter in this book.
70 See Schrumpf 1993 and 1996.

From full-time to part-time

Unpublised sources

- Forhandlingsprotokoll for Porsgrund Skolestyre 1890-1990. Porsgrunns byarkiv.
- Protokoll for Tilsynsutvalget ved Ulefos brugs Skole 1890-1920. Ulefos Brugs arkiv.
- Muntlige kilder:
- Hans Olsen Solvold, født 1865 på Ulefoss. Arbeiderminnesamlingen Universitetet i Trondheim.
- Torleif Albretsen, født 1910 i Porsgrunn. Arbeiderbevegelsens arkiv i Telemark.
- Isak Lindalens beretning om sin far, Ole Pedersen Lindalen, født 1859 på Ulefoss. Arbeiderminnesamlingen Universitetet i Trondheim.

Publised sources

- Dokument nr. 36 (1912-1913). Erhvervsmæssig arbejde blandt skolebarn i Kristiania.
- *Mohn, Jacob Neumann* (1875). Angaaende Børns og Unge Menneskers Anvendelse til Arbeide udenfor Hjemmet. I Stortingets forhandlinger 1883, del III. Kristiania.

Literature

Ambjørnsen, Ronny, (1981): "Barnets fødsel". In Clausen, C. (red)(1981). *Barndommens historie.* København.
Avdem, Anna og Melby, Kari, (1985): *Oppe først og sist i seg. Husarbeid i Norge fra 1850 til i dag.* Oslo.
Blom, Ida, (1984): "Barneoppdragelse". In Hodne, B. & Sogner, S. (red)(1984). *Barn av sin tid.* Oslo.
Blom, Ida, (1994): *Det er forskjell på folk før som nå. Om kjønn og andre former for sosial differensiering.* Oslo.
Bull, Edvard, (1953): *Arbeidervern gjennom 60 år.* Oslo.
Bull, Edvard, (1970): "Historisk vitenskap foran 1970-årene". In Edvard Bull (1981). *Retten til en fortid.* Oslo.
Bull, Edvard, (1984): "Barn i industriarbeid". In Bjarne Hodne & Sølvi Sogner (ed.). *Barn av sin tid.* Oslo.
Bull, Edvard, (1985): "Arbeiderklassen blir til". 1 in *Arbeiderbevegelsens historie.* Oslo.
Chudacoff, Howard, (1989): *How old are you? Age Consiousness in American Culture.* Princeton.
Coninck-Smith, Ning, (1992): "Copenhagen Children's Lives and the Impact of Institutions c. 1840-1920". *History Workshop Journal.*

Dahl, Tove Stang, (1978): *Barnevern og samfunnsvern. Om stat, vitenskap og profesjoner under barnevernets oppkomst i Norge.* Oslo.

Davin, Anna, (1982): "Child Labour, the Working-Class Family, and the Domestic Ideology in 19th Century Britain". In *Development and Change,* vol. 13. Number 4 October 1982.

Dokka, Hans-Jørge, (1979): "Barn i skolen". In *Forskningsnytt* nr. 4-1979. Oslo.

Finkelstein, Barbara (ed), (1979): "Reading, and Writing, and the Acquisition of Identity in the United States: 1790 – 1860". In Barbara Finkelstein (ed.)(1979). *Regulated, Children/Liberated Children. Education in Psychohistorical Perspective.* New York.

Fløystad, Ingeborg, (1979): "Vi lærte tidlig å arbeide!". In *Forskningsnytt* nr. 4-1979.

Gordon, Linda, (1988): *Heroes of Their Own Lives. The Politics and History of Family Violence.* Boston 1880-1960. New York.

Hareven, Tamara, (1982): *Family time & Industrial Time.* Cambridge.

Historisk Statistikk, 1968.

James, Allison & Prout, Alan (ed.), (1990): *Constructing and Reconstructing Childhood. Contemporary Issues in the Sociolocical Study of Childhood.* London.

Jordheim, Knut, (1984): "Skolens rolle". In Hodne, Bjarne and Sogner, Sølvi (ed.)(1984). *Barn av sin tid.* Oslo.

Löfgren, Orvar, (1982): "The Swedish Family": a Study of Privatisation and Social Change since 1880". In Thompson, Paul & Burchardt, Natasha (ed.)(1982). *Our Common History. The Transformation of Europe.* London.

Marx; Karl, (1983): *Kapitalen.* Oslo.

Olsson, Lars, (1980): *Då barn var lönsamma.* Stockholm.

Qvortrup, Jens, (1990): "Børn forgår barndommen består. På sporet af en barndommens sociologi": *In Dansk Sociologi* nr. 1, 1990.

Rudberg, Monica, (1983): *Dydige, sterke og lykkelige barn – ideer om oppdragelse i borgerlig tradisjon.* Oslo.

Sandmo, Erling, (1995): "Et virkelig mandfolk". Teorier om kjønn i det tidlig-moderne Europa. In *Svensk historisk tidskrift* nr. 4-1995.

Schrumpf, Ellen, (1993): "Synet på industrielt barnearbeid – et opgjør med elendighetshistorien": In (Norsk) *Historisk tidsskrift* nr. 2, 1993.

Schrumpf, Ellen, (1994): "Familien i erindring". In *Historie. Populærhistorisk magasin* nr. 2, 1994.

Schrumpf, Ellen, (1996): "Barnearbeid og vestlig arroganse". Kronikk in *Aftenposten* 10. januar 1996.

Schrumpf, Ellen, (1997): *Barnearbeid – plikt eller privilegium? Industrielt barnearbeid i to norske industrisamfunn omkring århundreskiftet.* Kristianssand.

Seccombe, Wally, (1993): *Weathering the Storm. Working-class Families from the Industrial Revolution to the Fertility Decline.* London.

Seip, Anne-Lise, (1984): *Sosialhjelpstaten blir til. Norsk sosialpolitikk 1740 – 1920.* Oslo.

Shorter, Edward, (1975): *The making of the Modern Family.* New York.

Slettan, Dagfinn, (red.) (1989). *Bondesamfunn i oppløsning? Trønderske bondesamfunn 1930-1980.* Trondheim.

Sutherland, Neil, (1993): *Growing up. Childhood in English Canada From the Great War to the Age of Television.* Upublisert manus. University of British Columbia.

Thompson, Edvard P., (1967): "Time, Work-Diciplin, and Industrial Capitalism". In *Past & Present* no. 38, 1967.
Thorsen, Liv Emma, (1993): *Det fleksible kjønn. Mentalitetsendringer i tre generasjoner bondekvinner 1920-1985.* Oslo.
Tønnessen, Joh. N., (1957): *Porsgrunns historie 1807 – 1920.* Oslo.
Ytterbø, S., (1957): *Holla II.* Skien.

Pirjo Markkola

"God wouldn't send a child into the world without a crust of bread" Child labour as part of working-class family economy in Finland, 1890-1920

Children's paid labour has come up in several studies on the relations between industrialisation and the family life of working populations. From the point of view of family economy it seems obvious that because of low wages, unemployment, illness or drunkenness many families were in need of children's economic contribution. Many unskilled and all female heads of household could not survive on the wages adult family members could make. The father's work and health were important factors explaining the employment of children.[1] Child labour was an essential part of working-class family economy during the early period of industrialisation. However, the story of child labour has very seldom been told from the point of view of children themselves. The aim of this article is to problematise the relation between child labour and family economy and to reveal working children as historical agents.

This article discusses three issues. First, I examine the limits of the family economy approach.[2] I argue that the emphasis on family economy has both advantages and disadvantages in the research of child labour. Especially study of family strategies – understood as implicit principles shared by family members – can even hide or ignore children's agency. With the help of oral history evidence I reconstruct children's strategies, which of course were closely related to the family economy, but which cannot be completely subsumed to the family's interests. I examine the ways in which the children of working-class families contributed to family economy and the ways in which they even acted independently. What meaning did the daughters and sons of working-class families give to their paid labour? Second, leaning on oral histories I show agency hidden by statistics and other 'traditional' sources. A study based on them reveals children's paid labour in industrialising towns only partly. I will concentrate on the period between 1890-1920, during which industrial child labour diminished in Finland. During that period children's work became less visible and more scattered in nature but did not disappear altogether. The third point I want to make is the contextualisation of the patterns of child labour. The local evidence from Finland suggests that there were remarkable differences between various localities.

Many studies of working-class family economy pay only limited attention to working children and their experiences. In spite of the serious interest in the history of child labour in many countries, the working children's own voice has hardly been heard. According to my understanding there are two major reasons: the questions historians ask and the sources available. Some historians studying child employment are mainly interested in the economic structures and patterns that determined children's work. Children's experiences are not a central question from the viewpoint of the macro level of social and economic history. My interests, however, are on the micro level – on the everyday life of the working families.

Historians striving to hear the voice of child labourers have to deal with the fact that there are very few sources produced by labouring children. There are, however, some examples that encourage historians to ask questions about children's experiences. Joy Parr, for example, has used family letters sent by the immigrant children in Canada at the end of the nineteenth century and the beginning of the twentieth century. Edvard Bull as well as Eva-Lis Bjurman and Lars Olsson have presented oral history evidence on child employment in Norway and Sweden. Also Steven Humphries, Elizabeth Roberts, Lynn Jamieson and Carl Chinn, among others, analyse oral histories of working-class women and men about child labour in Britain.[3] These sources – letters and oral histories – reveal some experiences of working children and their parents.

The voice of working children can to some extent be heard through oral history evidence. Despite the fact that oral history sources are adults' interpretations of childhood and child labour they do, however, reveal some otherwise hidden information about children's work in industrialising towns. They can help us to discuss attitudes and experiences, especially when people tell about their own work, their own youth. Edvard Bull has made a valuable point: people's descriptions of their first attempts to find work tell about the attitudes of the child labourers themselves.[4] Their answers to direct questions about attitudes to child labour are more likely apt to be biased by modern attitudes.

In this article I combine 'traditional sources' – for instance social statistics and investigations – with interviews with old working-class women and men who were born in the 1870s, 1880s and 1890s, some of them in the beginning of the twentieth century, and who spent their childhood and adolescence in the industrial town of Tampere. There are more than 200 people from Tampere who were interviewed in 1965, but I concentrate on the interviews that tell about childhood and youth and which also comment on the working life of the working population.[5] These interviews consist of two major groups, one of women who worked in textile factories, and another one of men in the printing trade.

As an industrial town Tampere, which grew rapidly from a small artisan village into a town of textile factories, represented a new era in Finnish history. The large factories – the largest of them being the cotton factory of Finlayson with more than 3000 workers and Tammerfors Linne- och Jern-Manufaktur with more than 2000 workers in 1900 – characterized the town. Due to its extensive textile industry Tampere was a town of child labourers after the mid-nineteenth century.

The population of this pre-industrial town could not satisfy the industry's demand for labourforce. The increase of its population was 26-fold from 1840 to 1920, i.e. from some 1800 to some 47800 inhabitants. The most hectic period of increase took place in the closing years of the 1890s (1896-1900), when the population increased by over 40 per cent.[6] Because of migration, the share of young and single people was high among the urban working population of the nineteenth century. However, from the 1870s on people with family constituted a clear majority of Tampere working population as a whole. This started a new phase, which signified the increasing growth of population, a formation of a second-generation working population and both demographic and social stabilisation. An increasingly large proportion of the young workers were children of Tampere working families still living at home.[7] In this article I focus on these children and their work.

Family economy

The study of family economy is not completely misleading regarding children's work. Important preconditions for child labour can be revealed in the analysis of family economy, which studies both the paid labour performed by family members outside the home and the work carried out at home – work which made paid labour possible and at the same time became possible by it. The emphasis lies on the conditions under which the families got the resources they needed and on the ways in which the families produced and used them. In the earning of a livelihood the family's power relations were also in the picture.[8] When we talk about family economy we do not imply that the decisions were unanimous or that there were no disputes or disagreements in the family concerning going to work or bringing the wages to the common coffer. Although there were contradictions, empirical findings support the view according to which, in the working families of the nineteenth century and even of the twentieth, the key issue in the family's subsistence questions was the interest of the family; especially the activity of the children was often subordinated to it.[9]

The concept 'family strategy' has been used to describe the ways men, women, and children acted for the good of the family. In 1978 historians Joan W. Scott and Louise A. Tilly published an important study "Women, work and family", that attempted to combine women's experience of work and family in an industrialising society. The notion of family strategy for them represented a tool which enabled them to think about how people make decisions in the face of changing economic circumstances. According to their study historical actors are best understood in terms of family position – as daughters and wives or husbands and sons. In another context Louise Tilly adopted Pierre Bourdieu's usage of family strategies as implicit principles that are felt and understood by all family members, even if and when they acted outside or against them.[10] Tilly and Scott's assumption was that a collective ethos informed the behaviour of individual family members. However, they do not deny the viewpoint according to which the emphasis on the family as a strategic unit does not give sufficient attention to the process by which family strategies were implemented.

It could be claimed that the Finnish factory inspector Vera Hjelt was inspired by the notion of family strategy in her investigation of Finnish working families in 1908–1909. Her statistics illustrate the family economy of a working population. She applied a household budget method. During a period of 12 months the families participating in the research daily recorded their incomes and expenditures. The method required the participants to show perseverance, and it therefore ruled out many families.[11] The research was participated in by a few Tampere working families, whose household budgets can be used to illustrate the diversity and multiplicity by which the workers survived from one day to the next and at times could even afford some small luxuries.

According to Vera Hjelt's view, in the families where all children were under 15 years of age the wife and children could not be expected to earn an income; the man had to carry the responsibility of supporting the family. "If he cannot support the family, the wife and children have to abandon their regular and natural habitat,"[12] Hjelt figured. Despite the selective nature of the research method, Hjelt's results do not reveal an idyllic family in which the mother concentrated on household management, the children on attending school and in which the father won the bread. Working families resembling the bourgeois family model were definitely exceptional.

One of the families was tried by the severe unemployment winter of 1908-1909.[13] The husband was an unskilled worker, the wife a market seller and washerwoman. They had six minor children, the eldest being 12 and the youngest one year old. The father's work was seasonal; in 1909 he was unemployed for seven weeks, and it was generally not rare for him to be unemployed for two months at a time. The man had been forced to give up many jobs due to his poor health. Despite the casual unemployment his earned income was the most important factor in the family's economy. The wife washed laundry and sold for example old furniture, bread, berries, apples and flowers at the market – however, despite all the work her income was only a fourth of the family's total income. The 12-year-old daughter quit primary school in the spring, most likely in order to look after her siblings while the mother went to work.

The family survived the hard times by hopes of better employment, a hope that the wife's market selling might turn more profitable, and that the children could in future relieve their parents' economic burden by participating in the family's common expenditures. Children's earned income was not included in the family's household budget in 1909. "The children often buy cakes and even candy with the money they have earned. They can spend their money the way they choose,"[14] Hjelt commented. The family told that the older boys (aged 8 and 11) sometimes even deposited their money in the bank. The oldest son of the family was due to get a job the next year and was moving out.

The 42-year-old father of another family worked as an unskilled worker in a cotton factory. The family had seven children, of whom the eldest was 12 and the youngest one year old. The family did not live on the father's earned income. "He must allow his wife and his eldest daughter, although she is only 12 years old, to get additional income for the family,"[15] Hjelt noted. In addition to occasional work the wife worked every Saturday as bath attendant in a sauna. The earnings of the wife and children amounted to 38 per cent of the family's income in money – which was quite a high share. The eldest daughter worked in the factory for five hours a day and attended school every second day in the third grade of the factory school. The 8-year and 11-year-old sons attended primary, school and the parents wanted the younger children to take primary school as well. The 8-year-old son of the family daily earned 20–30 penni, which he gave his mother, by selling newspapers. Hjelt made no mention of the eldest son's possible income.

A child of a single parent was more likely to go to work than a child with two adult supporters. In the schoolyear 1906–1907 every fifth child of a single mother among the pupils in Tampere elementary schools earned money for the family. Some 13 per cent of the children whose father was alive took up paid labour.[16] The family economy of a 43-year-old widow, who worked as a washerwoman, cleaner and seamstress illustrates the family life of a single parent.[17] The youngest one of the children had been born after the father's death, the other siblings were not yet at school when they were orphaned. In 1909 all of them still lived at home. The boys were aged 8 and 15 years, the girls 10 and 12 years. In terms of the family's subsistence the children were so old that the hardest times were about to belong to the past. The eldest son was old enough to work full days, but he did not have a regular job: the gross earned income of the children varied from 30 marks in January to one mark in December. The eldest daughter worked as an unpaid trainee in a photographer's studio, where she had an opportunity to become an apprentice earning 30 marks a month after a year of training.[18] In other words, this spelled a great improvement in terms of the family's subsistence, which was at the moment scant.

The records of the municipal poor relief in Tampere also reveal that single mothers found it difficult to cover the family's expenditures. In some cases even mother's factory work combined with the children's earnings did not lift the poorest families above the minimum level of subsistence. Widow Maria worked in a papermill and her 12-year-old son worked half days in a cotton factory. Matilda supported her three minor children by working as an unskilled worker in the summer and by washing laundry in the winter, until she got her 12-year-old son a half-day job at the factory. Josefina's 12-year-old son also got work at the factory and could help his mother, who did sewing at home, support the four younger siblings. Although the firstborns brought their salary home, the mothers nevertheless had to seek poor relief, which was the last straw people could clutch at if their own and their children's earnings were insufficient. The same records also reveal, that some children refused to support their parents, which was, however, clearly disapproved and condemned by neighbours, authorities and others involved in the case.[19] The common disapproval indicates the norm: it was children's duty to contribute to family economy.

The examples above illustrate the life situations of urban working population in the early twentieth century. The threat of unemployment was real and a job was not particularly secure. Women had earnings of many kinds, but their wages were low. Children strained the parents' economy, but at the same time they were an economic resource and even an investment through which the scant livelihood could later be made better. To have the oldest children turn 12 was an important phase in the lives of urban working families, because it spelled a relief in the perpetual concern about subsistence.

In terms of children's work the working families in Tampere had come up with three different solutions. The ordinary procedure was that children brought their earned income home to mother; secondly they looked after their younger siblings so the parents were free to go to work. The third practice was found in the six-child-family in which the children were allowed to spend their earned income themselves, and they even deposited some money in the bank. This fact reveals a more independent position and different role of the children in the family economy. The eldest son of the family was supposed to move out once he got himself a job. This could also be seen as individualisation, but maybe it was after all no more than the normal agrarian way of children easing their parents' subsistence concerns by moving out and working elsewhere.

In the study of family economy children's paid work becomes visible if children bring their earned income home, or if they refuse to turn it over to the family, or if the parents know about their offspring's an pocket money. In the examples above some children seem not to have had an income. Were they only consuming what others earned or is their paid labour hidden by the family economy approach? We can try to examine this by analysing children's work opportunities in an industrialising town.

Children's work

The children of working-class families had a variety of jobs in Tampere as well as in other industrial towns. Since 1890, workers under 18 were divided into three categories in terms of paid labour: those under 12 years of age were prohibited from working in a factory, those aged 12–14 were allowed to work 7 hours a day, i.e. half-days, and the working hours of youth aged 15–17 were restricted to 14 hours.[20] The number of children, i.e. those under 15 years of age and their share of the total factory labourforce in Tampere, is presented in Table 1.

Table 1. The number of factory workers under 15 years of age and their share of the total factory labourforce in Tampere, 1860–1920.

Year	number	share, %
1860	409	17,4
1865	597	25,6
1870	1001	28,6
1875	762	20,6
1885	555	14,0
1890	401	8,2
1895	267	4,6
1900	430	4,4
1905	437	5,0
1910	339	4,0
1916	504	4,4
1920	151	1,2

Source: Haapala 1986, Appendix Table 4.

The factory work of children reached its height in the 1860s and 1870s. In the beginning of the twentieth century historian Väinö Voionmaa wrote about "the sad fairytale town of a thousand and one factory children."[21] There were 1001 factory workers under 15 years of age in 1870 – they spelled some 28 per cent of the total factory labourforce. The first decisive turn in the children's share of factory workers took place before the passing of the Labour Protection Act in 1889. In the 1890s their share dropped to less than 5 per cent. The proportion of children was relatively high in Tampere compared to other industrial localities in Finland where the children's share of industrial workers at the same time dropped to less than 2 per cent. The number of factory children in Tampere remained a few hundred.[22] The industrial child labour diminished but did not disappear.

In the beginning of the twentieth century about 45 per cent of the factory children attended school, too. In the school year of 1906–07 a research was carried out on schoolchildren's work in Finland.[23] In Tampere there were 196 primary school pupils – 82 boys and 114 girls – under the age of 15 working in factories. With the exception of three 10-year-old boys all of them were between 12 and 14 years of age and they made up about 14 per cent of males and 20 per cent of females of their age group still at school.

Although the proportion of schoolchildren with industrial work is relatively low, the number of them nevertheless is high compared to Helsinki – the capital of Finland – where only 5 girls and 24 boys of the same age group were reported to work in factories. In Tampere the number was increased by the 217 pupils of the factory school. The Labour Protection Act of 1889 ordered that minor workers without the completed primary school curriculum had to be provided with tuition at least 12 hours a week. The factory school was meant for factory workers under 15 years of age, and it functioned as a part of Tampere primary school.[24] In the school year of 1906-07 there also were some pupils who were 15 years old. The factory school explains the difference from other towns: in the age group between 12-14 almost every pupil with industrial work attended factory school.

There were also some other local differences concerning schoolchildren's work. The work of primary school boys was most common in Helsinki, where a fifth of the schoolboys had an income. The work of girls was most common in Tampere, where 14 per cent of schoolgirls had an income, mainly outside the home. The work of Tampere boys amounted roughly to the same. Altogether 276 boys and 290 girls in Tampere told they worked besides going to school – two boys and one girl were only seven years old. Table 2 illustrates the number of schoolchildren past eight years of age with various paid employment in Tampere in 1906.

Table 2. Primary school pupils with paid employment at home or outside the home and their share of the age group still at school in Tampere in 1906.

age	number	boys %*	number	girls %*
8	6	1,8	6	1,8
9	21	6,7	7	1,9
10	22	7,6	11	3,3
11	33	12,0	16	5,3
12	38	16,0	30	12,1
13	70	32,3	63	29,9
14	51	54,3	67	62,6
15 -	33	59,0	89	70,7

* the share of the children with paid employment of the age group still at school

Source: Snellman 1908, 35. Paid employment here includes both paid employment at home and outside the home, of which the latter is clearly more common.

It was obvious that the age of the child or youth affected paid employment – and in particular the paid employment outside the home. The paid work of Tampere schoolchildren was increased by a relatively large group of youth past the age of 15 who attended night school (aftonskola).[25] Not nearly all children of sufficient age (12 years) were work while at school, but nevertheless work increased with age. Among Tampere girls the increase in paid employment outside the home was sudden when the girls turned 12. Four per cent of the 11-year-old girls worked outside the home, but 11 per cent of 12-year-old primary school girls were working already.[26] The paid employment of boys became more common in a steadier manner.

The growing industry employed both boys and girls, but outside the factories there were separate labour markets for male and female adolescents. In the research on schoolchildren's work the tasks of children were divided into several categories. In addition to industrial labour children's other occupations included selling and delivering newspapers, running errands, peddling odds and ends and various chores ranging from walking the dog to cleaning. Paid work at home was a category in its own right. The research also included participation in household management. Usually boys sold and delivered newspapers, sold cable news, ran errands and cleaned shoes at the streetcorners. Girls were often employed as domestics, or they could work in the neighbourhood by helping their neighbours. This could easily be interpreted as a different relationship between boys, girls and public space – streets – but on the other hand there were some jobs that sent girls to the streets as well. Many milliners and seamstresses had young girls as trainees, but sometimes their training actually consisted of running errands all the time. Girls delivered customers' dresses, hats and other clothes.[27] In this case it was not the space but the product that dictated the gender division of labour among children. It probably was more suitable for girls to deliver women's clothes.

Young boys between the ages of 7 and 11 were the most visible part of the working-class youth. They were too young to get industrial work, but according to the oral histories they also were in a constant need of pocket money or their families needed extra income, which also this age group could earn. Running errands was seldom counted as work by parents or by the boys themselves. Tyko Varto, for instance, who was a Working-Class boy born in Tampere in 1872, does not in his written memoirs count these kinds of jobs as work. According to his understanding his work began when he was recruited into a cotton factory at the age of 12. A similar difference can be found in the interview with a work man who was born in Tampere in 1890. After finishing primary school he had to begin to work at the age of 13 or 14. His father found him a job in printing industry. However, as a schoolboy he had delivered newspapers and sold both cable news and newspapers – "as schoolboys used to do at that time."[28]

In Tampere the primary school board had a survey made in the autumn of 1912 about the participation of primary school pupils in the distribution of newspapers.[29] According to the survey, the situation was not as bad as the authorities had expected. A scant fifth (18 %) of the upper primary school for boys took part in distributing the newspapers, mainly by selling them. In other Tampere primary schools distributing newspapers was not common. The teachers found altogether less than 400 newspaperboys or -girls, out of whom more than a half were pupils of the upper primary school for boys. One of the newspaperboys, who was born in Tampere in 1904, began to deliver newspapers at the age of 11. He was asked by work wives in his neighbourhood to take up that job. The distance from the neighbourhood to the town was about two kilometres. Every morning the boy walked to school and came back home during his lunchbreak. At six o'clock in the evening he had to walk downtown again to fetch the newspapers and come back to deliver them. During the summertime he also delivered another paper in the morning.[30]

Industrialisation grew a large-scale network of homework, which was one alternative to earn a livelihood, and in many countries especially women and children were involved in paid labour done at home.[31] In Tampere the most common work at home was sewing, but industrial homework was relatively limited. One match factory had all its boxes produced as homework; the production of matchboxes was typical homework for children. According to Tyko

Varto, the earnings were so small that even the most nimble-fingered worker could not make a fortune; nevertheless, there was some money in it. Other industrial homework was offered by a stockinet factory, which announced that one fourth of its production was produced at home. Also a few other factories provided homework either to their older workers or people pensioned from the factory.[32]

In the schoolyear of 1906-1907 about 2 per cent of Tampere primary school pupils were involved in various kind of paid homework.[33] However, the interviews with old Working-Class men and women tell very little about children's industrial homework in Tampere. There are some children who helped their parents, who worked as caretakers, and the interviews also mention children helping mothers in household management. With the exception of the production of matchboxes, the informants do not recall industrial homework. It has to be noted, however, that the people were not asked any questions about homework; the informants were free to tell about the most important memories of their childhood and youth in a factory town.

On the basis of this summary description of children's work in Tampere, we can conclude that children's labour market was very scattered in nature. There were many kinds of work for both boys and girls, but all the children could not work all the time. It is also possible to talk about unemployment among urban children.[34] The surveys made on child labour at the turn of the twentieth century gave cross-sectional information, which managed to note only a part of the working children – those children who happened to have some income during the research period, or who found it reasonable to give honest answers to interviews conducted mainly by teachers. What is interesting in these surveys is that they seem to take Working-Class children's work for granted. The same attitude can also be found in the philantrophists' activities in Tampere.

Through work into proper citizens

It was commonly accepted in Finland that the children of Working-Class families should work. The local philanthropists began to organize work for the children who dropped out from the children's labour market in town. The concern about begging inspired Tampere philantrophists to establish a children's workroom in 1881. It was meant for poor children from 3 to 15 years of age. In the workroom girls sewed, spun and wove cloth, boys whittled toys, wooden shoes and furniture. Small children tore bask or did some other simple tasks. Young workers were provided with meals and the poorest of them could also get clothes and shoes from a philanthropic association. The number of children was at its largest – 104 – immediately during the first month. Later the numbers diminished and the workroom had to be closed down in the autumn of 1900. The philantrophists accused the parents who were reluctant to bring their children to the workroom. A member of the workroom board suggested that one of the reasons for the diminished number of children was the improved economic situation.[35] This also makes it possible to conclude that the children came to the workroom out of necessity, not for their own pleasure. They preferred to work elsewhere or not to work at all.

The children's workroom was re-established in 1903. The difference to its predecessor was that the new institution was meant for primary school pupils instead of all the children who had been caught begging. The tasks of the children did not differ from those of the old workroom. The new one also taught work: sewing, weaving, carving, shoemaking, net weaving, basketry and the plucking of patches. Girls did the cleaning and washed dishes, boys sawed and chopped wood and helped in laying the table and cleaning. Already at the planning stage it had been emphasised that vocational education was to be a part of the institution's duties, as work weaned bad habits and secured the children an ability to support themselves as adults.[36] In addition to these future rewards w o r k children got their daily meals in the workroom, but they were not paid for their work. The meals eased parents' sustenance worries but did not strengthen the children's feeling of being wage earners. In that sense the workroom only represented the disadvantages of child labour: children had to work but they could not earn money.

While the establishment of the workroom in the 1880s had been motivated by the prevention of begging, the most weighty grounds in the early years of the twentieth century was the opposition to idleness. In Tampere – as well as other Finnish towns – a repeated complaint was that street life was a social disadvantage, which made even the children of good Working-Class homes adopt bad habits. The worst form of idleness was the street loitering of children and youths. Considering that the working population lived in one room or one room and a kitchen, it is not surprising that the children of the working population were a part of the street scene.

The investigation on child labour among schoolchildren revealed that street peddling, for example the selling of newspapers, was considered especially worrying by teachers and other authorities. In the teachers' opinion, the boys' leisure had to be reduced. According to an educational association, consisting mainly of teachers, the law of labourforce protection was harmful rather than useful: "The ones who have not completed primary school have been banned from the factories. Therefore they loiter on the streets. The best aid is work."[37] The interpretation of the factory act was based on the fact that not all factories were eager to employ children under 15 years of age who had not completed their primary school. The rules and regulations of many factories required from

Urban boys had a variety of jobs in the streets as well. Their street life was considered worrisome by teachers and other authorities. Many important elements of their concern are present in this picture; boys loitering in the street, a movie theatre and a café. (City Museum of Tampere)

minor applicants a diploma of "received learning". The requirement could for example be found in the rules and regulations of Tammerfors Linne- och Jern-Manufaktur company, which involved a linen factory, machinery shop and groundwood mill.[38] However, judging by the pupil numbers of the factory school the interpretation of the educational association of the connection between labourforce protection and children's idleness was oversimplified. It was possible to get a factory job without a primary school diploma, but then you had to attend school.

God would'nt send a child

These is one additional form of child labour that also deserves to be mentioned in this connection. In the beginning of the twentieth century the educational authorities began to organize vegetable gardens for urban youngsters. Gardening represented work that was proper and recommendable for children, suited to wean work family children from 'bad habits'. Local educational boards arranged gardening for ill-mannered children; initially for boys, later for girls as well. In Tampere the garden patches of the educational board were in the 1910s cultivated annually by some 300-800 children.[39] Gardening was the local administration's weapon against the youths' street life, peddling and idleness and a cure for the evils they were supposed to cause. From the point of view of the families these garden patches of children brought some extra food to the table. For children they represented a way to contribute to the family economy. A relatively high number of young gardeners suggests that children were willing to find work and to become economically significant members of their households.

Burden and blessing

The attempts to find a job play an important role in the stories of old Working-Class men and women. Those memories can be used to scrutinize the work children's interpretations of their life situation. Was it a burden or a blessing for a child to get a job? It seems to have been a common pattern that children finished their school at the age of 12 or 13 and began to look for work immediately. This impression is further confirmed by the age structure of primary school pupils in the schoolyear of 1906-1907 (figure 1).

Among the youngsters in Tampere – both male and female – factory work had a high status. Old work class women often comment on their difficulties in finding work and the struggles for steady employment. Many girls had to work as domestics before they were recruited into factories. These memories clearly show that children were eager to get a job, and they also did their best to get it, partly because it was expected of them.

There are many stories by children who were assisted by their family members, relatives or neighbours to get a job in a factory. It was even a common complaint in the working population that the factories only recruited the children of their own workers or applicants recommended by some reliable workers.[40] One woman remembered that her mother, who worked in a linen factory, managed to arrange a job for her in the same factory: "I was so happy. I knew my wages were of great importance for my mother."[41] A work man born in 1890 told that his father, who was a factory worker, had a chance to read

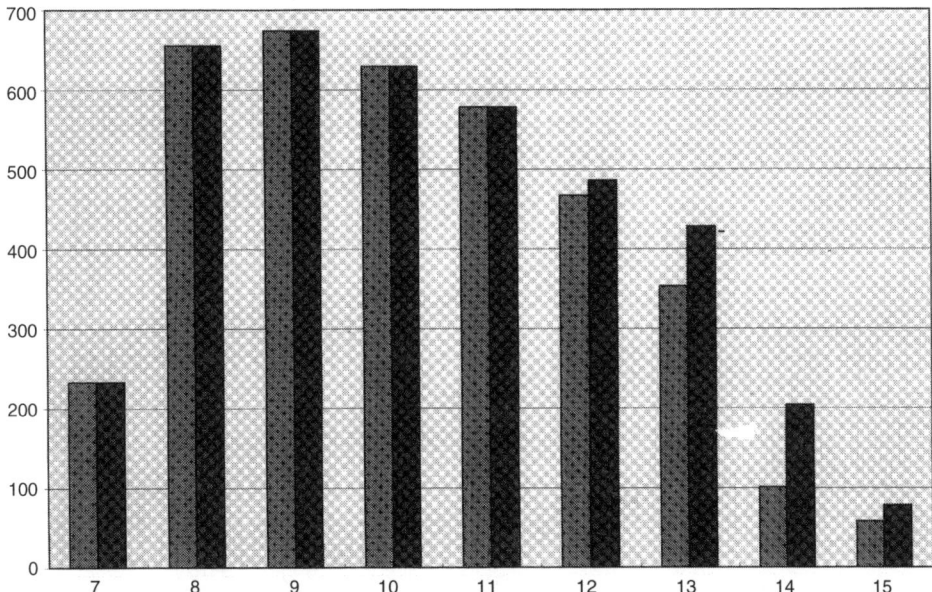

Figure 1. The age structure of Tampere primary school pupils in the school year of 1906-1907.

▨ number of pupils excluding factory school and night school

▨ number of pupils including factory school and night school

newspapers at work and one day he found a newspaper announcement of a trainee contract in printing industry.[42] The boy was the oldest son in a family of eight children, and it was very important for the family to find a job for him.

Some children worked very hard to ease their parents' economic burden. The Labour Protection Act of 1889 regulated the work hours of children but the regulations did not necessarily shorten the work hours of minor workers. Sometimes children worked overtime or they tried to find some extra income. A woman born in 1885 worked as a domestic servant before she began to work in a linen factory at the age of 13. When the work hours in the factory were restricted she continued the domestic service. In the morning she worked in a factory, in the afternoon as a servant or vice versa. At the age of 15, when she was allowed to work full-time in a factory, she gave up domestic service and became a weaver at a cotton mill.[43] In this family children's wages were necessary because their father had fallen ill and could not work anymore.

Many parents considered it to be a blessing if their children succeeded in finding a job. We have to note that most often this was the case when a child had finished school. In Finland urban Working-Class parents clearly attempted to keep their children in school if possible. This has been noted in many studies and also the interviews with working-class men and women confirm this conclusion. Most of the work class parents wanted their children to complete their primary school before they were sent to work.[44] Sometimes the family's economic situation nevertheless forced children to quit school and go to work.

All children who began to work before they had completed their schooling did not do so because of economic difficulties. Some of them independently tried to get a job in a factory. One 11-year-old schoolgirl was recruited into the cotton mill while she was on her way to school. This happened in September 1903. Other children persuaded the girl by telling her about a chance to earn money: "Don't go to school. Come and earn money!" Among many girls applying for a job she was chosen. She was told to bring a birth certificate, medical certificate and her parents' permission. According to the Labour Protection Act, children were not allowed to work unless a medical certificate guaranteed that work was not harmful for their health. This girl could easily get the needed official certificates, but she found it almost impossible to persuade her mother to give a permission to begin work in a factory. The mother insisted she should continue in school. Finally, encouraged and supported by the neighbours, the girl was allowed to become a factory worker at the age of 11. She had to complete the primary school curriculum in a factory school.

Child labour seems to have been a blessing and a burden for work children at the same time. Many Working-Class men and women have memories of hard work and long work hours, but these are often recalled with pride. Having been a young, hard-work labourer is remembered as a sign of respectability. The sufferings they may have confronted get a positive interpretation, and the work of a child signifies an initiation into adulthood. This was the case for boys as well as for girls. However, there is one interesting gender difference. Only women tell that in addition to paid labour they were burdened with housework too. When men tell about their early childhood, they tell about helping mother but as soon as they begin to tell about their paid work, they do not mention their housework anymore. Because of the scattered nature of the oral histories it is not possible to judge if they were freed from housework or if they did not find it worth mentioning. The results of the research into schoolchildren's work suggest that girls really participated in the household management more often than boys, but actually the gender difference in Tampere is smaller than in other Finnish towns. About 75 per cent of schoolgirls in other towns but only 62 per cent in Tampere helped at home. Of schoolboys in Tampere about 58 per cent were involved in domestic work at home, which was one of the highest percentages among schoolboys.[45] This would suggest that women tend to find their participation in household management worth mentioning, while men tend to forget it.

It was a girl's duty to participate in the domestic chores. Ida's father worked in a paper-mill and could provide his family with a relatively high standard of living. (Picture by photographer Bergius. City Museum of Tampere)

Private earnings or family purse?

Did the work children give all their wages to their parents or were they allowed to use their earnings themselves? It seems to have been a common practice that regular wages – from factory, newspaper distribution or some other relatively permanent job – were turned over to the family purse. Working children gave their earnings to mother who would sometimes give some pocket money for the child's own consumption. Nevertheless, it was also possible that a work child had incomes that were not a part of the family economy. They were earnings of a temporary nature.[46]

The children with regular wages could bring home a nice pay-packet. In Tampere half of the older pupils in primary schools in 1906 worked in factories, which also reflected on the wages. Only Tampere schoolchildren were able to assist their parents in supporting the family to a significant extent. In Helsinki and Turku every second working schoolgirl earned less than three marks per week, but out of the Tampere schoolgirls with an income, only a fifth earned so little. As many as 60 per cent of girls brought home 3-6 marks per week and the pay-packet of every fifth girl contained more than 6 marks. Boys had more jobs with poor wages, but they also began work at a younger age. Out of the Tampere work boys, 40 per cent earned less than 3 marks per week, a half earned 3-6 marks and one tenth reached a weekly wage of over 6 marks.[47] Converted into annual income, 6 marks per week is over 300 marks, which was a palpable contribution to the family economy. The amount of earnings is better understood when we know that the average annual income of an industrial worker was about 1000 marks in 1909–1913.

The teachers, who studied the distribution of newspapers in 1912–1913, stressed that the income was important for indigent families. Tampere primary school teachers, many of whom had a realistic picture of their pupils' living conditions, saw no alternative for the paid labour of schoolchildren. In the teachers' opinion three newspaperboys out of four spent their earnings on useful purposes and the remaining youth, on useless, if not harmful, purposes.[48] We can easily guess that the 'useless, if not harmful purposes' consisted of the boys' private consumption.

Some teachers feared that peddling would lead to dishonesty, if the parents demanded money from the children even if they had not been able to get any – the children were forced to cheat to satisfy their parents' demands. If there was any truth in the teachers' fear, it strengthens the view of the importance of children's income for work families. The situation in which a child tried to get a few coins to take home also illustrates the sense of responsibility and duty the children had towards the family.

The boy who began to deliver newspapers at the age of 11 didn't remember the amount of earnings because they were a part of the family economy. He brought every penny to the parents. However, it seems to have been a common practice that work boys had some means to earn pocket money they did not have to report at home. This industrious schoolboy sold newspapers downtown: "If I had to buy something that was the way to earn something."[49]

Sometimes young factory workers had secret reasons to find extra income. Tyko Varto gave his pay-packet to mother and got 10 pennies a week for private consumption. Being a 12-year-old boy he could not ask for money to buy a snuffbox he desperately needed. He solved the problem by gathering bones and selling them to a bonemeal factory.[50] These earnings he could use 'off the records'.

The children who grew up increased the mother's possibilities of having regular paid work, but on the other hand it was possible that the mother did not seek paid work outside the home if her children could earn enough money. When G.R. Snellman studied Finland's textile industry, he considered the usual case to be a family in which the mother managed the household of children who went to work without her having paid work herself. Snellman concluded that mothers participated in the breadwinning of the family through household management and could not therefore be considered dependent on others.[51] The solution was rational, also in the sense that the prospects of aging work women on the labour market were weaker than those of their children. For example, among the recipients of poor relief there were widowed mothers who had no income in addition to the income of their children.

In some work families children were completely responsible for the support of their parents and siblings. Out of the households living in the dormitories of Finlayson cotton factory in 1905, 8 per cent were the kind of household in which the principal breadwinner was the child or the children together. In factory families the paid work of children was common as a rule: in 1905 one out of three children living with their parents went to work; it is true that many of them were over 15 years old, but they still lived at home.[52] The salary of young work women or men was not nearly always consumed by them personally: instead, it was used to purchase bread – or at least coffee and coffeebread – for the whole family.

In the interviews of single women we often find a self-evident, as it were, mention of supporting the mother. A woman who was born in 1875 in the countryside surrounding Tampere moved to the town with her mother at the age of 13. Having served as a maid for a couple of years she got a full-time job at the factory, and the mother "worked elsewhere, in a variety of places." Eventually the daughter supported her mother and encountered economic difficulties: "Even if I worked, I never got rich work. The wage was small, and I had a mother whom I nursed after she got sick..."[53] Poor relief provided a small aid, but otherwise they had to make do on the daughter's income.

A similar story was told by a woman who moved to Tampere in 1906 from the neighbouring municipality. She also initially worked as a maid until she got a job at the factory. She lived in a four-room apartment of shared kitchen where she and her mother shared one chamber: "I took care of my mother all the way to the grave and supported her all along."[54] Both women had responsibility for a poor mother who had moved from the countryside and could no longer support herself. Old mothers managed their daughters' household as long as they could, but in the final years their strength was spent.

The examples above show the loyalty between aging parents and their children. The paid work of children could affect the family's power relations depending on the extent the household was dependent on the children's income. The children's income grew while they grew up themselves. Instead, the aging father had to be satisfied with a job that paid less. In this respect a worker household differed from a bourgeois household where the father controlled the resources.[55] In Tampere, for example, girls in the upper grades of primary school had relatively good earnings, but it is difficult to claim that factory work

God would'nt send a child

levelled the family's power relations for the benefit of the daughter. The daughter supported her parents because it was her duty, but her income could hardly make her head of the family.

Bettina Bradbury has an important remark on the Working-Class families in Montreal, which is applicable to Finland too: "There is no question that the fact of earning gave children a different power within the family. Yet offspring were tied to their parents by custom, shared experience, and mutual need."[56] Custom, shared experience and mutual need are clearly illustrated by the life stories of wage-earning daughters who supported their aging mothers.

Rural attitudes in an urban setting

In Tampere the rural background of the working population and the opportunities provided by a growing industrial town united.[57] Tampere workers of the latter half of the nineteenth century came from agricultural families whose scant livelihood required the work input of all family members. In the town everything had to be purchased with money, which the family members tried to come by. The rural nature of this working population manifested itself in the attitude towards work, family and earning a livelihood. Among agrarian workers the work of men, women and children was considered self-evident, an everyday life necessity. This had even been required by the social order of the ancient régime called legal protection (laga försvar) according to which every dependent man and woman past the age of 15 was obliged to seek work with farmholders or other independent people. The system, which was based on forced service, was abolished in the 1860s,[58] but 'forced service' continued as an economic necessity and a mental structure among the working classes. This background was also reflected in the children's perception of their rights and responsibilities. They did not question their going to work because it was based on collectively shared values.

In the beginning of the nineteenth century Tampere work families gained their principal livelihood through the father's earned income. The paid labour of the wife and children was nevertheless common, although more scattered in nature. Children went to work at 14–15 at the latest. The breadwinner model only gradually became a norm among the urban working population. In the mid-nineteenth century parents had appealed to the employer's benevolence and their own poverty when they had asked for a job for their children at the factory. In the early twentieth century factory inspectors repeatedly reported to have encountered children under the age of 15 work full days. Even then both employers and the parents of the minor workers made appeals to the family's subsistence: sometimes it was claimed to rest on the child's income. The appeals illustrate the parents' wish to keep their 12-14-year-old children in full-time work. Sometimes parents tried to lie about the age of the child in order to get the child a job or a full-time job at the factory or sawmill.[59]

The work parents' mode of thought was reflected by unskilled worker J.A. Silander in the Social Democratic Party convention in 1903. He commented that industrial workers had 'major privileges' compared to the agrarian working population: citydwellers could send their children to work as soon as the law permitted it (the age of 12).[60] The labour movement began to demand more extensive protection for the children and such living conditions for the parents that they could support and raise their children. Both the labour movement and the educated classes, who took an interest in the question of the working class often pitted primary school and children's paid work against each other and demanded a right for children to complete the primary school curriculum.[61] The desire of Tampere working-class parents to find work for their children in the early twentieth century was not contradictory to the education goal. The same parents who wished that their living conditions would improve through their children's earned income strove to keep their children in primary school until the end. The curriculum of primary school was completed at the age of 13 or 14 (sometimes at the age of 12).

Despite the continuities on the level of mentalities, the working-class childhood changed when the nineteenth century gave way to the twentieth. The working family stabilised as the duration of marriage lengthened decisively: more and more children had the opportunity to grow up in a home with both parents alive. While only every fourth marriage between worker couples born in the 1820s lasted at least 30 years, nearly half of the marriages of couples born in the 1840s and 1860s lasted at least 30 years.[62] The economic pressure of the families to take their children from school and send them to do paid work diminished. Working-Class children got more options but many of them nevertheless chose to take up paid labour as soon as they could get it.

Conclusion

Children and their parents in Finland as well as in other European countries knew the saying: "God wouldn't send a child into the world without a crust of bread."[63] At the turn of the twentieth century, however, urban Working-Class families had to wait for that crust of bread for over a decade. Children under the age of twelve usually managed to bring home a few crumbs of bread, but they could not make a significant economic contribution until they were well into their teens.

An analysis of the relationship between children's paid labour and family economy brings up several interesting aspects about the prospects of the family economy perspective to comprehend the history of children at work. The family economy perspective has distinct advantages. It helps us to understand the conditions under which Working-Class families solved their livelihood concerns. In changing situations it was necessary to consider which member of the family had the best earning chances, and which member could contribute to the mutual livelihood in some other way. The family economy perspective also brings children's work into the family context and thus provides one explanation as to why the children went to work.

The description of Tampere children's paid labour also suggests that strict concentration on family economy involves certain problems. First, from this perspective the children may appear more loyal than actually was the case. The poor relief records contain information according to which children did in fact not bring their earnings home but kept them, which resulted in the parents being forced to seek poor relief. If the family economy perspective is understood so that children's paid labour was dictated by the needs of the family, then the contradictions within the family are easily obscured. It will also be possible to reconstruct a harmonious image of a situation which actually could contain much tension. It is naturally feasible to take many of these factors into consideration in the research on family economy, although it may not always be easy. On the other hand, the needs of the family do not explain the whole of children's paid labour. Especially boys, in addition to the earnings they brought home, got additional income they used to satisfy their personal needs. Similarly, the decision of the Tampere girl who quit her school and went to work in a factory, despite the opposition of her parents, represents something that cannot be completely explained by the needs of family economy. Had I not happened to come across the interview revealing that the girl quit school of her own accord, I would undoubtedly have interpreted her employment to have been dictated by the family's needs.

Another interesting feature that emerges from the Tampere data involves the invisibility of children's work. Industrial work was relatively closely recorded and compiled into statistics in the large-scale 19th century industry; instead, children's work as domestics, newspaperboys or errand boys or girls for private people do not show in official sources. Furthermore, information about a multitude of minor earnings, like selling bones to a bonemeal factory or gathering scrap iron for a scrap metal merchant, have only survived as fragments in the memories of people or very randomly for example in newspapers or contemporary descriptions. It is yet more difficult to gain information about the ways in which the children spent their-pocket money and how they understood the division of their income for the family and for themselves. Data provided by oral histories is especially valuable in terms of tracing these aspects.

Finally, I would like to comment on local differences, which to my mind are well worth consideration in research on the paid labour of working-class children. The parents' relationship to the paid labour of their sons and daughters was not identical in all countries, or even all towns. While it has been clearly shown that in a few countries parents opposed girls' factory work, or at least had misgivings about it, the attitude in Tampere was the opposite. The parents considered factory work to be the most suitable for their daughters, even safer than other occupations. The esteem of factory work was high and the girls sought jobs expressly in factories. The esteem of domestic service was low, on the other hand, and the parents did not necessarily consider it a suitable career choice for their daughters at all.

Another factor that separated Tampere from the other major Finnish towns was the wage level of boys' and girls' paid labour. While primary schoolboys in other towns could bring home more money than primary schoolgirls, the situation was different in Tampere. There girls of 12–14 years of age could relieve the livelihood concerns of their parents even considerably. This could also be seen in the fact that a smaller share of Tampere primary school girls carried out domestic chores than primary school girls in other towns. In a textile industry town the chances of young girls to assist their parents in earning the family's livelihood were even better than those of boys at the same age. It was only upon reaching adulthood that the wage difference between the sexes turned to favour males.

Notes

1. Anderson 1971; Hareven 1984; Tilly & Scott 1987, 63-145; Heywood 1988, 108; Chinn 1988, 67-71; Bradbury 1990, 109-128; Rose 1992, 78, 166; Ross 1993, 149; Bradbury 1993, 118-151; Markkola 1994, 117-123.
2. The approach concentrating on family economy is also called household economics approach. The emphasis is on economic or other exchange relationships within the family and between family members and others. Cf. Anderson 1980, 65-84.
3. Parr 1994; Bjurman & Olsson 1979; Bull 1982, 223-231; Humphries 1981; Roberts 1984, 34-38; Jamieson 1986, 49-67; Chinn 1988, 67-71.
4. Bull 1982, 224.
5. The tape-recorded interviews at the Department of Ethnology at the University of Tampere.
6. Haapala 1986, appendix table 7; Rasila 1984, 181, 210; Statistisk Årsbok för Finland 1922, tabell 11.
7. Haapala 1986, 223-228; Haapala 1990, 402.
8. Anderson 1980, 65-66.
9. Roberts 1984, 40-44; Tilly & Scott 1987, 111-121; Chinn 1988, 67-70; Bradbury 1993, 118-151; Markkola 1994, 121-123.
10. Tilly & Scott 1987 (1978); Tilly, Louise, A., "Individual lives and family strategies in the

French proletariat." *Journal of Family History* 4/1979, 137-152; Tilly, Louise A., "Beyond family strategies, what?" *Historical Methods* 3/1987, 123-125.
11 Hjelt 1912; The household budgets of Working-Class families were studied in several industrial countries. However, many of the surveys consisted of material collected during a short period. A period of one year is followed for example in a German study *Erhebung von Wirtschaftsrechnungen minderbemittelter Familien im Deutschen Reiche* (Berlin 1909), in a Swedish study *Lefnadskostnaderna i Stockholm åren 1907–1908* (Stockholm 1910) and in a Danish study *Danske Arbejderfamiliers Forbrug* (Copenhagen 1900 – 1901); Van den Eeckhout 1993 is based on similar material from Belgium.
12 Hjelt 1912, 63.
13 Hjelt 1912, 124-127. 148-149; Kuusi 1914, 205-207.
14 Hjelt 1912, 126.
15 Hjelt 1912, 127-130, 150-151.
16 Snellman 1908, 30-32.
17 Hjelt 1912, 114-116, 140-141.
18 Hjelt 1912, 141.
19 Markkola 1994, 109-111.
20 Finlands författningssamling 18/1889.
21 Voionmaa 1907 – 1910, 683.
22 Haapala 1986, appendix table 4; Rasila 1984, 266.
23 Snellman 1908.
24 Finlands författningssamling 18/1889; Rasila 1984, 647-648.
25 Snellman 1908, 33-35.
26 Snellman 1908, 35.
27 Snellman 1908; Tape 31/1965.
28 Varto 1958, 104; Tape 98/1965.
29 Markkola 1994, 120-121.
30 Tape 98/1965.
31 Cf. Boris 1994.
32 Snellman 1903, 147; Snellman 1904, 157; Hjelt 1908, 53-54; Hjelt 1913, 14-17; Varto 1958, 81-82.
33 Snellman 1908, tabell 10.
34 Cf. Cunningham 1990.
35 Markkola 1994, 199-206; Rasila 1984, 650.
36 Markkola 1994, 202; Pulma 1987, 105-122.
37 Tampere educational association 8.5.1896.
38 Snellman 1908, 24-27, table 1.
39 Annual reports of Tampere educational board; 1911, 3; 1912, 3-5; 1913, 3.
40 Kanerva 1946, 128-132; Kanerva 1972, 33–35; Interviews with Working-Class men and women from Tampere. Department of Ethnology. University of Tampere.
41 Kanerva 1972, 34-35.
42 Tape 98/1965.
43 Tape 36/1965.
44 Haapala 1986, 188-189; Interviews with Working-Class men and women in Tampere. Department of Ethnology. University of Tampere.
45 Snellman 1908, 33-36.
46 Interviews with Working-Class men and women in Tampere. Tapes 25/1965, 27/1965, 28/1965, 31/1965, 35/1965, 36/1965, 37/1965, 38/1965, 82/1965, 98/1965. Department of Ethnology. University of Tampere.
47 Snellman 1908, 38-39.
48 Markkola 1994, 121.
49 Tape 98/1965.

50 Varto 1958, 107.
51 Snellman 1904, 132.
52 Talojen asukasluettelo 1905. Finlayson & Co:n arkisto I Bb 2. JMA.
53 Tape 25/1965; Kanerva 1946, 227.
54 Tape 35/1965.
55 Göransson 1988, 244; Van den Eeckhout 1993, 87-110.
56 Bradbury 1993, 147.
57 Haapala 1986; Haapala 1992, 233-241; Voionmaa 1907 – 1910, 676.
58 Markkola 1996, 91-93.
59 Kanerva 1946, 123-124; Yrkesinspektörernas berättelser 1905 – 1909: Naispuolisen ammatintarkastajan kertomus vuodelta 1905, kirj. Vera Hjelt, 96; Kertomus, maamme naispuolisen ammattientarkastajan antama vuodelta 1907, kirj. Vera Hjelt, 184; Kertomus, maamme naispuolisen ammattientarkastajan antama vuodelta 1908, kirj. Vera Hjelt, 136-137; Kotkan piirin ammattientarkastajan kertomus vuodelta 1909, kirj. Artturi Käpy, 152-153; Kertomus, jonka Viipurin ja Kotkan piirien naispuolinen ammattientarkastaja on antanut huhti-joulukuulta 1909, kirj. Jenny Markelin, 375-376.
60 Markkola 1994, 122-123.
61 Markkola 1994, 123.
62 Markkola 1994, 42-68.
63 This saying from Ross 1993, 131. The Finnish saying goes: "Lapsi tuo leivän tullessaan."

References

I
Talojen asukasluettelo 1905. Finlayson & Co:n arkisto. Jyväskylän maakunta-arkisto (Jyväskylä landsarkiv).
Tampere educational association. Minutes and annual reports. Tampereen kasvatusopillisen yhdistyksen arkisto. Hämeenlinnan maakunta-arkisto (Tavestehus landsarkiv).
Tapes 25/1965, 27/1965, 28/1965, 31/1965, 35/1965, 36/1965, 37/1965, 38/1965, 82/1965, 98/1965. Interviews with Working-Class men and women in 1965. Department of Ethnology. University of Tampere.

II
Tampere educational board. Annual reports 1911 – 1913. Tampere 1912 – 1914.
Finlands författningssamling 18/1889.
Statistisk Årsbok för Finland 1922.
Yrkesinspektörernas berättelser 1905 – 1909. Helsingfors 1904 – 1910.

III
Anderson, Michael, (1980): *Approaches to the History of the Western Family,* 1500 – 1914. Mac Millan. London.
Anderson, Michael, (1971): *Family Structure in Nineteenth Century Lancashire.* Cambridge.

Bjurman, Eva-Lis & Olsson, Lars, (1979): *Barnarbete och arbetarbarn.* Nordiska museet. Stockholm.

Boris, Eileen, (1994): *Home to Work. Motherhood and the politics of industrial homework in the United States.* Cambridge University Press.

Bradbury, Bettina, (1982): "The Fragmented Family: Family Strategies in the Face of Death, Illness, and Poverty, Montreal, 1860 – 1885." *Childhood and Family in Canadian History.* Ed. Joy Parr. McCLelland & Stewart Inc. Toronto 1990.

Bradbury, Bettina, (1993): *Working Families. Age, Gender, and Daily Survival in Industrialising Montreal.* McLelland & Stewart Inc. Toronto.

Bull, Edvard, (1982): "Industrial Boy Labour in Norway." *Our Common History. The Transformation of Europe.* Ed. Paul Thompson. Humanities Press. Atlantic Highlands.

Chinn, Carl, (1988): *They worked all their lives. Women of the urban poor in England, 1880 – 1939.* Manchester University Press. Manchester and New York.

Cunningham, Hugh, (1990): "The Employment and Unemployment of Children in England c. 1680 – 1851." *Past and Present* no. 126.

Göransson, Anita, (1988): *Från familj till fabrik. Teknik, arbetsdelning och skiktning i svenska fabriker 1830 – 1877.* Arkiv. Lund.

Haapala, Pertti, (1986): "Tehtaan valossa." *Suomen Historiallinen Seura and Vastapaino.* Helsinki- Tampere.

Haapala, Pertti, (1992): "Työväenluokan synty." *Talous, valta ja valtio. Tutkimuksia 1800-luvun Suomesta.* Ed. Pertti Haapala. Vastapaino. Tampere.

Hareven, Tamara K., (1984): *Family Time and Industrial Time. The relationship between the family and work in a New England industrial community.* Cambridge 1984.

Heikkinen, Sakari & al. (1983): *Palkat, toimeentulo ja sosiaalinen rakenne Suomessa 1850 – 1913.* Helsingin yliopiston talous- ja sosiaalihistorian laitoksen tiedonantoja 13. Helsinki.

Heikkinen, Sakari, (1992): "Aineen voitot – 1800-luvun elintaso". *Talous, valta ja valtio. Tutkimuksia 1800-luvun Suomesta.* Ed. Pertti Haapala. Vastapaino. Tampere.

Heywood, Colin, (1988): *Childhood in nineteenth-century France. Work, health and education among the 'classes populaires'.* Cambridge University Press. Cambridge.

Hjelt, Vera, (1913): "Det industriella hemarbetet." Föredrag. *Suomen Työväensuojelus-ja sosiaalivakuutusyhdistys.* Julkaisuja III,6. Helsingfors.

Hjelt, Vera, (1912): "Tutkimus ammattityöläisten toimeentuloehdoista Suomessa 1908 – 1909." *Arbetsstatistik XII.* Helsingfors

Hjelt, Vera, (1908): "Tutkimus koskeva ompelijattarien ammattioloja Suomessa." *Arbetsstatistik VI.* Helsingfors.

Horn, Pamela, (1994): *Children's work and welfare, 1780 – 1890.* Cambridge University Press. Cambridge.

Humphries, Steven, (1981): *Hooligans or rebels? An Oral History of Working-Class Childhood and Youth 1889 – 1939.* Basil Blackwell. Oxford.

Jamieson, Lynn, (1986): "Limited Resources and Limiting Conventions: Working-Class Mothers and Daughters in Urban Scotland c. 1890 – 1925." *Labour and Love. Women's Experience of Home and Family, 1850 – 1940.* Ed. Jane Lewis. Basil Blackwell. Oxford.

Kanerva, Unto, (1972): Liinatehtaalaisia ja "tehtaanmaistereita". *Pellava- ja verkatehtaan työoloja ja tehdastyöväen sivistysharrastuksia viime vuosisadan jälkipuoliskolla.* Tampere-Seura. Tampere.

Kanerva, Unto, (1946): "Pumpulilaisia ja pruukilaisia." *Tehdastyöväen työ- ja kotioloja Tampereella viime vuosisadalla.* Tammi. Helsinki.

Kuusi, Eino, (1914): "Talvityöttömyys, sen esiintyminen, syyt ja ehkäisytoimenpiteet Suomen suurimmissa kaupungeissa." *Taloustieteellisiä tutkimuksia XV.* Helsinki.

Markkola, Pirjo, (1996): "Den problematiska arbetarfamiljen. Familjeidealet och arbetarfamiljernas vardag i Finland, 1870 – 1920." Pylkkänen, Anu & al., *Statens beroende av familjen.* Publikationer av institutionen för privaträtt vid Helsingfors universitet. Helsingfors.

Markkola, Pirjo, (1994): "Työläiskodin synty". *Tamperelaiset työläisperheet ja yhteiskunnallinen kysymys 1870-luvulta 1910-luvulle.* Suomen Historiallinen Seura. Helsinki.

Olsson, Lars, (1980): *Då barn var lönsamma. Om arbetsdelning, barnarbete och teknologiska förändringar i några svenska industrier under 1800- och början av 1900-talet.* Tidens förlag. Stockholm.

Parr, Joy, (1980): *Labouring Children. British Immigrant Apprentices to Canada, 1869 – 1924.* University of Toronto Press. Toronto, Buffalo, London 1994.

Pulma, Panu, (1987): "Kerjuuluvasta perhekuntoutukseen. Panu Pulma – Oiva Turpeinen, Suomen lastensuojelun historia." *Suomen lastensuojelun keskusliitto.* Helsinki.

Rasila, Viljo, (1984): "Tampereen kaupungin historia." *Tampereen kaupunki.* Tampere.

Roberts, Elizabeth, (1984): *A Woman's Place. An Oral History of Working-Class Women 1890-1940.* Basil Blackwell. Oxford.

Rose, Sonya O., (1992): *Limited Livelihoods. Gender and Class in Nineteenth-Century England.* University of California Press. Berkeley – Los Angeles.

Ross, Ellen, (1993): *Love and Toil. Motherhood in Outcast London, 1870-1918.* Oxford University Press. New York – Oxford.

Sandin, Bengt, (1986): *Hemmet, gatan, fabriken eller skolan. Folkundervisning och barnuppfostran i svenska städer 1600 – 1850.* Arkiv. Lund.

Schybergson, Per, (1974): "Barn- och kvinnoarbete i Finlands fabriksindustri vid mitten av 1800-talet." *Historisk Tidskrift för Finland* 1.

Snellman, G. R., (1904): "Tutkimus Suomen kutomateollisuudesta." *Arbetsstatisk II.* Helsingfors.

Snellman, G. R., (1903): "Tutkimus Suomen tupakkateollisuudesta." *Arbetsstatistik I.* Helsingfors.

Snellman, G. R., (1908): "Undersökning af folkskolebarnens i Helsingfors, Åbo, Tammerfors och Viborg arbete utom skolan." *Arbetsstatistik V.* Helsingfors.

Tilly, Louise A. & Scott, Joan W., (1978): *Women, Work, and Family.* Routledge. New York – London 1987.

Van den Eeckhout, Patricia, (1993): "Family Income of Ghent Working-Class Families ca. 1900". *Journal of Family History* 2/1993.

Varto, Tyko, (1958): "Lapsuuteni Tampere. Kuvaus Tampereesta 1880 – 90 luvuilla." *Tampere-Seura.* Tampere.

Voionmaa, Väinö, (1907 – 1910): "Tampereen historia." *Tampereen kaupunki.* Tampere.

Mats Sjöberg

Working Rural Children.
Herding, child labour and childhood in the Swedish Rural Environment 1850-1950

In 1894, three pupils, Matilda, Vilhelmina and Frans, were in their second year in the village school in Högstorp. Högstorp – in the parish of Bolstad and county of Dalsland in the west of Sweden – was a school in a decidedly agricultural environment. Frans and Matilda were 12 years old and Vilhelmina was a year younger. Although the academic year was quite short, 100 days in total, the three children were not often in school. Matilda was present for a total of 55 days, Vilhelmina 45 and Frans was only in school for 9 days. The year was not exceptional in any respect – either regarding the weather or farming conditions. Indeed, the children's absence can scarcely be explained by rain, cold or poor harvests. The reason for the children's absence from school was that they had worked. Matilda, Vilhelmina and Frans had been herding animals.[1] Instead of being in school, these children had been taking care of cows belonging to their own and other families. They were herdmaidens and herdsmen.

Their level of absence was not unique either for Bolstad or for children in other similar rural areas in Sweden during the late 19th century. Their class mates also had a high rate of absence.[2] Nor was their reason unique. In fact in their reports from the 1860s until 1910, the state school inspectors could write that the most important competition to a high, regular school attendance was herding. The School Inspector for Dalsland – the district of which Bolstad was a part – was repeatedly forced to state that herding was very common and that it " spoiled " the school attendance and, what was considered even worse, the local school authorities did not bother about the problem, but rather seemed to accept the excuse.[3] The problem continued to exist for a long time. When in 1919 the local school authorities in Bolstad were asked to report to the central school authorities which factors produced absence without permission, child labour was the most important cause and, in particular, the use of children for herding of animals.[4]

For many years children's herding work seems to have been considered of great importance. This caused problems for both the school and the family as the children's work exposed different interests and generated conflicts around the children. This is therefore a good reason for us to study the work done by children in rural areas more closely. Besides the fact that opposing interests and conflicts seem to have been great and to have run deep, we have relatively little knowledge about agrarian child labour in general – and about the children's work as herders in particular.

Both Swedish and also international historical research has shown only a marginal interest in rural child labour. Typical for this situation is the fact that under the heading "Child labour" the Encyclopedia of Social History does not devote a single word to rural child labour.[5] Neither does Hugh Cunningham's recently published history of children and childhood consider this question.[6] In Pamela Horn's survey, the question of rural child labour is only just touched upon.[7] This is surprising because rural child labour was probably much more widespread than industrial, in the sense that it concerned a greater number of children. Some research has been carried out, however. In a study of English children in a rural environment, Pamela Horn has shown that during the late 19th century, children increasingly moved from full-time to part-time work.[8] Colin Heywood also points out the importance of the role work played in the lives of French country children and the wide range of tasks in which they were involved.[9] Lynn Jamieson and Claire Toynbee show us how the individual socioeconomic conditions of the agrarian families were reflected in the tasks that the children were expected to do and in their socialization.[10] Elliot West emphasizes the importance of the role that the work done by children had among the American settlers.[11] In Michael Mitterauer's research into the history of youth, both work and the special conditions prevalent in the countryside have a prominent place, which is also relevant for the younger age groups.[12] For children in the Norwegian countryside, it is particularly Dagfinn Slettan who has given prominence to the fact that children in the agricultural community maintained a central role in the family's work far into the 20th century.[13] However, the authorities for writing about the history of rural child labour are essentially different from those dealing with the history of industrial child labour. The work done by children in the countryside was never paid any attention by public statistics in most European countries. There are many sides to rural child labour that are now impenetrable, and it is therefore symptomatic of this particular research that the history of this work must be gleaned from interviews, jotted down memories and biographies as well as from "indirect" sources such as material from schools. The situation, both with regard to research and to sources for gaining knowledge and insight into rural child labour in Sweden, is very similar to that found in other countries. Matyas Szabo has given a lucid picture of the work done by country children using material from personal memories.[14] In a thesis, which was also based on biographical sources, Marianne Liljequist has studied children's work and socialization among the farmers and settlers in Northern Sweden and stressed the very central role work played in the children's upbringing.[15] Helene Brembeck reaches similar conclusions in her studies of children from western Sweden.[16] Through

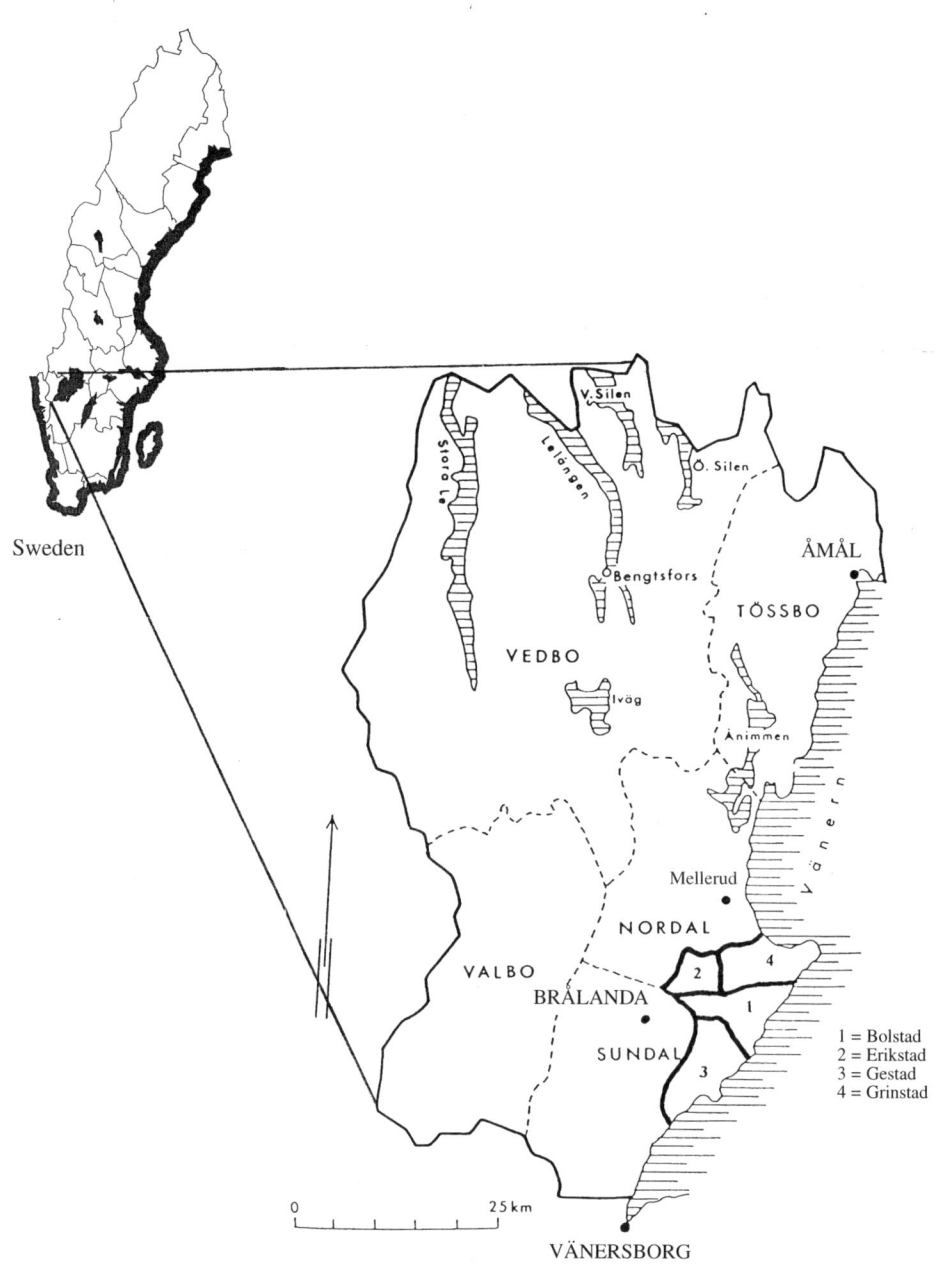

The county of Dalsland and the pastorate of Bolstad with its four parishes Bolstad, Erikstad, Gestad and Grinstad.

the research carried out by Anders Perlinge we encounter the work done by children during a later period than the aforementioned. The earlier studies focus on a period from the mid-19th century to a couple of decades into the new century, whereas Perlinge aims to highlight the years from 1930 onwards. Perlinge believes that children still had an important role to play until the Second World War. However, the mechanisation, which then began, had its starting point in the children's work and was done out of consideration for them. The jobs usually done by children were the first to be mechanized and, after this, the importance of their work decreased.[17]

One task commonly carried out by children, which has been the focal point of Nordic research, is the one mentioned in the introduction – herding. Matyas Szabo has studied the place of children in this organisation in a study into herding in Europe – although he focuses on the role of the adult in this institution.[18] Szabo touches upon specifically Swedish children's experiences in a short article in Fataburen.[19] With regards to Norway, Ingeborg Floystad has explicitly considered herding as a job for a child, and with this has emphasised the great importance children had for animal husbandry in earlier times.[20] Previous research into rural child labour in general, and herding in particular, leaves us despite everything with significant gaps in our knowledge and several unanswered questions. This situation is particularly typical for Sweden, but it also reflects the international scene. In some cases it is a matter of pictures where only the main outlines are drawn, and in others we have very detailed descriptions with few connections to the greater context. Changes and dynamics in the question of rural child labour are rarely the object of analysis, and the work done by children is not made problematic. Why, for example, did just herding become predominantly a child's task and such an obvious matter of conflict? What did the work mean to the children, to their families and to agriculture? What cultural values surrounded the children's work? How did rural child labour and values change with time?

The aim of this essay is not to give any definite or definitive answers to these questions. My aim is rather to suggest that a perspective based on the history of childhood can contribute to an understanding of the changes in both the rural villages and in childhood. My point of departure for this discussion is found in the four congregations making up the pastorate of Bolstad in the county of Dalsland.[21] This area was located on a plain and dominated by small and medium sized family farms, which tended to specialize in both grain and livestock. Agricultural mechanization moved relatively slowly; estates and larger farms were few and the region was thus representative of large areas of southern Sweden's farming communities. The area on which the research is based also had a similar population development. Until about 1880, there was, in principle, a growing population. From the mid-1880s, however, the region suffered from an accelerating decrease in population. Large groups of people –

mostly under 30 years of age – emigrated to the USA, Norway or moved to the growing towns in the west of Sweden. How did this agricultural environment affect the growing child, his relationship to work in general and to herding in particular?

Herding and Children

Elisabeth, Herbert, Hildur and Hilma were all born and grew up in the area we are studying around and immediately after the turn of the century.[22] What they all had in common is that they grew up in families who worked farms in the first decades of the 20th century. The farms were small or medium-sized and survived on the work that the family as a whole could put into it.

Elisabeth's family had a farm that comprised about seven hectares of arable land, a little pasture, three cows, a horse, some sheep and some hens. The farm could not support the family of two adults and four children, and the father was forced to work as a carpenter and smith on neighbouring farms. The mother took care of the household, the children, the work in the cowshed and, when necessary, in the fields. The oldest brother usually went to work with his father on the other farms and the oldest sister had various jobs, of which herding was the most common, on the neighbouring farms. Herbert was the oldest of six children. The farm was relatively big and comprised 25 hectares of land. Besides that there were ten to twelve cows, some young animals, pigs, hens and four or five horses. Herbert's mother died quite young with the consequence that he had to take on the responsibility of his younger brothers and sisters. As the oldest child, he was soon fulfilling the role of farm hand. Hilma was the youngest of five children, and she also suffered from an early loss of a parent – in this case, her father. The family owned their farm, which comprised 13 hectares. Hildur grew up on a smaller farm of about 4.5 hectares. This farm could only support three cows and a few pigs and hens, therefore, it was impossible to support a family of eight without the father periodically going to sea.

All these children – not only the ones mentioned but also their siblings – had to begin to work early in life. According to Herbert, this began as soon as the child could do something. Hildur began at the age of seven as a nanny, but she also herded cows. Elisabeth's first jobs were to fetch wood and water. Hilma's family situation was such that she had to begin work at a very young age. However, the recurring theme in all the early experiences of these children was herding. In Elisabeth' case, it was the animals on neighbouring farms. The few cows they had of their own were tethered. The neighbours often had many animals. Hildur and Hilma shared this experience, but Herbert herded the animals belonging to his own family's farm.

Berta and Anna Person from Lima in Dalarna bringing the animals back to the farm for milking 1906. (Photo: Hans-Per Persson)

The season for taking the animals out to pasture and herding them there began when the first grass began to appear in April. The cows were then kept out on pasture throughout the growing season until they were finally put into the cowshed – usually at the end of October – for the winter. This usually meant that the cows were herded throughout the season. They were sometimes tethered for shorter periods. There was a variation in this on Herbert's farm. There was a fenced-in pasture but this was too small to provide the animals with sufficient food for the whole season, and so herding was periodically necessary there too. The work of the herdmaids and boys began when the cows were released after the morning milking and consisted of taking the cows to places where the grass was plentiful, to look for new places, when the grass had been grazed down, and to try to keep the animals together. The choice of pasture was important as inferior grazing gave a poorer milk yield. If the choice of pasture was an important part of the job of herding, so was the task of trying to keep the animals away from growing crops, which had to be protected – such as grain growing in the fields or vegetables in the kitchen garden. One problem was that when there was poor grazing, the cows searched for food in ever increasing circles. To keep them together was a critical moment. Herding became a job demanding nimbleness and agility at such times, and the herdmaids and boys had to walk or run a lot. Another critical moment was to water the animals. This had to be done at regular intervals to prevent them from going off to look for water themselves. Watering meant that the animals had to be gathered and led to a pond or another source of water. At dinner time – in the middle of the day – the beasts had to be returned to the shed for milking. It was unusual for the cows to be milked out in the open in the pastures. After milking, the cows were taken back out to graze in the afternoon and then they were herded until the farmers called the herdsmaid or boy back home again with the cows. This could sometimes be late in the evening. Often, the animals' owners tried to keep them out to graze as long as possible to get a better milk yield. It gave a higher percentage of fat and therefore a better chance of making butter and cheese. The cows would then be milked for the third time and put inside for the night.

This daily routine was followed with little variation for about half the year. For Elisabeth, not even Sundays were free. Sometimes Hildur's father could take over the herding on a Sunday to allow the children to be free. However, on certain days the children should attend school. In the case of Hilma this problem was solved by her taking it in turns with her older sister, who had different school times. Another solution was to do what was done on Herbert's farm. While he was in school the animals were put into the fenced-in pasture, and when the school day was over Herbert took care of the animals again and herded them until it was time for the evening milking. Sometimes several children herded together and then the school/work conflict could be resolved. In many cases though no solution could be found – and then the child quite simply stayed at home and took care of his or her job.

When there was rich grazing and the cows had quenched their thirst, the herding might give room for other activities. Both Elisabeth and Hildur remember how they did their school work, knitted or made brooms on such occasions. The factor that most influenced the way they felt about the work was the weather. Hilma claimed that rain and cold made the work both bad for their health and miserable. Usually, the children looked after the animals alone and this contributed towards making the work boring. Sometimes the problem of isolation could be resolved by the children communicating with each other by singing. If the pasture was far away, the child was given a packed lunch, but otherwise they usually shared their meals with the other people on the farm.

Children who worked for others, in this case Elisabeth, Hildur and Hilma, were paid wages. The money went directly to the parents and into the family's common household economy. In Hilma's case her earnings were used to buy piglets, and in Hildur's case the mother used her earnings to buy clothes for the children. In Herbert's case it was a question of him "paying" for his own consumption, but furthermore – and this was largely true for the other children as well – it was also a matter of him learning for his adult life. By work they gained both work morals and also specific knowledge of work techniques. In this way, child labour served both short and long-term ends.

The experience of herding shared by these children is neither exceptional, dramatic nor even unique. They started to work at an early age. Their daily life was shared by many of their contemporaries – boys and girls alike – both in the area where they lived and also in Sweden as a whole. This statement cannot however be supported by any references to any contemporary statistics about the number of children who worked with herding in Sweden. There were no statistics about how much or how extensive rural child labour was, unlike the case of children who worked in industry. Support must be found elsewhere and for the situation in Sweden it is the records of absence, kept by the schools and the state school inspectors' reports, which provide us with the possibility of understanding how extensive rural child labour was. In the inspectors' reports for the years 1861-1910 herding is mentioned as the work causing most absence.[23] But herding was not extensive only in Sweden. In 1908, a survey into Danish schoolchildren's gainful employment was carried out. Child labour was more common in the country areas than in the towns, and the most usual job in the rural districts was herding. Two-thirds of the boys were occupied with herding, whereas it was rather less usual among the girls – and it was among these children that the longest work day could be found – eight hours or more.[24] In Norway, where it is possible to follow rural child labour in official statistics at certain periods, the situation was similar around the turn of the century. Among the children, who worked for somebody else, herding was the dominant occupation. Just as in Denmark, there were great regional variations in the extent of herding, but it could also be seen that herding was in decline.[25] In 1908-09 a large statistical survey was carried out in Austria to look into the question of school children work. Here too the care and herding of animals were seen to be the most important occupations.[26] Elisabeth, Herbert, Hildur and Hilma had their experience of herding animals in common with many other children in Sweden, the Nordic countries and Europe.

Herding in its context

From the description given above, the work done by the cowherds could seem a marginal occupation requiring no qualifications. But this work – and the work carried out by children as a whole – must be seen in a greater perspective. Herding must be considered in relation to both agricultural economy and family economy. The job of taking the cows out to graze – if seen in isolation –

most probably did not place any great technical demands upon the children. It could not really take a long time to learn the job, but if we take our starting point in the experiences of "our" four children, we must realise that it was necessary to have certain basic skills: to know how to keep the herd more or less together and to know when there was a risk for it separating. In addition – and perhaps even more important – it was imperative to try to protect and safeguard other farm resources – in particular the growing crops. The alternative – a partially destroyed crop – was very expensive for the farmer and his household. In addition, and very important in the long run, the children who looked after the animals had to see that the available pasture was used as efficiently as possible to ensure the best grazing. The grazing resources were very limited for many small farmers, and thus the most efficient use of the available pasture was a central issue.

The work of herding was part of the farmer's total economy. Cattle, and animals on the farm as a whole, represented a large economic investment. Good animal husbandry was therefore an important condition for good housekeeping in the short and long term. The animals were used to pull things and provided raw materials, which were of great significance to the household's economy as a whole: food, clothes and manure. Cows had a very special role in the area

Herding boys from Tärnaby in Lappland 1919. (Photo: Stellan Rosén)

studied. Their yield – milk – became increasingly important to the agrarian economy in the latter part of the 19th century. Since the 1840s, agriculture in the area had concentrated on the cultivation of grain – oats – for export. However, the slump in prices on the international market during the 1880s set a stop to the continued cultivation of export crops. Instead, a slow but clear transition to the production of dairy products – particularly butter and cheese – got underway.[27] After the first shock waves were over, farmers in the area consciously tried to diversify their production. Total dependence upon the cultivation of oats had put them in a very vulnerable position and so instead they went in for the care of animals. Urbanisation created markets for goods such as butter and cheese, and the hand-powered separator made it technically possible for even small-holders to become part of the production and selling of butter. The sales of butter and cheese to the growing towns and urban districts replaced oats as the farmers "cash crop". This led to cattle playing an increasingly important role in the region's agrarian economy. Their yield could be converted into cash and buying power. To get a high milk yield, it was important for the cattle to get as much fodder as possible and of as high a quality as possible. We know that the way in which the animals were kept improved because more fodder crops were grown, so that the animals could have greater food supplies – especially during the period when they were kept inside. The growing season was seen as something wholesome and useful and in part free and, provided it was used to the best advantage, could result in more and richer milk from each cow. In addition, grazing required less work than the extensive process of cutting, drying, transporting and storing the hay in barns. Consequently, herding came to play a central part in supporting the household even though the animals were kept inside for a long period of time. It is into this context of agricultural economics that the role of the children as cowherds must be set. The work of Elisabeth and the other children was not merely to "watch the cows". They protected and created important family resources. Development within the farming industry led to the greater importance of this work. The question however is, why did they herd their animals in the area under study at all? Why did they not keep them in enclosures instead?

Herding or barbed-wire

The herding of cattle had been the accepted way of dealing with the question of grazing during the outdoor season for a long time. There were also extensive common lands, which could be used by everyone in a village with animals. The principle, which was applied, was that fields and meadows were fenced off – not the animals. The animals were then looked after by special herdsmen, often grownups but children were also used for herding. Changes in the law brought this collective grazing culture to an end. Land ownership and grazing rights were individualised and the old herding system died out.[28] The new system found expression in the 1857 Bill of Protection, which decreed that pasture land – and thus the animals – should be fenced in. The Bill allowed the possibility of the animals being kept, either by herding or by tethering, so that they did not damage growing crops. The overriding responsibility for the animals not going into areas of growing crops was placed on the owner.[29] The earlier system of fencing with wood, stone, earth or twigs was expensive both regarding materials – this was especially the case for gardens – and/or the work required for its erection and maintenance. When the new fencing principle was introduced, it meant that many farmers – who were moreover animal owners – used the cheaper system of herding instead of the older, more expensive system of fences. In addition, access to large areas of pasture disappeared for many smallholders. They were directed to use, in part, the grazing areas available within the compass of their own farms, which were often likely to be very small and not enough to feed even a few cows – and, in part, to graze on land considered marginal because of impediments such as river banks, dykes and so forth.

The alternative, to building wooden or stone fences and walls, was to use barbed-wire fencing. Technically, this was in early use in the region – but among the bigger landowners. To put up a barbed-wire fence required two things, however. The first was to have the means to be able to buy it, which smallholders did not, and the second was to have an area of pasture land sufficient for the grazing needs of the animals and then to consider it a profitable investment. Most probably barbed-wire was a too expensive option for the large number of small farmers. Herding and tethering was for them the optimal – and perhaps only possible – alternative. In contrast, on larger farms it was possible to invest in barbed-wire and also, most probably, have access to larger areas of pasture. This is why children were used to herd animals in an early phase on the larger farms – and why they were later replaced by barbed-wire. The question is why children, rather than any other workforce, herded the animals?

Lack of manpower and "time capital"

Much of the Swedish countryside experienced a serious decline in the population during the last quarter of the 19th century. This was very much the case in Bolstad also.[30] One stream of this population drain took the form of emigration to the USA, in particular, but also to Norway. Simultaneously, there was an internal Swedish migration to the towns and industrial areas of western Sweden. This crisis was rooted in the drop in grain prices from the mid-1880s. The consequences of this population decline was a severe lack of labour. Even the number of children decreased noticeably. The response to the slump in the price of grain was to change over to an increased animal production. Keeping animals increased on the farms and the number of cattle, in particular, rose. This new direction – that farming was taking towards butter and cheese – was labour intensive, since it was in principle based on existing techniques – that is to say milking by hand. The only technical innovation was the hand separator, which made it possible for small farmers to make the transition to dairy production. The transition to animal production thus most probably led to an increase in the volume of work, which should in turn be shared by fewer workers, in principle. Production efficiency and mechanization only marginally lightened the labour equation in the area. The result was a lack of labour – in turn influencing the child's role as a source of labour. The increasing numbers of cattle, in combination with the prevailing fencing system, required herding and this was a solution that – at the end of the 19th century – had been applied for several decades. Children became more attractive as a source of labour – but the question remains whether children had any other advantages? Was there something children had that other sources of labour did not have?

The children's physical strength – their "physical capital" – and their knowledge – their "knowledge capital" – were the limits for the demands agricultural production made. Many jobs required great physical strength, which children were not considered to possess. This was something everyone was quite conscious of. Similarly, there were jobs requiring knowledge or many years' experience, which, again, children could not be expected to possess. In consideration of this, a systematic, conscious training of the children by the adults occurred. This usually happened informally by the child participating in different types of tasks. In this way, children gained both physical and knowledge capital. But children had another "capital" – time. Time was a resource children automatically had, and it did not demand any preliminary investment such as training or education. Children could therefore compensate for their limitations concerning physical and knowledge capital with their time capital. Time was the substitute for their other, limited resources.

Herding was, as we have earlier discussed, not merely an uncomplicated "guard occupation". It also took time. This is where the children came into the picture. The great competitive advantage that children had was access to time – a time not previously decided or claimed by other interests. The time that the adults had at their disposal was more clearly reserved for the obvious, foreseeable purposes of earning a living. Time was therefore much more something grownups did not have. It is in this context that – compulsory – schooling and school attendance came to mean a fundamental change as far as children were concerned – and to cause problems both for the school and for families. School and school attendance demanded the child's time and thus "encroached" upon the family's possibilities to have the child at their disposal for work, for example. The family got a competitor for the child and its time, which previously had not existed. It is because of this that the meeting between these two interests was so problematic – especially in the first phase of the establishment of the schools. This conflict was solved in Bolstad – and also in other regions – by the family giving work priority over school and keeping the children at home. However, families also tried other strategies – such as trying to persuade the local school authorities to organize their children's schooling so that it competed as little as possible with the work seasons. The clearest example of this was the introduction of part-time study in Bolstad – and other rural areas – and a variation of this called period study in which the older children went to school during the late autumn and winter but were free in the spring, summer and early autumn.[31] This free period coincided obviously with the peaks of the farming cycle and with herding, in particular.

"To live was to work"

Lack of labour and children's "time capital" are hardly enough explanations for the problem, which is being discussed here. Work and the ability, the will and the knowledge of how to work were conditions for life for the small farmers in the late 19th and early 20th centuries. Work was a condition and a means for earning a living but it also had a value of its own. This ideology about work was an attitude that consciously and unconsciously was conveyed to the children. This happened through the children being expected to participate and by their actual participation in the farm work. Work even became a form of culture for the children and young people. They trained and held competitions to practise strength and skills, which would eventually show their ability and qualifications for the work. Thus, the ability to do certain tasks at an early age became a point of honour. These tasks were usually different for boys and girls. On the other hand, inability to perform these tasks was an economic and cultural handicap. Growing up in a farming family therefore consisted mostly of work training and in being brought up to understand the necessity of work. By adjusting and gradually increasing the work in relation to the child's strength, age and maturity, the child was schooled to a future life as a farmer or farm labourer. In Bolstad, this ideology about work was also founded on religion. It was an orthodox Lutheran interpretation of religion in which the idea of a calling in life was strongly emphazised. The area preserved a strong belief in the church despite an increasing secularisation of Swedish society.[32] This religious ecclesiastical tradition supported the central place work had in everyday and family life. Children should therefore learn to participate in all the tasks necessary for earning a living from an early age. The spiritual message about work and family, which was incorporated in the regular, recurring church ceremonies, had a material correspondence in the family as a work agricultural unit. Thus, a strong identity and unity were created between daily work conditions – to a life beyond all that related to the "heavenly" aspect. Child labour was in this way granted cultural legitimacy. But how was this expressed in herding specifically?

The local legitimacy of herding

The unwillingness or inability to come to grips with a phenomenon with the available legal means ought to be regarded as a cultural acceptance of that phenomenon. Until the 1940s, rural child labour was not governed by law in Sweden.[33] The few attempts made, as with industrial child labour, to regulate by law a child's farm work, were dismissed and unsuccessful, although it was taken up seriously by the Parliament in 1915.[34] Child labour was accepted and had apparently significant support. To some extent, this was because life and work in the rural communities were not considered in the same way as the work carried out by children in an industrial environment. Time spent in the country and life there were considered to strengthen both body and soul. The work was usually done in the fresh air, the children often worked on the initiative of their parents, or at least in close contact with them. It was also technically very difficult juridically to create adequate instruments of the law, which could actually work in real life and be applied to the multifaceted work of farming. But it would also seem that the use of child labour in agriculture was too important for any intervention to be really possible. Any such decision would have lacked legitimacy and, for these reasons, no laws were passed.

Therefore, we understand that the work of herding was not regulated by any labour welfare laws and regulations. The only attempt to regulate herding in any way was a rule from 1734 in which society decreed that girls, rather than boys, should do the herding. In this case the misgivings, which produced this regulation, were the claim that boys would be tempted to commit bestiality. Before the changes and the 1857 Fencing Decree, herding was an activity discussed and organised on the local village level and, through the herder's institution, it had a formal status and legitimacy. As we have already discussed, after these changes herding and care of the animals during the grazing season were privatised, and children became almost exclusively responsible for this task. The herding of animals done by children was, as we have seen earlier, the only reasonable solution for many small farmers. But now children's work did not have the same formal sanctions or status. This was not discussed in village meetings or mentioned in village charters. It was not regulated as such and did not maintain the same official status. The work done by the children became invisible, but they did a necessary job.

The fact that the children's work herding animals had a local legitimacy is however revealed in how the question was resolved in Bolstad, for example. For a long time herding was most probably the single most important reason for absence from school. This absence was not combated locally because the local school authorities, mainly farmers, knew very well that this absence was a "practical necessity". The lack of any attempt to stem up for absenteeism must be interpreted as an insight into and a defence of the needs of the local community. In addition, the school's terms were adjusted and organized to suit the grazing season. The work done by the children was necessary – and as such it was treated with great local respect. The herder children of Bolstad – like those of other similar regions – had cultural legitimacy. Until the 1920s you could see advertisements in the local newspapers for "herdsboys" and "herdsmaids". These designations in themselves reflected a need and also a culture.

But the herding tradition also had its roots and ultimate legitimacy in religion and religious interpretation. The ecclesiastical and religious tradition in Bolstad was very faithful to the Bible. Daily life should be lived in agreement and consistency with the letter of the Bible. Even if it is reasonable to interpret the Bible on a metaphysical level, there is good reason to observe it to the letter as for the references and meaning of the shepherd motif. In the Gospel according to Saint John, for example, there is a simile to Jesus the "Good Shepherd" who "gives his life for his sheep." The literal – and naturally also symbolic – meaning of this and other "shepherd motifs" was brought to life in the people and local culture through religious ceremonies – in the child's case, this was especially strongly felt at its confirmation and preparation for confirmation. Confirmation can almost be considered as the school's "real examination". Much of the school's teaching was aimed to prepare the child for this vitally important event. Confirmation was required for marriage and was therefore the real – and culturally legitimized – starting point for the building of a family. Admission to confirmation was only granted when the child had successfully completed his or her schooling. It is through the local traditional and literal interpretation of the Bible by the church and the role of the school and confirmation that we must judge the weight and legitimacy of the shepherd motif. To herd cows and to be a "good shepherd" cannot have been as far apart as we might suppose from our modern point of view. Thus, herding had double legitimacy; partly, on a local level because of the structure of farming and, partly, through the letter and symbolism of the religious message. It was also in this local community that the child was to find his future. In this historical situation, other messages and other cultures – for example the new, progressive, industrial-urban, secularised and national – had difficulty in gaining local legitimacy.

The child's work and role in the division of family labour

The focus up to this point has been the herding work done by the children in its agricultural, technical and local cultural environment. There is however, a need to see the child's work as a herder in another context – the family's. We must therefore widen our perspectives to look more closely at the work done by children in general. Within the given framework children performed a series of tasks, which the demands to earn a living placed on the farming family. Herbert recalls in particular autumn threshing. By the age of 13 he had learned to plough alone with a horse, and many years earlier he had learned how to use a scythe. Elisabeth and her brothers and sisters "helped" the haymakers by gathering and binding the corn. When it was time to harvest the potatoes, it was a matter of mustering all the available family labour to safeguard the most important food of the winter and spring. Elisabeth, Hildur and Hilma all remember how they used to milk the cows every day, feed the pigs and the hens and look after their own or other families' small children. They also helped with the baking, butchering and cleaning. Because of his interest in horses, Herbert had a great responsibility to care for them and bring them in. All remember the endless number of times they had to bring in wood and water and the trips to the forest in the autumn to gather berries.

The fact that there was a clear – though not regionally similar – division of labour in the farming family is accepted knowledge. The family was a dynamic unit with relatively clear outer limits and flexible inner ones between the ages and sexes. This was especially true for the children. The limits between the sexes were quite mobile up to the age of about 12, although boys and girls had already developed certain work patterns specific to their sex.[35] Children had their given place, which could, however, vary from region to region and farm to farm with different production interests and economic conditions. They performed and participated in most of the work needing to be done in a farming household. Together with the adults, the children performed a whole series of tasks. They looked after the animals when they were kept inside, they helped with the spring work on the farm – work the land and sowing, and in the work of threshing and harvesting they had their given place. Spring and harvest times were critical periods in the farming production cycle since it was necessary to complete the work within a limited time. Because of this, the whole family had to contribute.

The children had, however, their own separate sphere of work or responsibility, which they carried out on their own initiative. Herding is the best and most obvious example. Picking up stones in the fields, spreading manure and keeping growing crops free from weeds were also purely children's activities. Keeping the household supplied with wood and water, and providing the family with berries and fruit were also often the child's responsibility. Another task was to mind and look after their younger brothers and sisters.

The Carlsson family from Grinstad in Dalsland harvesting timothy grass. 1920. (Photo: Oscar Carlsson)

Children had a complementary role in the family's division of labour, which probably considerably eased the burden of work and of making a living. In particular, the work done by the children made the family into a highly flexible production unit as they performed tasks that released other labour forces, particularly the father and mother, for work requiring the knowledge and strength the child could not yet have. They probably also made it easier to perform a whole series of jobs by helping the grownups in various tasks. Even if the time children spent work and their full-time work outside their own family decreased over the years, their work for someone else at certain times of the year could make it much easier for the family in question to support itself. Because they replaced hired manpower, work done by the family's own children was also economically advantageous.

It is from this perspective that we should understand the work, both herding and other tasks, which Elisabeth, Herbert, Hildur and Hilma carried out. Their work was done in relation to the contributions made by the other members of their families. It is neither particularly meaningful nor fruitful to take the child out of context and ask whether their individual contributions to the family's economy was greater than what they actually consumed.[36]

Child labour, school and childhood in change

In this article we have discussed rural child labour relating to a specific task and from a limited geographical area with a specific agricultural structure. There are several indications that the role of children in farming continued to be significant for several decades into the 20th century. One, perhaps the most important, was the conflict centring on the form and content of the rural school, which was fought in southern Sweden during the 1920s – and in which Bolstad played a very active part.[37] On the surface, it was a battle about the right to continue teaching Christianity – both content and quantity – according to the traditions of many years. A new, state curriculum in 1919 was the reason. However, the battle was ultimately about the opportunity and rights of a local community to create a school, which allowed for the fact that the child had important work to do on the farm. The determining question in the whole conflict was whether Bolstad could keep its part-time school. According to a decision reached by the Government in 1917, part-time study was not a satisfactory form of schooling. Only full-time study could fulfil the educational demands that modern, Swedish, industrial society placed upon its citizens. Full-time schooling would mean a doubling of the time children spent in school – and a similar decrease in the amount of time they spent at home. In this way, it would be much more difficult for the parent's to have the labour resources of the child at their disposal. The result was that both in Bolstad and in other rural areas the time-honoured school form – part-time schooling – continued and existed until the 1940s. The conflict was not limited to Bolstad but had extensive support in rural areas with a predominance of family farms all over the south of Sweden. The conflict was not simply about time and the right to have the child's labour potential at the parent's disposal but was rather a question of another attitude to children and to childhood in general. What was being fought for and protected was the deal of children and childhood.[38] A child was a work being, and in childhood it prepared for its work life – as a farmer or farmer's wife – through participating in work and in learning to work. This could not be done in a school. It could only be done out in the fields, in the cowsheds or in the kitchen. It is from this perspective that we ought to understand why many children in rural Sweden did not go to school more than they did. For them and for their parents, work was also a school.

There were much fewer children herding in the 1930s than in the 1890s. The use of barbedwire had spread and a part of the work usually done by the children had disappeared. Herding as such continued, but only to a certain extent in specific areas and in connection with smaller farms; it was one of the conditions of survival for these farms with very little pasture land, to enable them to own a few cows and earn money from selling milk. The spread of barbedwire was thus a first setback for the number of children herding. Another, more definitive decline took place as the number of smallholdings became fewer.

Despite innovations like barbedwire, threshing machines and milking machines, the family smallholding still had a few obvious jobs, which had to be done for a few decades. Agricultural mechanization certainly took over some of the work children had previously done but it also created new ones.[39] The children of farm owners still put in many hours' work. Around 1940, boys of about thirteen worked on average for more than 800 hours a year and girls of the same age about 500. In all 65% of the boys and 40% of the girls, whose parents owned and worked a farm, were work.[40] Moreover, a mentality and ideology survived, which decreed that country children ought to work.[41] To this must be added the fact that it was completely legal for farm children to work. It was not until the late 1940s that the government regulated their work with the Labour Welfare Laws. The agricultural work done by children has not been only governed by cultural values about work and childrearing but also by the economic situation of the time. When the availability of labour has been scarce or when high wages have made manpower expensive, children have been an acceptable alternative source of labour. This can be seen not least during times of national "crisis". It was very clear during the First World War. In 1916 certain changes were made to the labour welfare law, which enabled young children to be used to dig up peat.[42] There was also a demand from many rural areas to have school time reduced at harvest time – so that the children could help with the harvesting.[43] Farming was thus a daily experience and a way of life for many rural children for several decades into the 20th century.

The fight to keep part-time schooling – both in Bolstad and all the areas of southern Sweden, which strove to preserve part-time study in schools – has so far been used as an indicator of both the importance of the child as a source of labour in agriculture and as the expression of a basic appraisal of the child's socialization. The question is how to explain the fact that half-time schooling was in a state of serious decline from and including the 1920s and that full-time schooling became increasingly common – even in rural districts – during the 1930s and 1940s. Did the child's importance as a source of labour decrease – and did the cultural values, related to countrychildren and work – and thus life style, change? The spread of full-time schooling means that the child's labour resources were doubtless supplied with a new role, but also that the actual amount of work decreased in volume – at least in certain regions.[44] Mechanisation, a reduction in the number of small farms, state agricultural policy – in short, the rationalization of farming – changed the conditions for the contributions children were expected to make. Thus, families could combine an increased amount of time the child spent in school with the work of farming. This probably happened by rationalizing and making the family's and the child's use of time more efficient. The schooling of rural district children "was normalized" and life in the country began to take on a new shape. That the child had daily work continued, however, as most probably did the "work mentality". In a study into school children's free time carried out in 1946, it was shown how the schoolday – before and after school – was filled with daily chores. In some regions, daily chores took more time each day than did the lessons in school. [45] One could therefore say that farm children took their work into the classroom in the full-time school. How the clash between these two cultures was dealt with individually and collectively is an area full of interesting questions, which still has to be researched. Did the rural children turn the urban-industrial, formal school culture into their own – or did they live in two distinct cultural worlds – work/home and school? In other words, because the rural culture did not become the school's.

Even if this alternative did not become a reality, the fact remains that the scheduling of the Swedish school – especially its long summer holiday – originated in agrarian conditions. It was then that the countrychild was most needed to work at home – and the school had to relinquish its demands on the child's presence. Thus, we can even say that today's school – as far as external appearances are concerned – bears the mark of a completely different reality and ideology about children.

Notes

1. Dagbok för Högstorps folkskola 1892 – 1900, Bolstad's Parish records, PeBo.
2. Sörensen 1942, pp. 134-140; Sjöberg 1996, pp. 58-65.
3. See for example Berättelser om Folkskolorna i Riket 1905 – 1910, Karlstad's diocese, p. 53.
4. Sjöberg 1996, p. 131.
5. Encyclopedia of Social history pp. 105-107.
6. Cunningham 1995 pp. 138-145.
7. Horn 1994 pp. 25-27.
8. Horn 1974; 1985 pp. 82, 107.
9. Heywood 1988 pp. 17-60.
10. Jamieson & Toynbee 1993.
11. West 1989 pp. 73- 98.
12. Mitterauer 1988 pp. 144-163.
13. Slettan 1982, Slettan 1984, Slettan 1993. See also Svelmo 1982.
14. Szabo 1971.
15. Liljequist 1991, pp. 102-122.
16. Brembeck 1986.
17. Perlinge 1995 pp., 51, 58-59.
18. Szabo 1970 pp. 184-191, 231-236.
19. Szabo 1971.
20. Floystad 1982.
21. For more information about this area see Sjöberg 1996 pp. 26-33. See also the map at the end of this article.
22. The section about Elisabeth, Herbert, Hildur and Hilma is based on interviews made in 1993.

23 Sjöberg 1996 p. 106.
24 Danmarks statistik 1910.
25 Floystad 1982 pp. 261-262; Slettan 1984 pp. 69, 72.
26 Schiff 1912.
27 Sjöberg 1996 pp. 29-31, 127-128.
28 Szabo 1970, p. 234, claims, using Germany as an example, that the system of using children to herd the animals flourished when the commonlands were abolished.
29 Svensk Författningssamling (SFS) 1857:59; Sjöberg 1996 pp. 125-126.
30 Sjöberg 1996 pp. 28-29.
31 Bruce 1935 pp. 65-71.
32 Martling 1958 pp. 52-55.
33 Ettarp & Kvarfort 1981 p. 44.
34 Sjöberg 1996 pp. 199-201.
35 Mitterauer 1991 pp. 147-148.
36 Parts of the discussion about the child's contribution and costs for the family's economy are given in Macfarlane 1986 pp. 51-78.
37 Frediksson etc. 1950 pp. 52-79; Sjöberg 1996 pp. 219-231.
38 Sjöberg 1996 pp. 195-217.
39 Perlinge 1995 pp. 51, 58-59 argues the thesis that mechanization from 1930 had the good of the children in mind.
40 Nyberg 1995, note 24. From Nyberg's research we see that eleven-year-old boys worked 565 hours and eleven-year-old girls 224 hours per year. By the age of fourteen, the boys workload had tripled to 1660 hours, whereas the girls' had only increased by 20 % to 633 hours; Isacson 1994, pp. 118-129, also describes the participation of children in work on smallholdings in Dalarna in the middle of the 20th century.
41 For the situation in Norway, see Slettan 1984 pp. 70, 72-73.
42 Bruce 1940 p. 134.
43 Sjöberg 1996 p. 207. For an international comparison of the period of the Second World War, see Tucker 1994.
44 Isacson 1994 p. 129, claims that he can detect a decrease in the amount of child labour in Dalarna in the 1950s.
45 In some agricultural areas in the south of Sweden, children had a work day of four to five hours on top of their schooling, see Sjöholm 1948, table 1 and pp. 106-110. This can be compared with a total lesson time of about four hours per day.

Sources and literature

Unpublished sources
Bolstads kyrkoarkiv (Parish records); (Pastorsexpeditionen, Bolstad; PeBo)
Dagbok för Högstorps folkskola 1892-1900

Published sources and literature
Danmarks statistik (1910): "Skolesøgende Børns erhvervsmæssige Arbejde". *Danmarks statistik, Statistiske Meddelelser,* Fjerde række, Fem og tredivte Bind, første Hæfte. København.
Berättelser om Folkskolorna i Riket, 1905 – 1910. (Karlstad's Diocese)

Brembeck, Helene (1986): *Tyst Lydig Arbetsam. Om barnuppfostran på den västsvenska landsbygden*, (Lokalhistorisk identitet nr 5), Göteborg; Etnologiska institutionen.
Bruce, N.O. (1935): *Den svenska folkskolan och dess uppgifter*, Stockholm.
Bruce, N.O. (1940): "Det svenska folkundervisningsväsendet 1900 – 1920," in: V. Fredriksson (ed.) *Svenska Folkskolans Historia*, IV, Stocholm.
Cunningham, Hugh (1995): *Children & Childhood in Western Society since 1500*, London.
Encyclopedia of Social History 1994, P.Stearns (ed.), New York.
Ettarp, Lars & Kvarfort, Eva (1981): *Arbetsmiljöboken*, Stockholm.
Floystad, Ingeborg (1982): "Gjetarinnsats og gjetarkår," in *Heimen*, nr 4.
Frediksson, Viktor – Hofstedt, Lars – Paradis, Sigurd 1950: "Det svenska folkundervisningsväsendet 1920 – 1942," in: V. Frediksson (ed.) *Svenska Folkskolans Historia*, V, Stockholm.
Heywood, Colin (1988): *Childhood in Nineteenth-Century France. Work, Health and Education among the Classes Populaires*, Cambridge.
Horn, Pamela (1974;1985): *The Victorian Country Child*, Gloucester.
Horn, Pamela (1994): *Children's Work and Welfare, 1750 – 1880s*, London.
Isacson, Maths (1994): *Vardagens ekonomi. Arbete och försörjning i en mellansvensk kommun under 1900-talet*, Hedemora.
Jamieson, Lynn & Toynbee, Claire (1993): *Country Bairns. Growing up 1900 – 1930*, Edinburg.
Liliequist, Marianne (1991): *Nybyggarbarn. Barnuppfostran bland nybyggare i Frostvikens, Vilhelmina och Tärna socknar 1850-1920*, Umeå.
Macfarlane, Alan (1986): *Marriage and Love in England 1300 – 1800*, Oxford.
Martling, Carl Henrik 1958: *Nattvardskrisen i Karlstads stift under 1800-talets senare hälft*, Lund.
Mitterauer, Michael (1991): *Ungdomstidens sociala historia*, Göteborg.
Nyberg, Anita (1995): "Barnomsorgen – ett kvinnligt nollsummespel eller?" in: E. Amnå (ed.): *Medmänsklighet att hyra? Åtta forskare om ideell verksamhet*; Örebros.
Perlinge, Anders (1995): *Bondeminnen. Människan och tekniken i jordbruket under 1900-talet. Landsbygdens folk berättar*, Stockholm.
Schiff, Walter (1913): "Die Kinderarbeit in Oesterreich", *Archiv fur Sozialwissenschaft und Sozialpolitik*, b. 37.
Sjöberg, Mats (1996): *Att säkra framtidens skördar. Barndom, skola och arbete i agrar miljö: Bolstad pastorat 1860 – 1930*, Linköping.
Sjöholm, L.Gottfrid (1948): "En undersökning om folkskolbarns fritidssysselsättning och fritidsintressen", *Skola och samhälle. Tidskrift för uppfostran och undervisning*.
Slettan, Dagfinn (1982): "Barn i bondesamfunn", *Heimen*, nr. 4.
Slettan, Dagfinn (1984): "Barnarbeid i jorbruket", in. B. Hodne & S. Songner (ed.): *Barn av sin tid. Fra norske barns historie*, Oslo.
Slettan, Dagfinn (1993): "Barna og hamskiftet", *Heimen*, nr. 4.
Svelmo, Peter (1982): " Barnarbeid i jordbuket", *Heimen*, nr. 4.
Svensk Författningssamling (SFS) 1857 – 1859.
Szabo, Matyas (1970): *Herdar och husdjur. En etnologisk studie över Skandinaviens och Mellaneuropas beteskultur och vallningsorganisation*, Stockholm.
Szabo, Matyas (1971): "Barnarbete i agrarsamhället", *Fataburen*. Nordiska Museèts och Skansens årsbok.

Sörensen, Anna (1942): "Det svenska folkundervisningsväsendet 1860 – 1900", in: V. Fredriksson (ed.): *Svenska Folkskolans Historia*, III, Stockholm.
Tucker, Barbara M. (1994): "Agricultural Workers in World War II: The Reserve Army of Children, Black Americans and Jamaicans," in *Agricultural History*, 68:1.
West, Elliot (1989): *Growing Up with the Country. Childhood on the Far Western Frontier*, Albuquerque.

Ning de Coninck-Smith

The struggle for the child's time – at all time.
School and children's work in town and country in Denmark from 1900 to the 1960s

Introduction

During the First World War, the Copenhagen City Council conducted an occasionally spirited debate on the extent of schoolchildren's paid work. Copenhagen's Chief Education Officer wrote a memorandum at this time stating that he would endeavour to reduce the extent of children's paid work, since

> "The school system opposes in principle children carrying out paid work <u>before</u> school starts, because the children arrive exhausted for their educational work, which should be their main occupation..."[1]

Since then, school work and paid work have changed places in the lives of children in Denmark. Work used to come before school chronologically, whereas now the reverse is true. Paid work has been assigned to the time of day after school, a concrete expression of the fact that paid work is now considered secondary and school work primary.[2] During this process, some eras have been more decisive than others. The situation in the towns in Denmark changed in the 1900s to 1920s. In the countryside this happened in the 1950s.

Just as certain eras have been more important than others, some forms of work have been more controversial than others. From 1850 to 1900 legislators focused on children work in factories. Around the First World War, the reality of milk delivery boys disrupted the ideal portrait of a proper childhood. And when milk boys had nearly been removed, the focus was on children work in peat bogs. This conflict peaked during the Second World War.

This article has two themes. I review the legislation on and related regulation of child labour from 1900 to the 1960s. I also describe some of the social and cultural background that led to the new laws and regulations and the conflicts that arose when they came into force. For this purpose, I use two case studies of children's paid work that annoyed the adults: milk delivery and work in the peat bogs.

No Danish historian has previously studied any of these themes, as the previous work has focused on the time before 1914.[3]

From factory legislation to the regulation of children's work

Denmark's 1873 Regulation of Factory Labour Act prohibited people under 10 years of age from work in factories, and children were not allowed to work more than 6.5 hours per day including a 30-minute break. In 1901 the Act was made stricter. The minimum work age was increased to 12 years and the maximum hours reduced to 6 per day. The maximum distance allowed between work and school was 90 minutes, and the employer had to obtain proof of age from a physician's certificate. The Act also allowed its provisions to be applied to other forms of work. This was to be executed as bylaws prepared by local authorities in cooperation with the Ministry of the Interior and its expert group in such matters, the Labour Council. The regulations were only supposed to apply to children's work in towns and not agriculture, forestry, horticulture, fisheries and maritime work.

In addition to the Municipality of Copenhagen and the Municipality of Frederiksberg (a district of Copenhagen completely surrounded by the city of Copenhagen but a separate administrative entity historically and currently), bylaws on children's paid work were adopted for 24 provincial towns and one rural district between 1901 and 1923. Most of these bylaws were negotiated after the Regulation of Factory Labour Act was passed in 1901. A few new provincial towns were added when the Regulation of Factory Labour Act was made even stricter in 1913. Children were banned from factories, and this ban was extended to other types of work in the following years, including morning milk delivery. In 1925, the bylaws were repealed and replaced by national legislation (described later). The next section focuses on the adoption of the bylaws and the problems that arose when adults decided to restrict and regulate child labour in all of its diverse forms.[4]

Background

The first demands for legislative intervention in children's paid work other than factory work began to arise in about 1898-1899.[5] The authorities in Copenhagen considered it especially necessary to intervene,[6] and the probable reason was that the number of work schoolchildren increased drastically in the 1890s, especially boys from the public poor-schools (free of charge) and the public tuition schools, in which the school hours were allotted so that there was time for work.

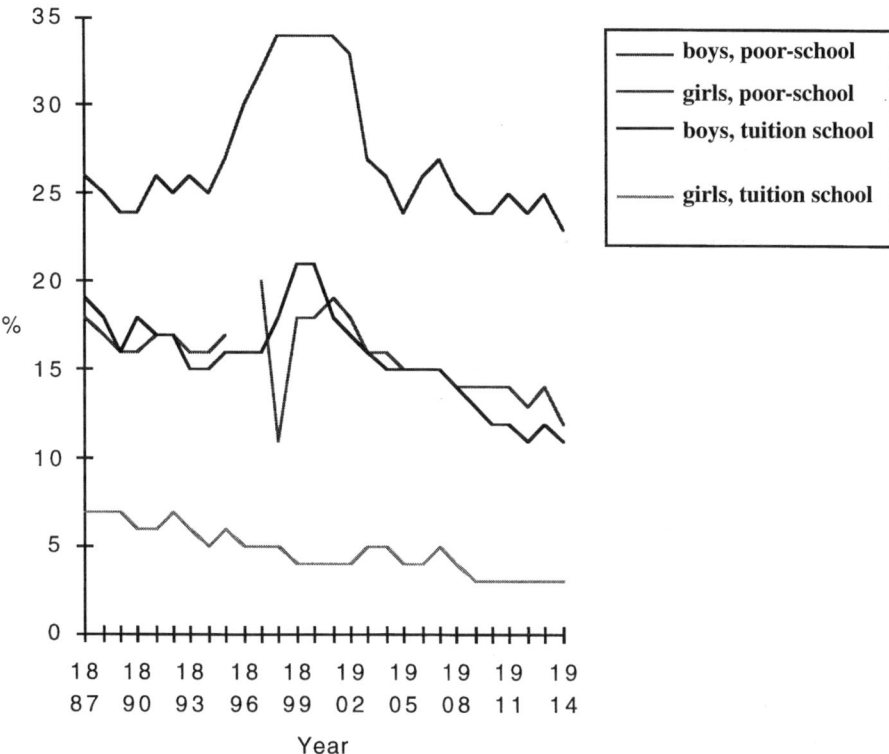

Figure 1. Percentage of public school pupils in paid employment in the Municipality of Copenhagen from 1887 to 1914 according to sex and type of school[7]

This trend upset the teachers in Copenhagen. Like their colleagues from the rest of Denmark, they had long hoped that children's paid work would no longer hinder their school work. Thus, the number of classroom hours had been substantially increased in many areas during the 1890s. The increase in school hours continued after a new Education Act was adopted in 1899, but especially schoolchildren in the towns got a longer school day.[9] The teachers thus desired to intervene in the free labour market, and the Danish Teachers' Association conducted the first national survey of schoolchildren's paid work in 1898-1899 to document the need for increased regulation.

The increase in the percentage of schoolchildren with paid work in Copenhagen[10] probably had several related causes. Paradoxically, the increase took place in a decade with increasing real wages. Nevertheless, the distribution of this increase was uneven: the skilled workers benefited, whereas single mothers and widows continued to suffer. In addition, increasing workers' real wages was hard work, since strikes and lockouts were as common as unemployment at the turn of the century. Thus, children's practical and financial contribution played a crucial role in Working-Class families. As late as 1910, the director of the National Bureau of Statistics claimed that each worker lost an average of 40 workdays per year from strikes and unemployment, equivalent to 150 kroner per year in lost wages, which was about the amount an errand boy could earn.[11]

The demand for children's labour was increasing in this period, probably because of the economic boom in the 1890s. Real wages were increasing and retail trade expanded. With a few exceptions, such as the tobacco and glass industries, especially retail trade absorbed the many new male labourers, whereas girls cleaned, washed clothes and minded young children. The new phenomenon of milk carts was also emerging. People previously bought milk directly from the farmers' carts or from the many home-distillers, who kept cows to consume the spent grains from distilling. In 1878, the first dairy company was formed: Copenhagen Dairy. The medical community supported this move; one purpose was to eliminate the diseases caused by contaminated milk, especially infant diarrhoea and tuberculosis. Copenhagen Dairy demanded a high standard of hygiene from its suppliers; they had to refrigerate the milk until it was collected. The milk was brought to a central dairy and was then distributed to the customers by milk carts.[12] Each cart was administered by a driver with five or six boys helping.

From adult laws to child laws

The first municipality that followed the recommendations of the state authorities was the Municipality of Copenhagen. At about the same time that negotiations on regulating children's work were proceeding in the Municipality of Copenhagen, the matter was taken up in the Municipality of Frederiksberg with the hope of coordinating the struggle against child labour, and especially against the milk boys. The large dairy companies that had formed since 1878 were located in Frederiksberg, and the school authorities wanted to adopt uniform regulations to prevent parents from speculating in differences between municipalities. As can be seen from figure 2 there had been a drastic increase in the number of working schoolboys during the 1890s at Frederiksberg.

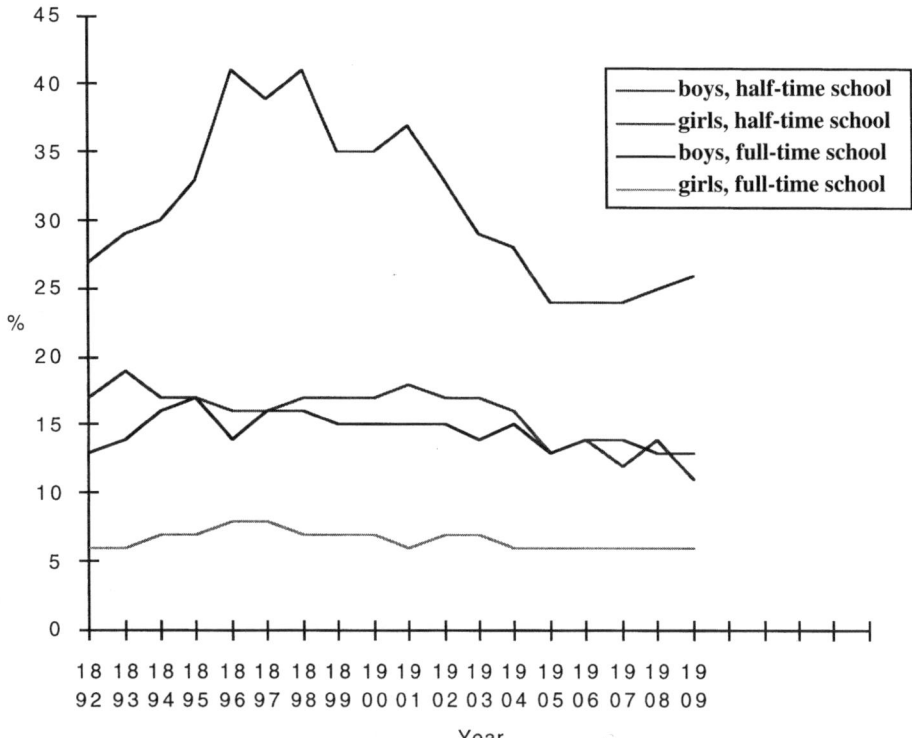

Figure 2. Percentage of public school pupils in paid employment in the Municipality of Frederiksberg from 1892 to 1909 according to sex and type of school[8]

The bylaws in Copenhagen and Frederiksberg set an example, as many bylaws were adopted elsewhere between 1907 and 1911. The lag reflects the fact that the struggle against child labour spread from Copenhagen to the provincial towns and finally to the villages, with a delay of about three decades. Two organizations played a key role in the surging regulation: the Association of Provincial Towns, which wanted identical bylaws for child labour to ensure

The struggle for the child's time

equal competition between the towns, and the Danish Teachers' Association, which had led a massive campaign since the late 1890s to strictly regulate (if not ban) children's paid employment.

From the late 1890s, it became clear that certain types of children's work demolished the ideal of a proper childhood more than others: industrial work, milk delivery, hawking and evening and night work at bars and in amusement parks.[13] But otherwise there was no opposition to children work as such, if it did not take time away from school work, because children's incomes played an important role in the finances of many families. And for the same reason the poor-law authorities in Copenhagen feared that far too restrictive legislation would increase the number of families seeking public assistance. Finally, many people felt that work kept children off the streets.[14] The Copenhagen bylaw from 1903 prohibited people under 12 years of age from selling milk, bread, cakes or newspapers, work at bowling alleys, bars or amusement parks, distributing beer or kerosene, or engaging in any other form of trade enterprise. Children were exempted from the provisions of the bylaw if they worked for their parents.

In the stipulations on which types of work were prohibited for children, the decisive criterion was the extent to which the work was considered to endanger their health. Nevertheless, some types of work in which the moral strain reinforces the potential physical harm, such as night work or work at a bar, were considered more hazardous than others. In contrast, many adults thought very highly of domestic work. If it was a proper home, then a girl could learn much that could be useful later in life. And in private employment, an additional advantage for the parents was that the child often received food and clothing instead of money.[15] Nevertheless, everyone did not agree with this viewpoint. And it was precisely this question that differentiated Copenhagen from the smaller provincial towns. In Copenhagen the main concern was work among the oldest schoolboys; the focus in the smaller towns was the youngest children, the girls and the work in private homes. These differences probably reflected the fact that child labour was more widespread among the youngest children and among girls in the provinces than in Copenhagen.[16] But the question was the extent to which legislation could cover private matters, including parents' use of their children's labour. And how young could the children be that were to be covered by such legislation? The work of the youngest schoolchildren usually comprised domestic chores or babysitting, and very often in private homes. For example, in Ribe, Senior Teacher Larsen found that the school had 19 girls and 16 boys under 12 years of age who had paid employment. Three delivered newspapers, and most of the rest ran errands, carried wood, cleaned, washed dishes and babysat.[17]

The Ministry of the Interior consistently refused to regulate private relationships. The urban middle class had the same opinion, often sending in petitions when the legislation approached their kitchen doors.[18] In the midst of a debate in the Vejle Municipal Council, one of the participants realized that

> "...on certain matters things have gone a bit too far. For example, I do not believe that there is reasonable cause to prohibit children from raising skittle pins. This does not have to strain them, and it will surely not be destructive to their moral fibre. And who else can be used to raise skittle pins if children may not?"[19]

The Regulation of Factory Labour Act solely regulated commercial employment and not private employment. This meant that most work by girls was not regulated. The first draft of bylaws in both Copenhagen and in several small provincial towns included regulation of cleaning and child-minding. Except for two bylaws, this provision was eliminated during the negotiations; one reason was that the Ministry of the Interior argued that these types of relationship were covered by the Master and Servant Act.[20] Nevertheless, in 1918 schoolchildren in the Cities of Copenhagen and Frederiksberg were prohibited from cleaning business premises not belonging to their parents.

The Regulation of Factory Labour Act specified a minimum age of 12 years. The various proposed bylaws submitted to the Ministry of the Interior before 1914 reflected the fact that it was not easy to maintain 12 years as a uniform minimum age. Boys and girls of varying ages worked in various places, but they all attended schools, as Denmark had implemented mandatory instruction for children at a very early stage. Many provincial towns therefore chose to equate children's paid work and the paid work carried out by schoolchildren. For example, as stated in the draft of a bylaw from Viborg in 1909:

> "Regardless of age, no schoolchild should work running errands if the school physician has any reservation about this."[21]

During the negotiations with the Ministry of the Interior, the Viborg Municipal Council, similarly to other municipal councils, had to concede the required age-specific regulation. But precisely because children's work was (and still is) perhaps more determined by function than by age, the old bylaws specify several different age limits: 10 years in some, 12 years in most and 11 in a few.[22] Another result of the adaptation of the bylaws to the existing Regulation of Factory Labour Act was that the local authorities could be certain that the Ministry would reject their proposals for prohibiting children's work before school.[23]

On the whole, the Ministry of the Interior wanted to avoid excessive interference in private employment relationships and the employment relationships in certain commercial sectors. They were therefore slower to give up the idea that

The struggle for the child's time

children were workers in their own right. This was in contrast with many local representatives of teachers, who advocated the interests of the schools during the molding of the bylaw proposals. For them, children were primarily schoolchildren.

Finally, there was the question of who would enforce the bylaws. Factory inspectors and the police enforced the Regulation of Factory Labour Act, but when the question of bylaws specific to children was first being debated in Copenhagen, the Chief of Police in Copenhagen discouraged any form of intervention in internal family affairs. He believed that the teachers and the school system should deal with this problem,[24] and many people agreed. The Ministry of the Interior received proposals from the provincial towns that the school boards should have the right to grant exemptions from the provisions of the bylaws and school physicians should have the right to issue prohibitions. But since the bylaws were drawn up pursuant to the Regulation of Factory Labour Act, the school had no role in supervision or enforcement. The bylaws thus did not contain provisions on supervision, but the police had the right to issue fines.

Nevertheless, the teachers continued to feel that they had a special responsibility to enforce the bylaws. The mayor responsible for schools in the Municipality of Copenhagen felt that the teachers should know the bylaws "as they know their catechism, so that they know precisely what may be demanded of the children and what may not be...".[25] The Municipality of Frederiksberg created a position in 1918 as supervisor of schoolchildren's paid work. The purpose of this was to regulate children's work amicably.[26]

This supervision came into force on 1 January 1919 and functioned until summer 1958. The first year there were 127 cases, and 27 of these were reported to the police. Most cases involved children who were not old enough to work or who had worked too many hours. Schoolchildren were employed to deliver for dairies, greengrocers, bakers and laundries, and nearly all were boys. Girls' babysitting and private cleaning jobs were not covered by the bylaw. The number of cases decreased by more than half in 1920. Until 1940 there were about 50 cases per year, with great variation between years. From the mid-1920s, almost no cases were sent on to the police.[27]

Thus, the trend was towards making supervision of children's paid work into a question of school policy and less a police matter. Frederiksberg had the only supervisory authority, and the question is how effectively the bylaws were enforced. During the First World War the Association for the Promotion of School Hygiene, especially referring to the situation in Copenhagen, claimed that the police were better suited to enforce the bylaws than were teachers, who often avoided intervening for social reasons. Nevertheless, the Association assessed that the bylaws had reduced children's paid work, especially by reducing the number of milk boys. The Association maintained that the main factor was the conversion of schools from half-time to a full-day in 1911 in Frederiksberg.

The Association said that this resulted in a massive flight of poor families over the border to the Municipality of Copenhagen.[28] But the full-day school was also coming in the Municipality of Copenhagen, starting in 1918.

The existing statistical material seems to confirm these assumptions. In Frederiksberg, 15-20% of the school-age boys and 9-10% of the school-age girls were work before the school hours were extended to a full day. Afterwards, the figure for boys declined to 12-13% and 5-6% for girls. In the Municipality of Copenhagen, about 16-17% of the boys and 7-8% of the girls were work during these years, until the full-day school was introduced. In the 1920s the figure declined to 3-4% of all pupils.[29] Thus, this implies that the full-time school played a role, but the declining number of children registered as having paid work could have resulted from an increasing number of children work surreptitiously as a result of the new bylaws: either they were too young or they continued in occupations prohibited for children. In any case, unemployment had an impact on many families, and many families needed the monetary contributions of children.

The trend in the number of registered milk boys in Frederiksberg showed that the 1903 bylaw alone could not prevent an increase in the number of milk boys in subsequent years. The decline first stabilized and became substantial after the school hours were increased. When the bylaw was revised in 1918, and boys were no longer allowed to be morning milk boys, there were hardly any left.

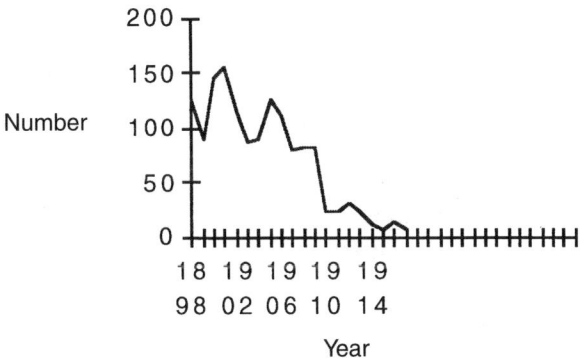

Figure 3. The number of boys employed for morning milk delivery in Frederiksberg, 1898 – 1917[30]

The struggle for the child's time

Milk boys – children who grew up too early

Among the many types of children's work in this era, morning milk delivery was the most controversial, especially among teachers but also among those who wanted the twentieth century to become The Century of the Child. The vigorous efforts to eliminate milk boys were not based solely on the fact that the boys were dead tired when school started at 1.00 p.m. after work from 5.00 or 6.00 a.m. until noon. The opposition was based on the efforts to prevent children from growing up too rapidly. And if anyone could provoke this fear, it was the milk boys. They participated actively in the strikes of their adult colleagues and were virtually hailed as heroes in the Working-Class press when they went on strike during the great Dairy Strike in November and December 1896, in which the workers at Copenhagen Dairy went on strike to win the right to organize themselves. The union paid strike benefits to the boys as well as the adults.[31] The milk boys were not alone in being active in the trade union movement; the tobacco industry was also hit by a wave of demonstrations and strikes by boys from the 1890s to the 1910s.[32]

Chants and songs from several milk boy strikes were supposedly written by the boys themselves. For example, a chant from a strike against the Pasteur Dairy in winter 1894: "Pasteur, Pasteur, that milk is sour!".[33] Or this chant from a strike at the Solbjerg Dairies in Frederiksberg in about 1905:

> We milk boys, we milk boys,
> we work only for the reddest gold,
> we will not bring the milk out
> until we get tips,
> we will party, really hearty,
> we will do what we please
> and not take any guff from a scab![34]

This activity spread like a wildfire. Some milk boys once stood in the school yard during school and said "Let us out! Let us out! Otherwise you will have a riot!". According to information collected during the great strike in late 1896 by Joakim Larsen, the Chief Education Officer at Frederiksberg, the boys had taken the trade union struggle with them into the schools. Under-age scabs and a boy who had not gone on strike were mobbed, and the milk boys had incited the other pupils to help them upset the milk carts. A few boys used the strike to get an extra day off school. The teachers did not hesitate to react; one teacher supposedly threatened to revoke school meal privileges from a girl whose brothers were on strike.[35]

Disrespect for school and all it implied along with trade union consciousness

Around 1898 the 9-year-old boy – far to the rigth on the milkman's wagon – had together with his parents and younger siblings moved to Copenhagen from the island of Funen. When he was 11 his father died, and he was as a milkboy helping to support his family. (Photo together with pensioner memoir no. 1908 in the Copenhagen City Archives)

were central aspects of the milk boy culture, according to the accounts of the former milk boys.

> "We always came to school with a milk boy shirt, cap and moneybag. But then they prohibited schoolboys from being milk boys. Then we had to go home first and change our clothes. When the teacher asked if we were milk boys, we lied."

> "In school we shirked often. Then the school officer came home and threatened us with the child protection services if we did not go to school. We did not feel much like going to school after work for seven hours. When they whipped us, we stuffed our cap into our pants, but this was usually discovered."[36]

The milk boys had a special status compared with the other boys. They had money; although their wages went to their families, they often got to keep the tips. Harald Nielsen, who started work as a milk boy in 1912, remembers:

The struggle for the child's time

"We had 12 children in our family. All my wages went to the family. I could keep the tips, but it wasn't much, 2 øre or 5 øre. One customer gave me 50 øre. Among the schoolchildren we were tycoons because we always had some money. The school officer sold gingerbread cakes, and we could buy them every day."[37]

The boys also had a high status at home solely because of their role as breadwinners, especially since they ensured a relative stability in the family income at a time of frequent, recurring unemployment. For example, a former milk boy remembers that, when his mother had finally accepted that he would leave the tobacco factory to become a milk boy, the sky was the limit:

"She asked if I could also get my brother a job and if I could then there would be two salaries and we would come home with 15 kroner in total plus tips, and Father could have an extra beer and we would be in the money! ... Mother got delusions of grandeur and bought a hat for Father..."[38]

Despite the job's high status among the boys and adult workers, as demonstrated by the fact that the Working-Class movement's own dairy Enigheden organized the milk boys to march in a parade, in the first Child Welfare Day in Copenhagen in 1905, and arranged annual parties for the milk boys,[39] the former milk boys agreed that it was hard work in all kinds of nasty weather resulting in lack of sleep and too many beatings and cases of detention in the school. Regardless of the bylaws, some of the boys started helping their older siblings as early as when they were 8-9 years old:

"My brother was two years older and was a milk boy for Trifolium Dairy. I helped him as well as I could although I was six years old and short and scrawny. It was hard on winter days at 5.00 a.m. with those cold bottles. When I got to school in the morning and sat next to the warm wood stove, I usually fell asleep listening to the teacher. He did not understand why I fell asleep, so at that time we got whacked in the head..."[40]

The teachers never tired of complaining about the milk boys. Either they were rascals with too much money or, as a teacher who lived in Frederiksberg said at a teachers' meeting in 1908:

"I had the opportunity to see the milk boys, pale, worn out and warped. They go to the baker's with their tips and play pitch and toss and what have you. The milk boys have too much money. Their wages are garnished for things that they break and then they have to steal from one another and fight... We teachers should not tire of struggling against this perversion. Childhood should not be a time for paid work..."[41]

Or they were innocent, misused children that had to earn their keep and that of drunken and unemployed parents. A school principal wrote in a letter to the Copenhagen School System in 1897:

"During winter it can also be very difficult, especially for the small boys, who are often hired out here, after several large dairies have come into existence, when they have to hang onto a cart in biting frost at night or run around with wet hands often full of chilblains and open wounds, so one can certainly say that the high wage, which tempts the parents, is dearly paid for."[42]

The fundamental problem with the milk boys was that they "arrive tired at school, which should be their main occupation," as Copenhagen's Chief Education Officer expressed it in 1916 during yet another set of negotiations on reducing children's access to the labour market.[43] And the complaints did not stop before in 1918 when boys could no longer be milk boys.

The world looked quite different when the dairies were asked for their opinion. They claimed in 1909-1910 that it was difficult to hire enough boys that had been through confirmation (13-14 years old), although the dairies tried. They also felt that work had some advantages that far exceeded the positive effects for poor children in attending school. According to the Copenhagen Dairy:

"...this work also has a moral aspect, as the act of the child helping his mother, who must work hard herself, to earn the absolutely necessary daily bread, will often help the child more in later life than the learning that perhaps is missed..."

And the director of Copenhagen Dairy continued to describe how the milk boy work was just an apprenticeship at an early age:

"We do not employ any boy unless our inspector in charge of supervising the milk boys has investigated the conditions in his home, and this man has no other task but to give the boys advice and assistance. Of course, we are often disappointed, but we also have many satisfactory results with our boys.

The work is out in the fresh air, and many, many boys who came to us hungry and neglected in all sorts of ways have left us healthy and improved, while a not insignificant number stay employed with us or obtain good positions elsewhere..."

The struggle for the child's time　　　　　　　　　　　　　　　　　　　　　*141*

Nevertheless, the dairies had to accept the extension of school from half-day to full-day in Frederiksberg in 1911, which made it almost impossible to use any school boy as a milk boy. But as early as 1903, the boys were forbidden to deliver milk on Sundays. The fact that they did it anyway (according to the accounts of former milk boys), dressed as adults, is another matter that emphasizes that the effect of the new bylaws was not that children stopped work but that it became illegal and especially literally invisible. From then on the boys were forced to dress as if they were adults if they wanted to continue working.

> "As milk boys of school age, we were not allowed to work on Sundays. When the police came, we had to hide; we were put in the cart or we were sewn a piece of cloth for our short trousers so it looked like they were long trousers. I also had a piece of cloth sewn for my trousers but it was another type of material so it probably looked pretty funny. On Sundays we got 1 krone, which we could not do without."[44]

In the Municipality of Copenhagen the full-day school was implemented in 1918-1919. The ban on milk boys, which came into force in the cities of Copenhagen and Frederiksberg in 1919, resulted in a wave of protests from the retailers, dairies and dairy workers' trade union. The union agreed that banning milk boys would make milk more expensive, make many people unemployed and eliminate an important source of income for the poorest part of the population in Copenhagen. The work would also become harder for the boys, as they would then have to deliver the milk after school using a basket or a bicycle.

Nevertheless, neither the city councils nor the civil servants could be persuaded otherwise. The report prepared by a joint committee with representatives from the cities of Copenhagen and Frederiksberg in connection with the revision of the bylaws on children's work stated that the proposed restriction of work hours for children was:

> "based on the main principle that, if school instruction is to fulfil its purpose, it is absolutely necessary that the child not be unable to follow the course of instruction with the necessary attention and to prepare for school because of excessive exertion from other forms of work. This consideration has led to the situation in which the members of the joint committee, who are inclined to consider it positive on the whole that children are occupied with work outside school hours instead of being left to a leisure life that can often harm them, can support the proposed additional restrictions, just as the consideration that children from poor homes to a lesser extent will have access to contributing to the support of their families must be secondary."[45]

There was no longer any doubt that the school was to be the children's main work-place in Denmark.

From local regulation to national legislation

The expectations towards childhood were not reduced after the end of the First World War. On the contrary, the horrors of war spawned ambitions on behalf of childhood, and the 1920s became a decade in which many of the thoughts of a good childhood, which were thought in the years before the war, were not merely revived but also carried out. This was expressed in the work of a national commission on education between 1919 and 1923, but new trends were also seen in the regulation of child labour. Ambitions were high, the regulations were to be uniform in the whole country and the regulations were also to cover the areas in which children worked most frequently: delivery and agriculture. But the regulations did not serve their purpose, and again it was necessary to use another method than worker protection laws: the schools.

The start was signalled by an international labour conference in Washington, DC in 1919. The conference adopted two international conventions on the minimum age for children work in industrial enterprises and the use of young people for night work in industry. The Rigsdag (Denmark's parliament) ratified these two conventions in 1921, and they were followed up by legislation in 1922, the appointment of a committee the same year and new legislation in 1925, which made the old bylaws superfluous.[46] Children were prohibited from work during school hours, and 14 years became the new minimum age – not only for industry but also for craft and transport.

Children's work in agriculture and fisheries and their work in retail trade, even for their parents, was not covered by the new legislation. Nevertheless, 10 years had already been established as the minimum age for hazardous work in agriculture in the Regulation of Factory Labour Act of 1913. All other agricultural work by children was covered by the Regulation of Farm Labour Act of 1921: "It is prohibited for children to be employed during the time that they are to be attending school or confirmation instruction, and the necessary time for preparing therefor shall be allowed...."[47]

In connection with the preparatory work for the 1925 Act on the paid labour of children and young people, the Ministry of Health, which was responsible for these matters for a short period, approached the municipalities and informed them that the old bylaws needed to be revised. Very few municipalities replied to this letter. One of the replies prompted the Ministry to discuss whether it was appropriate to develop a model bylaw that could cover both agricultural and delivery work. As mentioned previously, the justification for this was that these areas were not covered by the new act, but also that the number of accidents among children work in agriculture had been increasing and the increasing urban traffic was considered a hazard for delivery boys. There were also special moral hazards for them, as Head of Section Hansen wrote in his report:

> "Delivery boys are considered a special type of child in school, and it turns out that they are very easily influenced in a wayward direction..."

Hansen believed that the revised bylaws of 1918 from the cities of Copenhagen and Frederiksberg could be considered as models. This would make 12 years the normal minimum age and establish a maximum of four hours per day and a national ban on children delivering milk in the mornings. Hansen also proposed that children should not be allowed to drive or ride alone, and they should be prohibited from using a scythe or other hazardous tools.[48]

The proposal was tabled higher in the system, and the result was that two new provincial towns adopted bylaws that covered children's work in fisheries and horticulture as well as delivery work.

Nevertheless, the civil servants of the Ministry of Health were not alone in their opinion that general guidelines on child labour were needed. This matter was discussed in connection with the work of the national commission on education between 1919 and 1923, and the new Primary and Lower Secondary Education Act of 1937 stipulated that children were prohibited from paid work outside the home before school starts each day. Simultaneously, the municipal councils were urged to adopt a special bylaw on children's work together with school authorities, parents and teachers.[49]

At a meeting with the country's school advisers shortly after the Act was adopted, the Ministry of Education's adviser on educational matters Kaalund-Jørgensen explained that the provisions were actually obsolete, since morning milk delivery work, which was the main target of the national commission on education, had virtually disappeared. The problem in the late 1930s was in a completely different place: the countryside. And there the new provisions protected only the salaried help, whereas "the master's son may well move the cows before he runs to school."[50]

A few years later another problem arose: many rural districts still had half-time schools and most of these had instruction in the afternoons, which meant that many children theoretically had the whole morning available for work. In 1939, a school board in northern Jutland thus asked the Ministry of Education whether the Act could be interpreted as meaning that children were allowed to work in the morning if school started at 12.30. In this district, several 10-year-olds were employed milking cows and started work at 6.00 a.m. in the summer and 7.00 a.m. in the winter.

The Ministry of Education was split on this question, as the most important factor was that the children not be tired when they arrived at school, even though the rule applied to all children regardless of whether they attended school in the morning or in the afternoon. But, according to a civil servant in the Ministry:

> "...it is, however, difficult to carry out. For a farm boy or girl to be prohibited from participating in the morning milking the day they are to attend school – and are surely awake anyway at the usual time and can then sit down with their hands in their pockets and watch the master and mistress milking like crazy..."

Thus, Kaalund-Jørgensen concluded "...that the violations of the regulations that occur must be without the Ministry's blessing", and the Ministry of Education therefore decided to do nothing in this case.[51]

The uncertainty about the interpretation of the section of the Primary and Lower Secondary Education Act on work by schoolchildren was based on the differences between town and country. Towns had universal full-time schools, whereas many rural municipalities had very different conditions. Work came first in these areas, also chronologically. This trend became even stronger from the 1930s to the early 1940s.

The Second World War: the reserve army of child labour

In May 1944, the Ministry of Education issued a circular that authorized the local school authorities in the countryside to suspend the oldest classes "in consideration of the necessity of using children for light agricultural work..." Just as during the First World War, in which the Ministry had issued a similar permit in 1916, the justification was a lack of adult labour power.[52] This time the supposed cause was the normal migration from agricultural areas in combination with the forced work for the German occupation forces. In addition, work in the lignite pits and peat bog attracted many workers, as the wages were considerably higher than in agriculture.[53]

The Ministry of Labour had asked the Ministry of Education to speed up this matter in April 1944. The Ministry's pedagogic adviser strongly advised against

> "...closing schools to free children for agricultural work. Most village schools have only 18 hours of instruction, and very few have 30 or 36 hours, that is, full-time schooling, while some have 24 hours per week.

The struggle for the child's time

> There is thus ample time to participate in agricultural work outside school, and the Employment Office must be adequate for this..."

Nevertheless, the circular was ready to be printed in early May. Pupils could be away from school for 3 weeks in addition to the planned school holiday if they were 12 years old and could document that they were going to work. The reasons for this were very simple, according to a civil servant in the Ministry of Labour:

> "Since Danes based on their own interest must be interested in agricultural work being carried out, educational considerations must probably yield to the considerations on which the application from the Ministry of Labour is based..."

Another civil servant, who participated in the preliminary work, added that it was probably best that the entire class be suspended rather than individual pupils were dismissed, as

> "otherwise farm boys will have to do the work, while the children of farm owners go to school, and this would not be appropriate. We must therefore grant district councils and school boards general authority to dismiss the relevant classes when the employment office requests it. When one thinks about the work that is being done in Finland and partly in Sweden to produce food, the measures being considered are a small sacrifice for the school..."[54]

The Ministry had intended that children would especially be used for weeding beetroot fields, picking peas, digging up potatoes and miscellaneous harvesting work. The year after the circular came into force (1945), reports were requested from rural districts in the whole country. The reports showed that 93 of Denmark's 107 rural districts had taken advantage of this scheme, and that the children had been used for light agricultural work similar to what the Ministry had envisioned.

It is difficult to assess now the extent to which this scheme alone contributed to increasing children's paid work during the Second World War. In Denmark until the 1950s parents were fined if their children failed to attend school without justifiable cause. But many school authorities considered the amount of the fine to be too small and ineffective in preventing parents from regularly

> "...keeping their children at home during harvesting, butchering, threshing, cleaning beetroots, spreading manure, rounding up animals, driving to market etc. etc...."[55]

This is confirmed by the available absence lists from rural schools. During harvest and Christmas, frequent reasons for absence included "helping Father", "healing Mother", "at work", "helping at home", "minding brother", "in the pea field" and "in the beetroot field."[56]

It is thus perhaps more reasonable to say that the scheme legitimated this practice for a brief period.[57] It was reintroduced in 1946 and 1947 but ended after that.[58] But the old habits did not die. For example, this complaint was included in a 1956 report to the Ministry:

> "...With regard to the reasons for the numerous absences, many pupils are participating in harvesting potatoes....And the reason that the school board for as long as possible has avoided giving the maximum fine for absence from school without an excuse is that even the maximum fine is so small compared with the pupils' opportunities for having an income in potato harvesting that it will probably not suffice to stop the absences but will actually be symbolic..."[59]

The negotiations on absence from school for work purposes is but one example of how pupils were used more or less legally as a reserve army of labour during the Second World War to an extent that challenged an ideal picture of childhood.

This did also happen in the towns – the inspector responsible for supervising child labour in Frederiksberg registered a clear increase in children's work during the war – but it especially happened elsewhere, and that was in the peat bog.

Children work in the peat bog

After 1945, statistics showed that 2,500 to 3,000 people younger than 14 years of age had worked in extracting and processing peat, and two-thirds of these were boys.[60] Peat work had traditionally been children's work. Children mostly worked together with women in blocking, drying and processing peat bricks: that is, stacking them and transporting the finished bricks from the bog.[61] This work was classified as agricultural work pursuant to a decision in 1904 and was therefore not covered by the provisions of occupational safety and health legislation.

The documentation from this era is therefore quite free of children. Nevertheless, during the Second World War, the Ministry of Labour and the public began to question whether this type of work was compatible with an ideal childhood.

The uncertainty spread from the bottom up as the local inspectors assigned

Work in the peat bog was traditionally undertaken by the whole family. The boy in the middle is 13 years old and he is getting ready to take the peat bricks to the stacks. Kærby, Jutland 1920. (Private photo)

to supervise the production of peat discovered that children were also used to transport raw peat from the bogs to the processing plant. But the National Labour and Factory Inspectorate concluded that this matter was not to be pursued for "reasons of production".

In spring 1944, this matter came to a head: the Inspectorate had leaked to the press that, because of labour shortages, the Inspectorate would not prevent children from work in the peat bogs, and several cases were reported from bogs in various parts of Denmark of children as young as 8-10 years being employed to transport raw peat. Several inspectors opined that this not only made the children miss school but it was also a case of child abuse and greed. According to the inspector for the Kolding district:

> "...the fact that children have been shown to be work in several of the cases must clearly be considered to be misuse of the children's labour power. It is especially disheartening to discover how poorly self-regulation functions; as soon as law enforcement slackens, immediate widespread misuse occurs. And the parents' attitude is often such that it does not include any protection for the misuse of children. For example, when a farm owner, as shown here, lets three of his children (of which the youngest is a child of 10 years) work in the bog for a total weekly wage of 270 kroner, one would not hesitate to consider this as greed..."[62]

In all these cases, the Ministry resolved that, as long as the children were 12 years of age or older and the work day did not exceed 9 hours, the situation would be tolerated. Of the 16 cases reported in Kolding, 15 were still illegal (and therefore supposedly intolerable), according to this interpretation.[63]

The inspectors were not alone in their outrage; the various parents' organizations also protested.[64] The attitude of the political parties was more tolerant, however. Thus, an editorial in *Socialdemokraten*, the newspaper of the social democratic workers' movement, carefully expressed the hope that children's work could be reduced as much as possible. The conservative newspaper *Berlingske tidende* supported the tolerance of child labour in the interests of youth and the nation.[65] Not surprisingly, the peat manufacturers supported this attitude and added that children's work in the peat bog was in accordance with the nature of agriculture and children:

> "After all, older children have always participated in the light tasks associated with peat work, and they nearly fight to get down to the bog, where the work is really like a child's play. When they are not assigned work that is too exhaustive, they are not harmed by being useful. It is therefore justified to let the laws to protect children rest, especially because strict enforcement of its provisions can risk reducing peat production, which it is essential to maximize."[66]

The 1950s: child labour and extending the school day in the countryside

The available sources do not show how long it was common practice to use children for peat work. The archives of the National Labour and Factory Inspectorate have no more cases on children in the peat bogs after 1944. But the county school advisers continued to complain about illegal absences, one reason was that children worked in the peat bogs. Thus, an inspector described the situation in a municipality in northern Jutland in 1950:

> "The most important reason for these absences is to be found in the use of children by their families as labour power in the peat bogs and in potato harvesting in the summer...."[67]

The winds of change were sweeping the rural schools in Denmark. In the early 1950s, the schools were changed from part-time (either half-day or every other day) to full-time schools. The new Primary and Lower Secondary Education Act passed in 1958 made the formal educational requirements identical in town and country.

The reports from the county school advisers show that many parents pro-

During the 2nd World War the shortage of energy made it possible to make good money from producing peat bricks besides keeping the family warm during winter. Between 2500 and 3000 children below 14 years of age were working in the peat bogs, mainly boys. (Photo from the Royal Library's collection)

tested the introduction of the full-time school; as a school board responded to the Ministry of Education, which had complained about a very high number of absences without excuse in 1952:

> "...We consider the numerous absences to be a transitional phenomenon resulting from a certain amount of irritation in the population about...the curriculum, which introduces <u>full-time instruction for all pupils</u>, in contrast to the previous instruction every other day or 4 days per week. Thus, this meant that older children could no longer be counted on for help at home on the farm on certain days of the week. This aroused some opposition among the parents, who could not understand why their children should attend school every day when the parents knew that many areas here in Vesthimmerland had not yet set up full-time instruction. Why should our children have more time in school than children elsewhere? ...The school board has therefore accepted a transitional period throughout this process....After this it was assumed that the problem would solve itself...[since it involves] relatively few families. The school board has spoken with these

families and explained to them that children have a duty to attend school. This also seems to have had some effect."[68]

Just as the school board had chosen a careful approach in this case to avoid confronting the parents more than necessary, some teachers preferred to go with the flow instead of laying down the law.[69]

Nevertheless, during the 1950s the idea that the school is the children's primary work place spread throughout the countryside. For example, this is proved by the preserved statistical material, which shows that an increasing number of children remained in school after the mandatory 7 years of education.

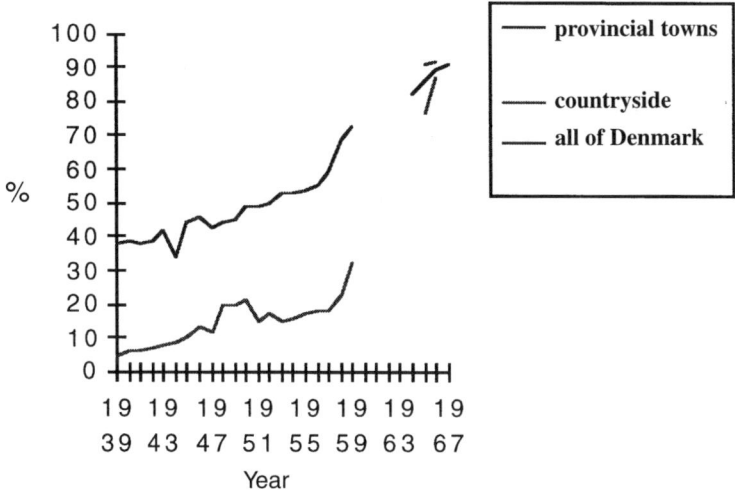

Figure 4. The percentage of pupils continuing in school after the 7th grade in Denmark 1939 to 1967 (percentages rounded off)[70]

These changes in the view of childhood and children's time were also incorporated in the legislation on occupational safety and health, which was revised in 1954. Agricultural work was covered by this legislation for the first time, but agricultural interests succeeded in reducing the minimum age for hazardous work from 16 in other sectors to 14 for agriculture, and children 10 years or older could carry out relatively hazardous tasks as long as the parents were nearby. The 1954 legislation restricted delivery work to two hours per day and only after school. This provision had been in force in Copenhagen since 1939. The new legislation also prohibited children under 12 years from carrying out delivery work.[71]

This extension of the coverage of the legislation on occupational health and

The struggle for the child's time   *151*

safety was associated with an increasing level of attention focused on child labour among the inspectors of the National Labour and Factory Inspectorate. The interest in the children work in the peat bogs in the 1940s was followed by an interest in children in fisheries in the 1950s, including their work in herring smokehouses. A case on Bornholm showed that children as young as seven years old were work with their mothers in the peak season. After this case was reported to the Inspectorate, the fishermen were instructed that all workers had to be older than 14 years.[72]

Conclusion

This article has had two themes: the regulations of children's paid work in Denmark from 1900 to the 1960s and the social and cultural conflicts related to two types of children's paid work, milk delivery in the early twentieth century and work in the peat bogs during the Second World War.

The investigation of the trends in regulation suggests that the regulation of children's paid work changed from being a local, primarily urban concern to a national one. The local bylaws were repealed and replaced by national legislation. Nevertheless, the question is how significant this was for the decline of and changes in children's paid labour in the period being studied. Based on my investigation, I believe that the effects were limited. First, the two jobs that were probably most common among children, farm work and urban delivery services, were largely untouched by the new legal restrictions. Second, children's work for their parents and in private domestic service was exempted from any form of legal intervention. Third, enforcement initiatives were few and irregular. Only the Municipality of Frederiksberg had an inspector supervising child labour; it is not known what measures were undertaken elsewhere. A factor that has been far more important for the development of the modern and largely work-free childhood in Denmark is the role of schools and the extension of school hours from half-days or every other day to full time. This process took place in the cities and the provincial towns in the 1910s and 1920s and four to five decades later in the countryside. An additional factor, which is outside the scope of this article, is the question of the interaction between trends in children's paid work and the living conditions of their families at all times. These conditions include the changes in real income and its distribution among families, but also the distribution of income within families and the related changes in family roles over time. For example, the development of the single (male)-breadwinner family model could have increased the burden of daily domestic chores for children within the family.

Child labour went on partial retirement but did not disappear. The historical evidence implies that the protective legislation and the spread of full-time education made the remaining paid work among children to become illegal and by that invisible. Children's work was more or less consciously ignored at the time, as illustrated by the milk boys and peat workers. This also helps to explain the lack of records that could document the conditions, the lack of statistical material on children's work and the lack of studies of childrens participation in the labour force over time.[73]

Another question is whether a special labour market for children has gradually been established, or whether the boundaries between childrens and adults' occupational areas have been (and still are) fluid. Except for certain occupations that have been prohibited for children under 14 years of age, the difference between childrens and adults' work seems to comprise less the type of work than the number of hours and the lower hourly rate for children. This emphasizes once again that the primary occupation of children under 14 years is school work. Because adults feel that school ought to come before work, eliminating work before school has been their special focus – from politicians to teachers. The struggle against milk boys was a clear example of this, but the introduction of full-time schools in the countryside in the 1950s had the same purpose.

This investigation of the changes in children's work during the twentieth century shows that a modern childhood, which is ideally full of play and learning, took time to become a reality. The lofty ideals of a modern childhood were more ignored during some periods than in others. This was especially flagrant during the Second World War, when children were drafted as a reserve army of labour, especially in agriculture. The changes in childhood did also happen later in the countryside, because of the adults' varying interests in the children's labour power.

The twentieth century has thus been the stage for a struggle for the child's time – at all times.

Sources

See the footnotes for citations.

Notes

1 A memorandum prepared by Copenhagen Chief Education Officer Niels Bang in about 1916, reg. no. 138, 1916, Municipality of Copenhagen Department 1, Copenhagen City Archives. Emphasis in original.
2 In Denmark, 35% of schoolchildren aged 10-17 years had regular paid employment in 1992 and 5% had more sporadic work. Thus, 200,000 children aged 10-17 years were in employment; of these, 20,000 were 14 years or younger. The mean work hours are about 4-6 per week, corresponding to the daily work hours for children in 1900. Source: *Betænkning afgivet af kommissionen om børn og unges erhvervsarbejde* [Report of the Commission on Children's Paid Employment], 1993, pp. 64-66 and 77-78.
3 Nissen (1973) and Eklund Hansen (1987) have studied child labour in the Danish countryside. Albeck Nielsen (1988) reviews the legislation on factory work in Denmark. Ferdinand & Thomsen (1982) describe children's paid work in a medium-sized provincial town in Denmark. International surveys relevant to these themes include Tucker (1994), Horn (1983) and Elder (1974).
4 The bylaws have been found at the National Archives in the journal of cases for 1901 – 1918 from the Division of Municipal Affairs, Ministry of the Interior, and then in the journal register for 1919 – 1926 of Division 1 of the Ministry of Social Affairs. In 1926, this division was transferred to the Ministry of Health. The child labour bylaws have been assigned number 22. Additional sources include local historical material from Vejle, Odense, Copenhagen and Frederiksberg, and the collection of printed records of the proceedings of town councils of the Royal Library.
5 *Købstadsforeningens Tidsskrift* [Journal of the Association of Provincial Towns in Denmark], issue 2: 75-76 (1907).
6 *Københavns Borgerrepresentations trykte Forhandlinger* [Proceedings of the Copenhagen City Council] 59: 1655 (1898 – 1899).
7 *Beretning om Kjøbenhavns Borger- og Almueskolevæsen* [Annual reports of the Copenhagen City School System], 1887 – 1914. The figure for the girls in the poor-schools in 1898 was probably 21% and not 11% as reported in the official statistics. The figure for poor-school girls in 1896 was missing from the official statistics.
8 *Beretning om Frederiksberg kommunale Skolevæsen* [Annual reports of the Frederiksberg City School System], 1892/1893 – 1909/1910.
9 de Coninck-Smith (1996, p. 197).
10 The national survey of schoolchildren's paid work in 1898 – 1899 conducted by the Danish Teachers' Association did not consider the trends in the previous decade. It is thus not possible to determine whether the increase in children's work in Copenhagen also took place in other towns or in the countryside. Closer study of the available local statistical material might assist in this enquiry.
11 Jensen (1910, p. 17).
12 *Salmonsens leksikon* (1924, vol. 17, p. 551); Nielsen et al. (1922, p. 3-4); Lebech (1970, pp. 58-73); Borch (1878). Girls delivered the milk in Sweden and Finland. It is not known why boys were preferred in Denmark and girls in Sweden and Finland, but the differences reflect how social and cultural conditions influence the division of labour according to sex, also for children.
13 Response from the school principals in the Cities of Frederiksberg and Copenhagen to a question from the chair of the Dairy Association Hans Christensen in autumn 1897: Municipality of Copenhagen Division 1, reg. no. 1693, 1901 (Copenhagen City Archives).
14 Letter from the Mayor of the Municipality of Copenhagen, Division 3 to Division 1, on 3. January 1902, Division 1 reg. no. 1693, 1901 (Copenhagen City Archives).
15 Reply from the Principal of Ryesgade Friskole on 9 October 1897. See also the reply from the Principal of Skt. Hansgade School on 8 October 1897, cf. note 11.

16 This is documented in the national survey of children's paid work in 1898 – 1899 by the Danish Teachers' Association (de Coninck-Smith, 1996, chapter 7).
17 Ministry of the Interior, Division of Municipal Affairs 1908, reg. no. 745, calculation of 19 March 1909 (National Archives).
18 Ministry of the Interior, Division of Municipal Affairs 1907, reg. no. 519; 1910, reg. no. 293; and Odense Municipal Council reg. no. 153, 1908 (National Archives).
19 Cited in the *Vejle Social-Demokrat*, 12 March 1908.
20 See negotiations with the Holbæk City Council, Ministry of the Interior, Division of Municipal Affairs 1909, reg. no. 1316, 1911, reg. no. 790, 1915, reg. no. 518 (National Archives) and a report in Municipality of Copenhagen, Division 1, reg. no. 138, 1916 (Copenhagen City Archives).
21 Ministry of Interior, Division of Municipal Affairs 1909, registration no. 1833 (National Archives).
22 Ministry of the Interior, Division of Municipal Affairs 1908, reg. no. 745 (National Archives); *Uddrag af Ribe Byraads Forhandlinger og Regnskaber m.v. for Aaret 1909-1910* [Excerpts from the proceedings and accounts of the Ribe Municipal Council for the year 1909 – 1910], pp. 27-28 (Royal Library).
23 Ministry of the Interior, Division of Municipal Affairs, 1912, reg. no. 2998 (National Archives).
24 Letter of 30 November 1901, Municipality of Copenhagen Division 1, reg. no. 1693, 1901 (Copenhagen City Archives).
25 *Københavns Borgerrepresentations trykte Forhandlinger* [Proceedings of the Copenhagen City Council], 1916 – 1917, column 2902 (Copenhagen City Archives).
26 Frederiksberg School Board, reg. no. 85, 1917 (Frederiksberg City Archives).
27 *Aarsberetning fra Frederiksberg Skolevæsen* [Annual report of the Frederiksberg School System], various years.
28 *Tidsskrift for Dansk Skolehygiejne* [Journal of Danish school hygiene], 1916, pp. 23, 51; *Folkeskolen* [Magazine of the Danish Teachers' Association], 1911: no. 6.
29 *Beretning om Kjøbenhavns Borger- og Almueskolevæsen* and *Københavns Skolevæsen* [Annual reports of the Copenhagen City School System], various years; *Beretning om Frederiksberg kommunale Skolevæsen* [Annual reports of the Frederiksberg City School System], various years.
30 *Beretning om Frederiksberg kommunale Skolevæsen* [Annual reports of the Frederiksberg City School System], various years.
31 *Socialdemokraten* [The Social Democrat], 20, 21 and 22 November, 1, 2, 4, 6, 9 and 10. December 1896 and 1 January 1897.
32 de Coninck-Smith (1996, p. 226).
33 *Nationaltidende*, 22 November 1896.
34 Told by Karl Rasmussen (born in 1897) and cited in Haugbøll (1979, p. 244).
35 A file on the milk boys' strike, 1896, including a report from Chief Education Officer Joakim Larsen on 14 November 1896 and various materials on a complaint on revoked school-meal privileges, Frederiksberg School Board cases, 1896 (Frederiksberg City Archives).
36 Told by Carl Johansen (born in 1904), cited in Haugbøll (1979, p. 43-44).
37 Haugbøll (1979, p. 40).
38 Copenhagen City Archives, pensioner memoirs no. 143, a man born in 1903.
39 *Mælkeriarbejdernes Fagforening gennem 60 år, 1897 – 1957* [The Dairy Workers' Trade Union throughout 60 years, 1897 – 1957], 1957, pp. 30-31; *Mælkeriarbejdernes Fagforening, Festskrift 1897 – 1922* [The Dairy Workers' Trade Union, Festschrift, 1897 – 1922], 1922, pp. 35-37.
40 Copenhagen City Archives, pensioner memoirs no. 268, a man born in 1903.
41 *Referat af Lærermøderne paa Skt. Hansgade Skole* [Minutes of teachers' meetings at Skt. Hansgade School], volume 1 (1908 – 1910), meeting on 31 January 1908 (Copenhagen City Archives). See also Mælkedrengene – Et Opraab, underskrevet af Lærere og Værgeraadsmed-

lemmer [The milk boys – an appeal, signed by teachers and members of the Child Protection Council], *Politiken*, 5 April 1908. In 1910, the teachers in Copenhagen circulated petitions at the schools in the Cities of Copenhagen and Frederiksberg to appeal for a total ban on milk boys. Copy, Frederiksberg School Board, reg. no. 30, 1910 (Frederiksberg City Archives).
42 Reply of 9 October 1897, City of Copenhagen Division 1, reg. no. 1693, 1901 (Copenhagen City Archives).
43 Municipality of Copenhagen Department 1, registration no. 138, 1916 (Copenhagen City Archives).
44 Haugbøll (1979, p. 40).
45 *Betænkning af 17.2.1917* [Report of 17 February 1917], p. 8, Ministry of the Interior, Division of Municipal Affairs, reg. no. 584, 1917 (National Archives). This also includes the statements of the dairy companies.
46 Act No. 145 of 18 April 1925 on the paid labour of children and young people; Act No. 313 of 10 July 1922; Report, 1924; *Rigsdagstidende* [Proceedings of the Rigsdag], 1920 – 1921, supplement A, columns 2849-5704 and 1921 – 1922, supplement A, column 3226; Ministry of the Interior, Division of Social Affairs, Committee of 25 October 1922 on the paid labour of children and young people in craft, industry, transport and similar enterprises, committee protocol etc. (National Archives).
47 Cited in Eklund Hansen (1987, p. 20.)
48 Report of 6 December 1926 in the Ministry of Health, Division 1, reg. no. 22,2, 1926 (National Archives).
49 Section 57, Primary and Lower Secondary Education Act of 18 May 1937; National Labour and Factory Agency, reg. no. A7028, 1948 (National Archives).
50 Ministry of Education, Department 1, Division 1, 1941, package: discussions on the instruction in primary and lower secondary schools. Minutes of meetings with the country school advisers on their conditions and on the Primary and Lower Secondary Education Act 1935 – 1942, meeting on 23 September 1937 (National Archives).
51 Ministry of Education, Department 1, Division 1, reg. no. 972/1939, report of 26 June 1939 and letter of 5 August 1940 (National Archives).
52 Ministry of Education, Department 1, Division 1, reg. no. AS 1646, 1916 (National Archives).
53 Hansen (1996, pp. 35-38) discusses the trends in employment and economics during the Second World War.
54 Ministry of Education, Department 1, Division 1, reg. no. 919, 1945, statements of 24 and 27 April and 1 May 1944 (National Archives).
55 Tjæreby District School Board, letter of 18 March 1945, Ministry of Education, Department 1, Division 1, reg. no. 919/1945 (National Archives).
56 School absence lists, Stenløse-Fangel School, June 1943-December 1947 (Regional Archives in Odense).
57 Ministry of Education, Department 1, Division 1, reports from rural districts gathered by the county school authorities, reg. no. 13/56, Maribo County, special report of the county school adviser for 1944 (National Archives).
58 Ministry of Education circular of 3 June 1947.
59 Ministry of Education, Department 1, Division 1, reports from rural districts gathered by the county school authorities, reg. no. 14/56, Ålborg County, letter of 15 May 1956 (National Archives).
60 Anonymous (1946, p. 387).
61 Mortensen (1990, pp. 39-48) discusses the history of peat work in Denmark.
62 National Labour and Factory Inspectorate, reg. no. A 70 21, 1944, report of 11 July 1944 (National Archives).
63 National Labour and Factory Inspectorate, reg. no. A 70 19, 1944, A 70 21, 1944 (Kolding district), A 70 17, 1944, A 70 16, 1944, A 70 15, 1944, A 70 14, 1944, A 70 11, 1944 (National Archives).

64 *Forældrebladet* [Parents' magazine], May 1944; *Tidsskrift for Danmarks Forældreforening* [Journal of the Danish Parents' Association], no. 6, 1944.
65 *Socialdemokraten* 22 April 1944; *Berlingske tidende* cited in *Tørveproducenten* [Newsletter of the Association of Peat Manufacturers in Denmark], no. 10, 15 May 1944.
66 *Tørveproducenten* [Newsletter of the Association of Peat Manufacturers in Denmark], no. 9, 1 May 1944, p. 5.
67 Ministry of Education, Department 1, Division 1, reports from rural districts gathered by the county school authorities, reg. no. 14/56, Ålborg County, letter of 4 January 1952 (National Archives).
68 Ministry of Education, Department 1, Division 1, reports from rural districts gathered by the county school authorities, reg. no. 14/56, letter of 15 December 1953 from the school board in the Municipality of Ranum-Mølle (National Archives). Emphasis in original.
69 Ministry of Education, Department 1, Division 1, reports from rural districts gathered by the county school authorities, reg. no. 20/56, Randers County, letter of 15 November 1956 (National Archives).
70 Sources: *Meddelelser om Folkeskolen m.m.* [reports on primary and lower secondary education in Denmark], 1939 – 1959; *Statistik 1972 – 1973, Folkeskolen m.v.* [Statistics on primary and lower secondary education etc. for 1972 – 1973], published by the Ministry of Education, March 1974, p. 51. Information is lacking for 1960 – 1965. National information only exists from 1965, and from 1967 the information on the countryside and the provincial towns no longer exists.The number of mandatory years of education was increased to the current nine years in 1972.
71 Drachmann (1956, pp. 249-271) reviewed this act.
72 National Labour and Factory Inspectorate, reg. no. A 70 23, 1952 (National Archives).
73 The extent of children's paid work has been surveyed in the twentieth century in 1908, 1987 and 1992. The Commission on Youth, which functioned between 1945 and 1951, also surveyed this back to the late 1930s.

Laws and reports

Lov nr. 71 af 11.4.1901 om Arbejde i Fabrikker og dermed ligestillede Virksomheder samt det offentliges Tilsyn dermed [Act No. 71 of 11 April 1901 – on work in factories and similar enterprises and the public supervision thereof (Regulation of Factory Labour Act)].

Lov nr. 143 af 29.4.1913 om Arbejde i Fabrikker og dermed ligestillede Virksomheder samt det offentliges Tilsyn dermed [Act No. 143 of 29 April 1913 – on work in factories and similar enterprises and the public supervision thereof (Regulation of Factory Labour Act)].

Lov nr. 145 af 18.4.1925 ang. Børns og unge Menneskers Arbejde [Act No. 145 of 18 April 1925 – on the paid labour of children and young people].

Undervisningsministeriets Cirkulære Maj 1944 og 3. Juni 1947 angaaende Lukning af Skoleklasser for større Børn af Hensyn til Børnenes Anvendelse til lettere Landbrugsarbejde [Ministry of Education Circulars of May 1944 and 3 June 1947 – on the suspension of instruction in school classes for older children in consideration of the use of these children for light agricultural work].

Lov nr. 226, 227 og 228 af 11. juni 1954 om almindelig arbejdsbeskyttelse og arbejderbeskyttelse indenfor handels- og kontorvirksomhed, landbrug, skovbrug og gartneri

[Acts No. 226, 227 and 228 of 11 June 1954 on normal occupational safety and health within trade and office enterprises, agriculture, forestry and horticulture].

Betænkning afgivet af Udvalget angaaende Børns Arbejde [Report of the Committee on Child Labour], Copenhagen, 1924.

Betænkning afgivet af kommissionen om børn og unges erhvervsarbejde [Report of the Commission on Child Labour], October 1993 (Betænkning nr. 1257, 1993).

References

Albeck Nielsen, Lizette, (1988): Det industrielle børnearbejde og årsagerne til dets ophør [Children's work in industry in Denmark and the reasons it ended]. *Arbejderhistorie*, 31: 49-63.

Anonymous, (1946): Beskæftigelsen i Tørvemoser og Brunkulslejer under Krigen [Employment in peat bogs and lignite pits during the Second World War]. *Socialt tidsskrift*, 22: 384-388 (1946 A+B).

"Beretning om Frederiksberg kommunale Skolevæsen" [Annual reports of the Frederiksberg City School System]. In: *Beretning om Frederiksberg Kommune* [Annual reports of the Municipality of Frederiksberg], various years.

Beretning om Kjøbenhavns Borger- og Almueskolevæsen [Annual reports of the Copenhagen City School System], various years.

Borch, G., (1878): En ny Plan til Kjøbenhavns Mælkeforsyning [A new plan for Copenhagen Dairy]. *Ugeskrift for læger* [Journal of the Danish Medical Association], XXV(3. række, no. 10): 145-150.

de Coninck-Smith, Ning, (1996): *For barnets skyld. Om byen, skolen og barndommen 1880-1914* [For the sake of the Child. Urban childhood and education, 1880-1914]. Unpublished manuscript, Odense University.

Drachmann, G., (1956): Børns og unge menneskers arbejde. En oversigt med særlig henblik på arbejdsforholdets indgåelse og dets indhold [Children's paid work. An overview focusing on the terms and content of the work]. *Socialt tidsskrift*, 32 (9-10, Afd. A): 249-271.

Eklund Hansen, Anette, (1987): Børnearbejde på landet 1879 – 1940 [Children's work in the countryside in Denmark, 1879 – 1940]. In: *Arbejderklassens børn* [Working-Class children], report from an SFAH seminar, Andebølle Ungdomshøjskole, 13-15 November 1987, pp. 12-25.

Elder, G.H., (1974): *Children of the great depression: social change in life experience*. London.

Ferdinand, Ida & Bodil Thomsen, 1982. *Byens børn* [Urban children]. Åbyhøj, Denmark.

Folkeskolen [magazine of the Danish Teachers' Association], various issues.

Forældrebladet [Parents' magazine], various issues.

Hansen, Per Henning, (1996): Dansk økonomi under besættelsen. Ved vi nok? [Denmark's economy during the Nazi occupation. Do we know enough?] *Den jyske historiker*, 73 (July): 33-54.

Haugbøll, Charles, (1979): *Svajerne* [Messenger boys]. Copenhagen.

Horn, Pamela, (1983): The employment of primary schoolchildren in agriculture 1914-1918. *History of education*, 12(3): 203-215.

Jensen, Aldolph, (1910): *Skolebørns erhvervsmæssige Arbejde i Danmark* [Children's paid work in Denmark]. A lecture in the Dansk Forening for Arbejderbeskyttelse (Danish Association for the Protection of Workers), 11 February 1910. Copenhagen.

Københavns Borgerrepræsentations trykte Forhandlinger [Proceedings of the Copenhagen City Council], various issues.

Københavns Skolevæsen [Annual reports of the Copenhagen City School System], various issues.

Købstadsforeningens Tidsskrift 1907.[Journal of the Association of Provincial Towns in Denmark], issue 2: 75-76.

Lebech, Mogens, (1970): *Solbjerg 1895 – 1970* [Solbjerg district, 1895 – 1970]. Copenhagen, Aktieselskabet Det danske Mælke-Compagni.

Mælkeriarbejdernes Fagforening gennem 60 år, 1897 – 1957, 1957 [The Dairy Workers' Trade Union throughout 60 years, 1897-1957]. Copenhagen.

Mælkeriarbejdernes Fagforening, Festskrift 1897 – 1922 , 1922. [The Dairy Workers' Trade Union, Festschrift, 1897 – 1922]. Copenhagen.

Meddelelser om Folkeskolen m.m. [reports on primary and lower secondary education in Denmark], 1939 – 1959. Copenhagen, Ministry of Education.

Mortensen, Niels, (1990): Tørvegravning på Skive-egnen var også børnearbejde [Peat extraction in the Skive area was also child labour]. *In*: *Jul på Skive-egnen* [Christmas in the Skive area], pp. 39-48.

Nielsen, N.F. et al., (1922): *Jubilæumsskrift i Anledning af A/S Mælkeriet Enighedens 25 Aarige Stiftelsesdag* [Festschrift on the occasion of the 25th anniversary of the founding of A/S Mælkeriet Enigheden]. Copenhagen.

Nissen, Gunhild, (1973): *Bønder, skole og demokrati* [The rural population, education and democracy]. Copenhagen, Royal School of Educational Studies (English summary).

Statistik 1972 – 1973, Folkeskolen m.v. 1974. [Statistics on primary and lower secondary education etc. for 1972 – 1973]. Copenhagen, Ministry of Education.

Tidsskrift for Danmarks Forældreforening [Journal of the Danish Parents' Association], various issues.

Tidsskrift for Dansk Skolehygiejne [Journal of Danish school hygiene], various issues.

Tucker, Barbara M., (1994): "Agricultural workers in World War II: the reserve army of children, black Americans, and Jamaicans." *Agricultural history*, 68 (1, Winter): 54-73.

Tørveproducenten. Eneste officielle Medlemsblad for Sammenslutningen af Tørveproducentforeninger i Danmark 1941 – 1945. [The peat producer. The only official newsletter of the Association of Peat Manufacturers in Denmark], various issues.

Ólöf Gardarsdóttir

Working Children in Urban Iceland 1930-1990. Ideology of Work, Work-Schools and Gender Relations in Modern Iceland

I. Introduction

In late September 1958 most of the large employers involved in fish processing in southwestern Iceland sent a letter to the city council in Reykjavík requesting that the beginning of the school year be postponed for pupils in the upper compulsory classes. They substantiated their request by claiming that around half of the workforce employed in freezing plants in the capital area were schoolchildren above the age of 12. In their argumentation, they referred to the practice in fishing towns in other parts of the country where it was – as they put it – "quite common to exempt pupils from school under extraordinary economic conditions." Their proposal was discussed in the city council and by the Reykjavík school board. The local educational authorities came to the conclusion that although they could sympathize with the immediate needs of the export industry, they could hardly agree to exempt whole age groups from school. They pointed out that, although a considerable proportion of the workforce in freezing plants were pupils in compulsory schools, these only made up about 10 per cent of the respective age groups. Delaying their school start for several weeks would therefore make it quite difficult for school authorities to find "suitable tasks" for those who were not employed in the freezing plants. The school board did however agree to allow headmasters to free individual pupils, or entire school classes, from attending school for a short period, if they asked permission to work in fish processing.[1]

Nowadays, it may appear odd that less than 40 years ago employers should forward such a request in the capital city, where the economic life surely was more diversified than in other parts of the country. However, the fact that school attendance was regarded as less important than work sheds light on the peculiarities of labour requirements in Iceland's most important industry. Teenagers formed an important part of the labour force, which could be seasonally mobilized. The Icelandic economy is characterized by considerable fluctuations, and a temporary need for surplus labour has therefore occurred regularly during periods of economic growth. In this context, the employers' request is hardly surprising – considering the fact that the late 1950s and early 1960s marked the beginning of the longest expansion period in Icelandic economy, which lasted until 1967.[2]

The standpoint of the educational authorities is much more perplexing. The fact that no one questioned that schoolchildren were work full-time in freezing plants is noteworthy. No one ever referred to the child protection legislation passed in 1947 which prohibited the employment of adolescents below the age of 15 in factories.[3] This was evidently no concern of the school authorities involved, they seem merely to have worried about the possible idleness of those pupils who could not find work.

The fear of children's idleness – threatening the social order during early industrialization and urbanization – has surely been a common theme in European history.[4] In Iceland, the concern about the idleness of young people manifested itself regularly in public discourse throughout the twentieth century. Several scholars have pointed out that work has been valued more highly in Icelandic culture than in the other European societies.[5] Several cross-national opinion polls have, furthermore, revealed that Icelandic parents value hard work more highly in bringing up their children than parents in other European countries.[6] In this context it is important to note that the summer vacations in Icelandic schools last longer than in most western countries, between three and four months.[7] Furthermore, it is interesting that the extension of the school year has not been seriously discussed until just recently. During their summer holidays, pupils in the upper compulsory classes are expected to participate on the labour market. The example presented above confirms that there has certainly been need for young labour reserve during periods of economic growth. It has been more difficult to solve the problem of excessive "surplus labour" during periods of economic recession. Under such conditions, how was it possible to provide adolescents with "suitable tasks" in a society where work was so highly esteemed?

The main objective of this article is to assess the contribution of local authorities in their attempt to provide schoolchildren with work during the summer. In all larger townships in Iceland, so-called work-schools have been operating for several decades, in some villages since the economic depression of the 1930s, in others since the late 1940s. My analysis focuses on the Reykjavík Work-School reports,[8] although different contemporary sources, discussing the participation of adolescents on the labour market, have also been used. By analysing the number of participants in the Reykjavík Work-School during the period 1948-1992 according to age and sex, and by assessing the tasks performed by the children throughout the years, I intend to shed light on the changes and continuities in attitudes towards children and child labour in a changing society. Due to the distinctive features of the Icelandic economy, I shall pay special attention to the social discourse regarding economic fluctuations and try to assess its influence on the construction of childhood and child labour. My other main objective is to clarify the different views regarding the activities of girls and boys on an obviously gender-divided labour market. Because the work-schools are only for adolescents aged 13-15, I shall focus mainly on this transitional period between childhood and adulthood.

II. Socioeconomic development in twentieth-century Iceland

Traditionally, the growth of the fishing sector in the late nineteenth century was regarded as an industrial breakthrough in Iceland. In modern historiography, however, there has been a tendency to focus on continuity rather than change in this respect. The transformation from a rural society to an industrial one, is thus supposed to have taken place in successive stages between 1880 and 1930.[9] Although the fisheries only constituted the main livelihood of a fraction of the population before the 1880s, they provided an important subsidiary income in most regions of the country. Despite the growing importance of the fisheries in the national economy in the late nineteenth and early twentieth century, historians have recently stressed the value of agriculture for the urban population during the transitional period.[10] This is perceived in the importance of agricultural activities in semi-urban settings, and also in the seasonal migration of the workforce to agricultural areas during seasonal unemployment in coastal towns and villages. During the first half of this century, most inhabitants in urban areas had only recently migrated from farming areas. Although they were principally deriving their livelihood from urban industries they had been brought up and trained to work in a rural setting. The close socioeconomic ties with rural areas, probably slowed the modernization process both economically and culturally. In fact, the cultural ties with the countryside were preserved and most parents in towns and villages continued to send their children to rural areas during summer vacations well into the 1960s or 1970s.[11] That choice was generally motivated by the argument that work in the countryside would prevent young people from the idleness characterizing the urban areas.

The first decades of the twentieth century in Iceland were characterized by a gradual disappearance of a household-based economy, and the emergence of a society where wage work outside the home became more and more important. This change did by no means occur quickly and was not a direct consequence of migration from rural to urban areas. Thus, although the growth in the fishing sector surely promoted the growth of a modern society, fish processing in many villages was often closely connected to the household-based economy where both women and children took active part in the production.[12]

The Icelandic economy has during the last decades been characterized by a faster economic growth than that of most other western countries. Another important aspect of the modernization process in Iceland is its economic dependency on a single resource – fish.[13] Fish products are by far the most important export article. As presented in Figure 1, it was only after 1950 that more than 60 per cent of the working population derived its livelihood from other industries than farming, fishing or fish processing. In many ways this has had a wide-ranging impact on the prevailing work ideology. The dependency on one resource has made the country prone to economic fluctuations. This is true both regarding the fluctuations between different years and seasonal fluctuations. Due to the seasonal aspect of different types of fishing, during the wintertime the labour market in coastal areas has often been characterized by seasonal unemployment,[14] whereas during the summer the demand for labour often surpassed the supply. Thus, the seasonal work characterizing this traditional rural society has at least to some extent prevailed in modern Iceland. Other important industries, such as the construction industry and road building, were also affected by the fact that their labour requirements were most intensive during the summer.

Figure 1. Occupational structure in Iceland 1910-1990

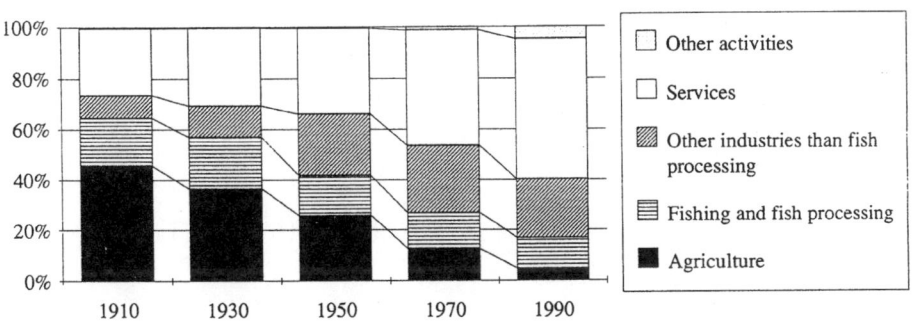

Source: Hagslunnd Icelandic Historical Statistics. 1977

During the past two or three decades, fluctuations in demand for labour have diminished substantially.[15] This is due to the relative growth in the service sector (see Figure 1) but also to technological innovations in other industries. In fishing for instance, large freezing vessels and the growing importance of fisheries in international waters have entirely changed the work arrangements of the population involved. Comparable changes have to a large extent also occurred in the construction industry. Thus, the Icelandic economy has only relatively recently become more or less independent from the need of seasonal reserve labour. The question is how this socioeconomic development has affected the construction of Icelandic childhood and child labour.

III. Theoretical considerations

In a recent volume on new trends in the study of childhood, the editors Allison James and Alan Prout maintain that childhood is socially constructed and reconstructed according to economic and social conditions.[16] Thus, childhood cannot be observed as a universal phenomenon defined by unchangeable biological features, but as a concept that varies cross-culturally according to time and place. Furthermore, they stress that factors such as sex, class and ethnicity are important when studying childhood in a given culture. They also maintain that children themselves are actively contributing to the construction and reconstruction of childhood.

This idea of childhood as a social construct is a useful approach when evaluating the importance of work in children's life. The concept of work is of course also constantly constructed and reconstructed according to various economic, social and cultural factors. Consequently, the ways in which we perceive children's work also vary according to several socially constructed categories such as gender and age. To illuminate this, I would like to refer to a simple example. Recently an old fisherman was interviewed on the Icelandic television and questioned about his childhood in a small fishing village in northern Iceland. He affirmed:

> I started fishing with my father at the age of nine. However, I did not begin to work until I was 12 or 13 years of age.

We can hardly presume that the tasks this boy performed at the age of 13 differed considerably from the tasks he carried out at nine. That he perceived himself as having begun to work at the age of 13, is probably based on the fact that by that time he first received "a part in the catch". By the age of 13 or 14 adolescents, in the rural or the semi-urban Icelandic society, seem to have been regarded as adults in terms of their work capacity. Thus, by the age of 13 or 14, most individuals have been given an occupational status in the Icelandic censuses at the beginning of the twentieth century.[17]

Presently, the concept of work is often narrowly defined. People are only defined as work if they are engaged in paid labour outside their home, and thus contribute directly to the national economy. This narrow definition of work excludes a majority of the working population from the process of work. Several scholars studying childhood in the twentieth century have criticized this narrow definition of work and maintained that although children in western societies are not directly contributing to the family's economy, they are still "useful" and by no means "useless" in modern society. The sociologist Jens Qvorttrup is one of these critics. He maintains that children are in various ways constantly "producing wealth" with their "school labour".[18] Anne Solberg claims that children in modern Norwegian society are the "new homestayers" – they have been left alone at home since both parents work on the open labour market. Solberg maintains that

> letting their children manage on their own for periods of the day, parents will probably change their conception of their children, seeing them as more capable and independent than before.[19]

Solberg furthermore points out that children generally take active part in various types of housework and thus contribute to the family's economy. She shows that girls contribute far more to the housework than both boys and men.[20]

It has been noted that historical research on childhood often ignores the gender aspect,[21] and it has been criticised that scholars often perceive children as "phenomena." Solberg's findings on the gender-neutral division of children's housework reminds us of the importance of taking into account the gender aspect when studying children's and adolescent's work in general. The socialization of children as well as their own cultural and economic contribution to the environment clearly bears the mark of a gender-divided society. When assessing the importance of gender in children's work, I shall particularly try to evaluate to what extent the tasks regarded as suitable for boys and girls are defined in terms of how they relate to the sphere of production, on the one hand, and that of reproduction on the other. This is an approach the social anthropologist Unnur Dís Skaptadóttir has used to explain changes in the concept of women's work in the emerging middle-class society in Iceland during the first decades of this century.[22] With the growing importance of wage work the women became ever more defined as caretakers of children and reproducers of social values – not as active participants in the production. The ideology of the male breadwinner versus the female housewife emerged in Icelandic society. This ideology probably affected the socialization of children in different ways. Boys were seen as future breadwinners, girls as housewives in the new urban society.

The main focus of my study of the Reykjavík Work-School is on paid child labour. Paid labour entails a direct contribution to the national economy, but this is by no means the only factor by which the concept of work can be defined. Other factors of importance are, for instance, gender and age. Since the work-schools were only intended for adolescents aged 13-15, it is likely that their work, although paid for, was not regarded as equally important as the work of adults. It is also probable that the tasks carried out by the adolescents in the work-schools changed over time, as has the general public's evaluation of its importance.

IV. The Reykjavík Work-School

The modern Reykjavík Work-School was established in 1948 and intended for pupils in the upper compulsory classes. The same year school-gardens were established for younger pupils.[23] Together these two institutions have formed an important part in the formalized socialization of children and adolescents in the capital. The Work-School has since the late 1940s provided work during summer for those pupils who have been unable to secure a job on the open labour market.

Originally, however, the Icelandic Work-School idea dates back to the 1930s, when several local communities experimented with such establishments for a couple of years.[24] Both cultural and economic factors explain the foundation of the work-schools. Economically they can be seen as a reaction to the unemployment during the Great Depression. The cultural ingredient, however, can be perceived as a peculiar mixture of international educational theory and the prevailing positive attitudes towards work. The late 1920s had been marked by economic growth in Iceland. New markets for fish products and new methods in fish processing accelerated the urbanization process.[25] During this period the cultural tension between urban and rural areas became more and more evident. The towns and villages were by many considered places of idleness, where the most important values of the old rural society were neglected. In this discourse the positive attitude towards work was by far the most appreciated moral value of the "old society".

One aspect of the modernization process in Iceland during the late 1920s and early 1930s was the strengthening of the school system and a growing professionalization of the teachers' core.[26] During this period, several secondary schools had been founded in urban areas, many of them paying more attention to vocational education than the traditional academic-oriented secondary schools.[27] The foundation of the work-schools can without doubt be seen as an important factor in those experiments concerning the secondary school system in Iceland. One of the international theories which had an important impact on the foundation of the work-schools, was the "Activity-school idea" or "Arbeitsschule" in German. This theory had its origin in the United States and in Germany. Several Icelandic schoolteachers spent some time studying in Germany and the Nordic countries and were well aware of the new currents in educational theory. The main aspect of the Activity-school idea was a growing emphasis on vocational education, or practical and life-related education. Traditional schoolteaching was criticised for paying too much attention to abstract concepts, disregarding to prepare children for future participation in society.[28]

The ideological background of the work-school experiment in Reykjavík in the early 1930s is firmly rooted in the Activity-school idea. As a matter of fact the term "vinnuskóli" is a translation of the German term "Arbeitsschule" and the term "skólagarðar", is a translation of the German term "Schulgarten". The "Schulgärten" were a part of the "Arbeitsschule-theory" developed by Georg Kerschensteiner in Munich.

Since the mid-1930s the organization of the work-school and the "ideology" on which it is based has gradually been developing and changing. The Work-Schools of the 1930s were for boys older than 14 having completed compulsory education. During this period the work-schools were run all year round and trained boys in various tasks. The Work-School experiments were of course first and foremost a reaction to the unemployment of the economic depression. But there was also a social aspect in the foundation of the work-schools. The public discourse during this period thus reflects major changes in the societal structure. The Work-Schools were in this respect intended to rescue young people from the evils of the urban environment and prevent them from idleness, which was also perceived to be one of the worst consequences of city-life.

The running of the first Work-Schools came to an end at the beginning of the Second World War, shortly after the British army occupied Iceland in 1940. The war completely changed the economic situation in the country. Growing demand for fish products in Europe and the construction operations of the occupational force effectively eliminated the unemployment problems of the 1930s. Thereby the basis for the continuation of the work-schools was removed. In fact, the demand for labour often exceeded the supply in Iceland during the war. The Reykjavík Work-School was temporarily revived for two summers in the early 1940s, when the city council of Reykjavík put into effect a labour demanding plan to use hot springs to heat houses in the city.[29] Because of labour shortage, the local authorities organized work for boys in the upper compulsory classes during the summer holidays.

The end of the war again dramatically changed the economic situation in Iceland. The first years of the postwar period were thus marked by general unemployment, and in 1948 the Reykjavík Work-School was started again and has been operating during the summer months ever since.

Although the ideology of the work-schools and the school-gardens clearly bear the marks of the Activity-school ideology, it is important to stress that the Icelandic Work-Schools have never become a formal part of the regular school system. It is difficult to explain why this is the case. A contributing factor has certainly been that the work-schools are run by local communities, while the formal school system is chiefly financed and run by the State. Furthermore, only part of the adolescents who were entitled to work sought employment in the work-schools. The reason for this is the fact that during the first decades of its existence a large proportion of adolescents could find work on the conventional labour market.

Figure 2. The proportion of 14- and 15-year-old boys and girls enrolled in the Reykjavík Work-School 1948-1992 (compared to the population in the same age groups in Reykjavík)

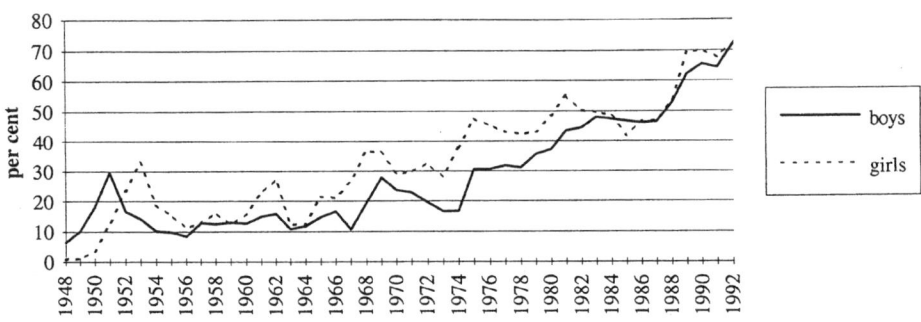

Sources: CAR. Reykjavík work-school annual reports

Figure 2 reveals that the total number of participants in the Reykjavík Work-School remained relatively stable until 1967. After that, the development has in general been characterized by a gradual increase in the number of participants, both in absolute numbers and proportionally. There seems, however, to be a relatively close correlation between major economic fluctuations in Iceland and the number of participants in the Work-School. Thus, the number of participants remained few during the economic growth of the late 1950s and the 1960s. The number increased considerably during the unemployment years between 1967 and 1970. The economic growth of the early 1970s was again characterized by a diminishing number of participants, but after the mid 1970s the number has increased constantly, and today the majority of adolescents are employed in the work-school. When considering the number of participants ac-

Figure 3. The number of 13- and 14-year-old boys and 14-years-old girls in the Reykjavík Work-School 1954-1992

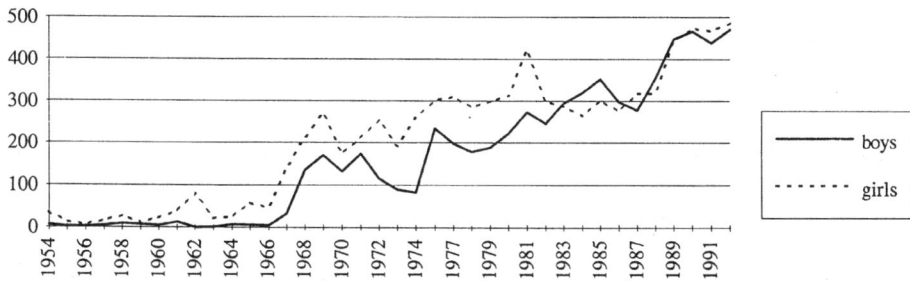

Sources: CAR. Reykjavík work-school annual reports

Figure 4. The number of 15-year-old boys and girls in the Reykjavík Work-School 1954-1992

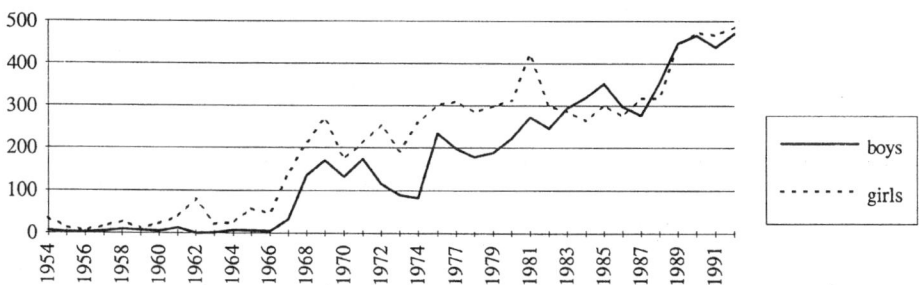

Sources: CAR. Reykjavík work-school annual reports

cording to age and sex (Figures 3 and 4) it becomes clear that the number of 15-year-old boys shows a far closer correlation with economic fluctuations than is the case when considering the number of the girls and the younger boys. Thus, the 15-year-old boys almost disappeared from the Reykjavík Work-School during the 1960s, and in the early 1970s their number decreased faster than was the case with the other groups. This shows that boys in this age group could easily provide themselves with work on the conventional labour market, where the wages were considerably higher than in the Work-School. The population growth in the capital area and expansion of the construction industry related to it probably explains why this group disappears from the school to such an extent.

When comparing the number of participants according to sex, it appears that until the early 1980s girls were generally more numerous than boys. This, and the fact that the number of girls shows fewer fluctuations than the number of boys, can probably be explained by the gender-division on the labour market.

V. Gender-division in the work-schools

During the 1930s the work-schools were for boys only. Although girls have participated in the Reykjavík Work-School since 1948, local authorities had, when planning this activity, not intended it for girls.[30] They were, however, forced to reconsider their position because already in the first year girls showed a keen interest in participating. But why did the local authorities not plan this school for both sexes? Were girls not faced with unemployment problems? Did their idleness not threaten the social order? The answers can be found in the socioeconomic changes that have occurred in Iceland since ca. 1920.

Above, the growing importance of public education was referred to as one of the main characteristics of the emerging modern Icelandic society. Another important feature was the growing importance of wage labour and the separation of the two spheres of activities, the spheres of production and of reproduction. Unnur Dís Skaptadóttir has studied gender relations in Icelandic fishing villages. She has pointed out that the first decades of the twentieth century were characterized not so much by radical changes in the women's contribution to the production, but rather in how female work was defined. Despite the fact that women in the fishing industry often continued to perform similar tasks, their work became redefined according to gender-related values. They were defined almost exclusively in connection with the sphere of reproduction. Men, on the other hand, were more and more defined as producers outside the sphere of the household. The male breadwinner versus female housewife ideology emerged in Iceland. One aspect of this changing construction of gender relations was the establishment of several home economic schools in Iceland during the 1930s.[31]

This process affected the socialization of boys and girls in different ways. Whereas one can identify a continuity in the ideological perception of the aims of upbringing as for the girls, a new attitude emerged towards the socialization of boys. In the rural society, both boys and girls were expected to leave home by the age of 14-16 to become servants. Their time of service was regarded as a suitable preparation for active participation in society. The technological and socioeconomic changes that occurred in the first decades of the twentieth century made the need for this kind of labour more and more "superfluous". The rise of a more or less urban society increased the demand for female servants in middle-class homes. According to the organizers of the original Work-Schools, there was plenty of work for girls inside the household – both at home and in the households of others. There they could be properly trained for their future role as housewives. Accordingly, it was more important to create new opportunities to prepare boys for their role as breadwinners. The work-schools were regarded as an ideal solution to this problem.

Thus, the slow emergence of an urban society, with more and more emphasis on wage work outside the home, resulted in a new social construction of work. It also resulted in a new construction of gender relations regarding work – emphasising the male breadwinner and the female housewife. Having analyzed the extent of unemployment in Reykjavík in 1935, before starting the Work-School, the local authorities came to the conclusion that

> a minority of those having registered were unemployed girls. Considering the extensive demand for female work in the homes, it can hardly be considered reasonable to take any measures as regarding these girls.[32]

This statement was made although girls in the respective age group constituted about 30 per cent of those registered in the unemployment records. As referred to above, once the Work-School was restarted in 1948 it became clear that the girls needed work no less than the boys did – and indeed they quickly outnumbered the boys. One might at first sight conclude that this fact reflects a uniform socialization of boys and girls. In reality, however, there was a clear gender-division of labour in the Work-School right from the beginning. Boys were thus employed in road building and some of them had the opportunity to work on a school ship where they were taught basic skills concerning the fisheries. The tasks performed by girls were traditional female tasks such as fish processing and child care in play-schools. Both boys and girls worked in parks and public gardens, but this work was also gender-divided to a large extent. Work involving the operation of machines was, in the first decades of the Reykjavík Work-School, almost exclusively performed by boys. They were employed in mowing the lawn, whereas girls planted flowers or picked weeds. This shows that the gender-divided labour market was also reflected in the tasks performed in the Work-School.

In one important way, the Work-School differed from the gender-divided labour market. On the open labour market, women as a rule received lower wages than men but in the Work-School both sexes were paid equal wages. This fact was criticized by the Work-School authorities. They argued that it was morally wrong to pay equal wages since the girls performed less important tasks. Furthermore, they complained about the fact that girls were outnumbering the boys and explained this by "the fact that boys' received "abnormally" low wages."[33]

Girls working in fish-processing in the Reykjavík Work-School during the 1950s. Photo by S. E. Vignier. (Vinnuskóli Reykjavíkur – Reykjavík Work School)

The relatively stable number of girls in the Reykjavík Work-School in relation to economic fluctuations may be explained in this context. As a matter of fact, the wages paid in the Work-School were probably in general relatively close to wages paid to girls on the open market for traditional women's work.[34] This fact hardly motivated girls to seek work on the open labour market. Furthermore, a part-time job in the Work-School can easily be combined with other typical female tasks often performed by girls during summer vacations. Here, I am mainly referring to child care traditionally performed by girls. The pedagogue Helga Pálmadóttir has recently analyzed the extent to which 11 and 12 year old children work. Her study reveals that although Icelandic girls spend more time work than boys, they receive lower wages. She points out that most girls in these age groups take care of children during the summer months.[35] A study which I carried out among the oldest pupils in the upper classes of one of Reykjavík's primary school's in the spring of 1994, revealed similar results.[36] Figure 5 reveals that although boys nowadays quite often take care of children, they almost exclusively attend to children related to them by blood.[37] On the other hand, besides taking care of children related to them, most girls prefer to mind unrelated children as well. The fact that child care is common among Icelandic girls, can be explained by the fact that daycare facilities in Iceland have not been developed to meet the demand for their services. Thus, although in a

Figure 5. Child-care performed by 15-year-old teenagers in Reykjavík 1993

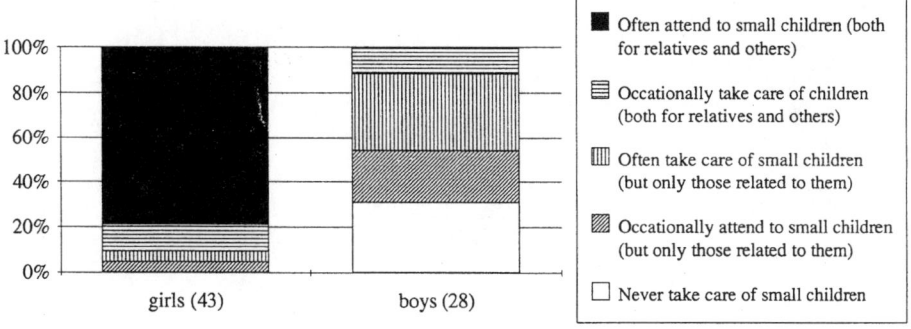

Sources: Réttarholtsskóli 1993

majority of cases both parents work outside the home, married couples have only been able to provide their children with half daycare in play schools.[38] This fact, on the other hand, can be seen as helping to preserve the gender division in the social construction of childhood. Thus, in spite of the general participation of women on the labour market, girls are still being socialized for motherhood and "housewifery". In terms of social construction of gender according to the concepts of reproduction and production, the most common task performed by girls is thus still defined as part of the sphere of reproduction.

The development of the Reykjavík Work-School during the last decade or so goes against this construction. Thus, the Work-School authorities have attempted to counteract the gender-division on the labour market by providing girls and boys with uniform tasks.[39] Another relatively recent feature of the Work-Schools is a general change in the tasks provided for the children. Initially, the work-schools main objective was to make the children directly acquainted with the nation's most important industries. Today, on the other hand, jobs in the work-schools are to a large extent separated from regular adult work. Children's work in the Work-Schools is thus mostly restricted to work in public gardens, and their instruction regarding other industries is restricted to visits in companies or to day trips to the countryside. Furthermore, work hours have been cut down to three hours a day, and each adolescent is currently only employed in the Work-School for six weeks each summer.[40] In the public opinion the work done in the Work-School is clearly not regarded as equivalent to regular adult work. The high proportion of adolescents in the Reykjavík Work-Schools during the past decade reflects the fact that there has been relatively limited demand for the labour capacities of adolescents on the conventional labour market. The gradual increase in the number of adolescents in the Work-

Picking the weeds. A typical girls' occupations in the work-schools during the 1970s. (Vinnuskóli Reykjavíkur – Reykjavík Work School)

School and the change in tasks performed can therefore be considered to reflect changes in the social construction of childhood. Although work and the participation of children on the labour market are still regarded as positive values in Icelandic society, "immaturity" has more and more become an issue in the discourse on youth.

Oddly enough, it was during the economic growth of the 1960s – when the boys aged 15 almost disappeared from the Reykjavík Work-School – that this changed construction of childhood, and child labour became apparent in Icelandic society for the first time.

VI. Continuity and changes in attitudes towards children and child labour

The historian Eggert Þór Bernharðsson has maintained that a modern urban middle-class society had not been established in Reykjavík before the early 1960s. He comes to this conclusion from studying various societies established in the capital for persons originating from particular districts of the country (átthagafélög). These organizations were involved in several activities intended to strengthen the ties between the members and their rural native region. The members of these organizations were quite many during the postwar period, and Bernharðsson points out that most of them took an active part in all activities. After 1960 the importance of these organizations seems to have diminished, the members became fewer and fewer, and their activities were reduced to one children's Christmas party a year.[41] According to Bernharðsson, this shows that the urban population no longer needed links with its rural past. By the 1960s most persons perceived themselves, in cultural terms, as town dwellers, who had exchanged the values of the rural society for those of an urbanized middle-class one.

This change towards an urban middle-class society is in various ways manifested in a social reconstruction of Icelandic childhood. There is, however, also a clear continuity in the attitudes towards youth in Iceland as well as in the living arrangements of Icelandic youth. The continuity is manifested in increased child labour during the mid 1960s. The example referred to at the beginning of this article occurred on the eve of the most extensive period of economic growth in post-war Iceland. The growing importance of the herring fisheries and the increased catches of other species during the 1960s made the seasonal employment of women and adolescents a necessity if the fishing industry was to cope with processing the catches. In the summer of 1965, most newspapers in the capital city discussed extensive child labour at Reykjavík harbour. The labour union for unskilled workers in Reykjavík (Dagsbrún) complained about the fact that boys and girls, many of whom were only 11 years of age, were work more than 10 hours a day.[42] During the mid-1960s, several left-wing politicians in Parliament maintained that child labour was widespread in Icelandic factories, while it had already been prohibited in other "civilized countries" in the nineteenth century. One member of Parliament maintained that the

> public opinion about child labour is still so positive that many foremen in freezing plants have complained about their difficulties when sending 12-year-old children home after full-time work. In some cases the children's parents have started serious quarrels with foremen, criticizing them for not allowing their children to work overtime.[43]

Child labour was often discussed in Parliament during the mid 1960s, when a new child protection legislation was passed. Although the critics of child labour were not many in Iceland by this time, the discussion *per se* surely suggests changes in society since the opposition towards children's work appears to have been a previously unknown phenomenon in Iceland.[44]

Mowing the lawn. Boys' occupation in the work-schools during the 1970s. (Vinnuskóli Reykjavíkur – Reykjavík Work School)

In fact, some socio political issues discussed both in the Parliament and the city council of Reykjavík are an indication of structural changes in society. At the parliamentary level this is manifested in various bills concerning labour legislation, child protection and major changes concerning education.[45] The 1960s were marked by a vivid discussion in Parliament concerning all those issues. This points towards changes in the perception of childhood. A social consciousness was emerging in which children and adolescents were more and more defined in terms of their immaturity but less as active participants in the production. It must, however, be stressed that this discourse does not necessarily reflect the opinion of the majority of the population about children and child labour. Neither does it reflect the children's point of view. In fact, only a fraction of left-wing politicians fully agreed with the standpoint that children should by no means take active part in the production and get to know the nation's main industries through direct contact. In general, the majority of the population seems to have approved of children work. This is reflected in the discussion in the newspapers referred to above. Several journalists partly agreed with the point of view of the labour union maintaining that a 10-hours work day was too long for adolescents. Most of them, however, said that the work the children were doing at the harbour was by no means too difficult for them. When interviewing the children one detects an admiration for the adolescents' hard work. This was especially the case when considering the attitudes towards girls employed in some typical boys' job. When questioning three 13-year-old girls on their work at the harbour, one journalist pointed out that they perceived themselves as lucky to have work and hoped to be able to work at the harbour for the rest of the summer. They said that their wages were four times higher than was the case in the Work-School. This made it possible for them to spend more money on hobbies. These girls intended to go on a skiing tour in the autumn.[46]

When discussing clauses in the new child protection legislation concerning the restriction of child labour (during the 1960) many politicians at the centre of the political arena pointed out that it was hardly realistic to prohibit full-time labour of adolescents. Notwithstanding whether or not politicians regarded it suitable for adolescents to work, both parents and adolescents demanded work for the youth.[47] The standpoint of the authorities could therefore be in direct conflict with the prevailing attitudes towards the moral value of work.

The 1960s were thus marked by a slowly growing cultural tension in society owing to the redefinition of children and child labour. This redefinition was accelerated by the depression of the late 1960s. The complete failure of the herring fisheries in 1967 caused unemployment in all regions of the country.[48] Although this situation lasted only about three years, it resulted in important changes in the attitudes towards child labour. As pointed out before, this resulted in an increasing number of participants in the Reykjavík Work-School.

But, this was also manifested in structural changes of the Work-School. Instead of providing adolescents with work six to seven hours a day, they were now only intended to provide half-time work (four hours a day). One of the members of the Work-School board stated in the Work-School report of 1968 that this was a "suitable length of work time" for adolescents. He continued by saying that

> if the economic depression continues, and it does not become easier to provide adolescents with work on the open labour market during the summer months, we must seriously begin to consider the extension of the school year.[49]

The extension of the Icelandic fishing zone in 1972 improved the economic conditions in Iceland and created a renewed demand for labour. This probably postponed a serious debate on the extension of the school year.

The need for seasonal labour in the fisheries, especially in the southwestern and western parts of the country during the early 1970s, led to an interesting discussion in Parliament at the same time as Parliament debated changes in the primary education legislation.[50] Thus, three members of Parliament from the Reykjanes constituency (in southwestern Iceland), all somehow involved in fish processing, put forward a bill intended to make the upper classes in the primary school and high school more flexible and better designed to meet the needs of the labour market. They in this respect referred to the experience of two secondary schools in the capital area, "where the headmasters had kindly enough agreed to exempt several of the youngest pupils, 16 and 17 years old, from school in May so that they could work".[51] This proposal was hardly discussed in Parliament, which by that time was concentrating first and foremost on the new legislation for primary education, which was passed in 1974.

This incidence brings us back to the example referred to in the beginning of this article. When comparing the two incidents, occurring with an interval of 15 years, they in a way reflect a changing construction of childhood. In 1958, an additional meeting was organized of the Reykjavík school board, following the employers' request to exempt pupils from school so they could work. Although the 1970s were still characterized by a considerable participation of adolescents on the labour market during summer, members of Parliament were not inclined to discuss a proposal to exempt pupils from school so that they could work. On the other hand, they discussed at length bills calling for improvements in primary education. The changing priorities of the authorities clearly reflect changing attitudes towards childhood and adolescence. The modern schoolchild was gradually replacing the work child of the 1950s.

VII. Conclusions

I have shown that although the concept of childhood in Iceland has undergone major changes as society has changed, there are important continuities regarding the importance of work in children's lives. The socioeconomic development in Iceland during the twentieth century has in general been characterized by growing material wealth and structural changes of the society. One aspect of this was the emergence of a modern primary school system, which already by 1907 obliged children in the age group 10-14 to attend school part of the year. The school system has gradually been strengthened during the twentieth century. Despite this, work has generally been highly valued in the upbringing of children. Other countries often faced social tensions in relation to the extension of the primary school and the introduction of laws prohibiting child labour.[52] In Iceland a strong educational system has been regarded as desirable, although there has been a consensus favouring that children and adolescents should work during the relatively long summer holidays. The existence of the work-schools during summer holidays has surely helped to preserve this consensus about the work adolescent. The fact that the work-schools have provided all those adolescents with work that could not find jobs on the open market has prevented the idleness of young people during the long summer holidays. The establishment and the existence of the work-schools besides a modern educational system can mainly be explained by the peculiarities of the Icelandic economy. The prevailing economic fluctuations have thus had a great impact on the construction and reconstruction of Icelandic childhood. Seasonal fluctuations on the labour market in an emerging modern society have helped preserve the image of the hard-working child.

Although the number of participants in the Reykjavík Work-School shows a clear correlation with major economic fluctuations, the general development of the Work- School has been characterized by a gradual increase in the number of participants during the past decades. Currently about 70 per cent of Reykjavík schoolchildren in the age groups 14-15 are employed in the Reykjavík Work-School during the summer. This shows that there is indeed only an insignificant need for the work capacity of young people on the open labour market and, in fact, only a minority of adolescents get to work on the conventional labour market before they leave the primary school system. Thus, although the majority of adolescents 14 and 15 years old are involved in paid labour in the Work-School during the summer, their activities have become more and more separated from the adult world. In this respect adolescents have more and more become defined in terms of their immaturity and not as active participants in the production. Thus, part of the year adolescents of the 1940s, 1950s and 1960s were more or less involved in work on the open labour market, whereas their counterparts in the late 1970s and 1980s have few possibilities for competing with adults on the labour market.

While, the organization of the Reykjavík Work-School in the beginning reflected the gender division on the labour market, the development in the school during the past two decades has been characterized by a uniform socialization of boys and girls. The gender division is, however, obvious when considering the activities of boys and girls outside the Work-School. Childcare is an activity performed mainly by girls, and the fact that it is quite difficult to provide small children with adequate childcare in play schools results in a high demand for young girls in childcare. The general participation of married women on the labour market since the 1960s has contributed to changes in the construction of childhood. Thus, a majority of Icelandic children and adolescents are left alone at home part of the day. In this context, they may be defined as the new homestayers.[53] In this respect many children and adolescents are faced with great responsibility as many of them need to take care of younger siblings. This is especially true for the girls. Although the life of adolescents has more and more become separated from the adult world, the Icelandic child is still perceived as having obligations at home, often involving responsibility for a younger sibling and being expected to carry out paid work during the summer holidays.

Acknowledgements

When writing this article, I benefited greatly from valuable discussions with my supervisor Gísli Ágúst Gunnlaugsson, who died last year. He supported me in various ways both as a friend and as a colleague. I would furthermore like to thank Unnur Dís Skaptadóttir, Guðmundur Jónsson and Guðmundur Hálfdanarson for useful comments on earlier versions of the article.

Guðni Baldursson at the Statistical Bureau kindly provided me with some statistical information.

Notes

1 City Archive of Reykjavík (hereafter CAR). Letters of the Reykjavík city council and minutes of the Reykjavík school board.
2 See for example Magnússon M.S. 1993 and Snœvarr 1993, chapter 1.
3 It is noteworthy that the appropriate clause of the child protection legislation had been passed without discussion in Parliament in 1946. *Stjórnartíðindi* 1947, A-deild, pp. 29-39; *Alþingistíðindi* 1946, B- deild, pp. 1441-1538.
4 On this discussion see for example: Cunningham 1990; Cunningham 1991, chapter 3; Sandin 1986; Davin 1982. In Icelandic context see for example Hálfdanarson 1986 and Magnússon S.G. 1993.
5 On this discussion see Magnússon F. 1990 and Ólafsson 1990.
6 Jónsson and Ólafsson 1991. These opinion polls have been performed by the Institute of Social Sciences (University of Iceland) in cooperation with the "European Value Systems Study Group" (EVSSG).
7 In 1988-77 per cent of all schoolchildren in Iceland went to school for 9 months a year, 13.5 per cent for 8 1/2 months, 9.3 per cent for 8 months and 0.1 per cent for less than 8 months. *Alþingistíðindi* 1989 – 1990, þskj. 748. On length of school year in Icelandic schools, see furthermore *Nefnd um mótun menntastefnu* 1993.
8 Those reports are preserved in the City Archive of Reykjavík, uninterrupted since the establishment of the modern Reykjavík Work-School in 1948. Some reports are preserved from the 1930s, but no reports have been found from the years of World War II. CAR. Reykjavík Work-School annual reports.
9 In his doctoral thesis, Magnús S. Magnússon has divided the modernization process in Iceland before 1940 into four stages and stresses that "the industrial breakthrough" can only be noted after the large-scale mechanization of the fisheries during the period of 1910 – 1930. Magnússon M.S. 1985. *On socio-economic development in Iceland*, see furthermore Gunnlaugsson 1988; Magnússon M.S. 1993; Hálfdanarson 1993; Snœvarr 1993.
10 On agricultural activities in urban areas see: Valdimarsdóttir 1986; Gunnlaugsson 1988; Garðarsdóttir 1993.
11 Little research has been done on children's work in farming areas. In 1962, the Reykjavík school board carried out a study on adolescents' work during summer. The study revealed that around 60 per cent of 12-year-old boys and 35 per cent of 12-year-old girls worked in farming areas during summer. See CAR. Reykjavík Work-School, annual report 1963. On the discussion on children's work in farming areas see Garðarsdóttir, forthcoming.
12 See for example Skaptadóttir 1993.
13 Magnússon M.S. 1993 and Snœvarr 1993 .
14 *Statistics of Iceland* II,82 1984, pp. 61-62.
15 Statistics on unemployment show that even if unemployment rates still show some seasonal variations, the unemployment rates have stabilized during the past decades. Magnússon M.S. 1985, pp. 152-158; *Statistics of Iceland* II,82 1984, pp. 61-62, *Statistics of Iceland* III, 5 1991, pp. 72-76.
16 Prout and James 1990.
17 A brief study of several districts in the Icelandic census of 1901 reveals this. NAI. The Icelandic census 1901.
18 Qvortrup 1995.
19 Solberg 1990, p. 131.
20 Ibid, 124-126.
21 See for example Blom 1982.
22 Skaptadóttir 1993, chapter 6.
23 School-gardens were, along with work-schools, established in several towns and villages during

the 1940s and 1950s. Their main objective was to teach those children, who could not work in rural areas during summer, basic tasks in agriculture. In the beginning, the school gardens were for pupils 9-12 years of age. The children were supposed to stay in the school gardens for 2-3 hours a day. Recently children in the Reykjavík School Gardens are allowed to register in the school gardens already at the age of 7. CAR. Annual reports of the Reykjavík School-Gardens.

24 Sigurdsson 1991.
25 Magnússon M.S. 1993 and Snœvarr 1993.
26 This can be observed in various factors, for instance in the growing number of pre-school teachers. This is also manifested in building of schools, and discussions about a new school system. The teachers' union started a new scholarly journal *Menntamál* where current international educational ideas were introduced. (Among these was the Montessori method for pre-school children (Steingrímur Arason), and the Activity School idea (Arbeitsschule, École active) put forward for example by J. Dewey (USA) and Kerschensteiner (Germany). See for example *Menntamál* 1925, 1 (6); 1925 1(7); 1926 2(4), 1926 2(8); 1927 3(4-5). During this period school attendance became more and more common both in rural and urban areas. On school attendance and the Icelandic school system in general during this period see Guttormsson 1996; Gardarsdóttir 1996b; *Statistics of Iceland* 1967; *Statistics d'Islande* 1922; *Alþingistí dindi* 1926.
27 See for example *Alþingistídindi* 1927, A-deild, þskj. 9; *Alþingistídindi* 1929, A-deild, þskj. 24; *Alþingistídindi* 1930, A-deild, þskj. 334; *Alþingistídindi* 1933, A-deild, þskj. 224.
28 For a discussion on the Activity-school idea see, for example, Ness 1965 and Ness 1989, pp. 201-208.
29 CAR. Reykjavík Work-School annual report 1970 and Arnfinnur Jónsson 1996.
30 CAR. Annual reports of the Reykjavík Work-School 1948 and 1949.
31 See for example *Alþingistídindi* 1937 (1), A-deild, þskj. 77, 203, 271, C-deild, pp. 702-705 and 752- 755. *Alþingistídindi* 1937 (2), A-deild, þskj. 52, 66. *Stjórnartídindi* 1938, pp. 83-85.
32 CAR. Annual report of the Reykjavík Work-School 1935.
33 CAR. Annual report of the Reykjavík Work-School 1953.
34 The wages in the Reykjavík Work-School have been about 50-70 per cent of unskilled labourer's wages. CAR. Annual reports of the Reykjavík Work-School.
35 See Rafnsdóttir 1990.
36 Réttarholtsskóli 1993.
37 Here I am referring to siblings and the children of older sisters or brothers.
38 See for example *Social Security in the Nordic Countries. Scope, expenditure and financing 1993*, 1995 (2), p. 58.
39 Arnfinnur Jónsson 1996.
40 Ibid.
41 Bernhardsson 1990.
42 Tíminn 21.7.1965.
43 *Alþingistídindi* 1964, C-deild, pp. 95.
44 In Parliament there was a vivid discussion on child labour in 1965 and 1966 in connection with the new child protection legislation, which was passed in 1966. *Alþingistídindi* 1964, C-deild, pp. 84-158, *Alþingistídindi* 1965, B-deild, pp. 1330-1351.
45 In this respect one can refer to discussions and preparation of new compulsory education legislation (passed in 1974) and the establishment of a "Research Division of the Ministry of Education and Culture" (skólarannsóknarstofa) in 1966. *Alþingistídindi* 1965, 1972, 1973. Wolfgang Edelstein 1988, part I.
46 Tíminn 21.7.1965.
47 *Alþingistídindi* 1964, C-deild, pp. 84-158.
48 *Statistics of Iceland II,2*, 1984, pp. 61-62.
49 CAR. Reykjavík Work-School annual report 1968.
50 The new primary education legislation was passed in 1974, after having been in preparation for several years. *Alþingistídindi* 1972, 1973. *Stjórnartídindi* 1974.

51 Alþingistíðindi 1974, A-deild, þskj. 74, C-deild, pp. 702-703.
52 See for example Bolin-Hort 1989, chapter 10; Sjöberg 1996.
53 Solberg 1990.

References

Unpublished sources

NAI (National Archives of Iceland)
Manntal á Íslandi 1901.

CAR (City Archives of Reykjavík)
Letters of the city council.
Minutes of the Reykjavík school board 1958.
Reykjavík School-Gardens, annual reports 1950 – 1993.
Reykjavík Work-School, annual reports 1935 and 1948 – 1993.

Interview
Arnfinnur Jónsson 1996. Interview with the principal of the Reykjavík Work-School. September.

Published sources and secondary works

Alþingistíðindi (Parliamentary records) 1926, 1927, 1929, 1930, 1933, 1937, 1946, 1964, 1965, 1972, 1973, 1974, 1989-90. Reykjavík, Alþingi.
Bernaharðsson, Eggert Þór, (1990): "Römm er sú taug. Aðlögun innflytjenda í Reykjavík að lífinu á "mölinni"," *N'y saga* 4, 39-52.
Blom, Ida, (1982): "Socialisering av barn i Norge på 1800-talet. Teori, metode og kildebrug," *Dugnad* 8, 23-39.
Bolin-Hort, Per, (1989): *Work, Family and the State. Child Labour and the Organization of Production in the British Cotton Industry, 1780 – 1920*. Lund, Lund University Press.
Cunningham, Hugh, (1990): "The Employment and unemployment of Children in England ca. 1680 – 1851", *Past and Present* 126, 115-150.
Cunningham, Hugh, (1991): *The Children of the Poor. Representations of Childhood since the Seventeenth Century*. Oxford, Blackwell.
Davin, Anna, (1982): "Child Labour, the work Class Family and Domestic Ideology in 19th Century Britain," *Development and Change*, 633-654.
Edelstein, Wolfgang, (1988): *Skóli – nám – samfélag*. Reykjavík, Iðunn.
Garðarsdóttir, Ólöf, (1993): *Á faraldsfæti. Fólksflutningar og félagsgerð á Seyðisfirði 1885 – 1905*. Unpublished BA-paper. Reykjavík, Institute of History, University of Iceland.

Garðarsdóttir, Ólöf, forthcoming "Redefining Childhood and Child-Labour in a Changing Society. Gender Division in Children's Work in Urban Iceland 1950 – 1990", forthcoming in *Det 5. nordiske kvinnehistorikermøte, rapport*. Oslo.

Garðarsdóttir, Ólöf, unpublished. "Compulsory Education in Twentieth-Century Iceland." Unpublished paper. Reykjavík, Institute of History, University of Iceland.

Gunnlaugsson, Gísli Ágúst, (1988): *Family and Household in Iceland 1801-1930. Studies in the relationship between demographic and socio-economic development, social legislation and family and household structures*. Uppsala, Historiska institutionen Uppsala Universitet.

Guttormsson, Loftur, (1996): "Kennsla heima og í skóla. Þáttur heimila í barnafrœðslu á Íslandi 1907 – 1926," *Uppeldi og menntun. Tímarit Kennaraháskóla Íslands* 5, 9-22.

Hálfdanarson, Guðmundur, (1986): "Börn – höfuðstóll fátœklingsins?" *Saga* 24, 121-146.

Hálfdanarson, Guðmundur, (1993: "Íslensk þjóðfélagsþróun á 19. öld", pp. 9-58 in Guðmundur Hálfdanarson and Svanur Kristjánsson (eds.) *Íslensk þjóðfélagsþróun 1880-1990. Ritgerðir*. Reykjavík, Félagsvísindastofnun og Sagnfrœðistofnun Háskóla Íslands.

Icelandic Historical Statistics, (1997): Reykjavík, The Statistical Bureau.

Jónsson, Friðrik H. and Ólafsson, Stefán, (1991. *Úr lífsgildakönnun 1990: Lífsskoðun í nútímalegum þjóðfélögum. Ísland, Danmörk, Finnland, Noregur, Svíþjóð, suður og vestur Evrópa (samanlögð) og Bandaríkin*. Reykjavík, Félagsvísindastofnun Háskóla Íslands and European Value System Study Group.

Magnússon, Finnur, (1990): *The Hidden Class. Culture and Class in a Maritime Setting Iceland 1880 – 1942*. Århus, Århus University Press.

Magnússon, Magnús S., (1985): *Iceland in Transition. Labour and socio-economic changes before 1940*. Lund, Ekonomisk-Historiska föreningen.

Magnússon, Magnús S., (1993): "Efnahagsþróun á Íslandi 1880 – 1990", pp. 112-214 in Guðmundur Hálfdanarson and Svanur Kristjánsson (eds.) *Íslensk þjóðfélagsþróun 1880-1990. Ritgerðir*. Reykjavík, Félagsvísindastofnun og Sagnfrœðistofnun Háskóla Íslands.

Magnússon, Sigurður Gylfi, (1993): *The Continuity of Everyday Life. Popular Culture in Iceland 1850 – 1940*. Unpublished doctoral thesis. Carnegie Mellon University.

Menntamál 1925, 1 (6); 1925 1(7); 1926 2(4), 1926 2(8); 1927 3(4-5).

*Nefnd um mótun menntastefnu*1993. *Áfangask' yrsla*. Reykjavík.

Ness, Einar, (1965): *Arbets- og aktivitetsskole i Norge, Europa og USA*. Oslo, Pedagogisk Forum.

Ness, Einar, (1989).:*Det var engang. Norsk skole gjennom tidene*. Oslo, Universitetsforlaget.

Ólafsson, Stefán, (1990): "Vinnan og menningin. Um áhrif lífsskoðunar á vinnuna", *Skírnir* 164, 99-124.

Prout, Alan and James, Allison, (1990): "A New Paradigm for the Sociology of Childhood? Provenance, Promise and Problems", pp. 7-34 in Prout and James (eds.) *Constructing and Reconstructing Childhood: Contemporary Issues in the Sociological Study of Childhood*. London, Falmer Press.

Qvortrup, Jens, (1995): "From Useful to Useful: The Historical Continuity in Children's Constructive Participation," *Sociological Studies of Children* 7, 49-76.

Rafnsdóttir, Guðbjörg Linda, (1990): "Vinnuþrælkun eða velmegun?", *Þjóðlíf* 6(10), 52-53.
Réttarholtsskóli, (1993): A study on adolescents' work in Reykjavík 1993.
Sandin, Bengt, (1986): *Hemmet, gatan, fabriken eller skolan. Folkundervisning och barnuppfostran i svenska städer 1600 – 1850.* Lund.
Sigurðsson, Benedikt, (1991): *Hugmyndafræðilegur grundvöllur unglingavinnu og Vinnuskóli Reykjavíkur 1951 – 1984.* Unpublished BA-paper. Reykjavík, Institute of History, University of Iceland.
Sjöberg, Mats, (1996): *Att säkra framtidens skördar. Barndom, skola och arbete i agrar miljö: Bolstad pastorat 1860 – 1930.* Linköping, Linköping Universitet (Tema Barn).
Skaptadóttir, Unnur Dís, (1993): *Fishermen's wives and Fish Processors. Continuity and Change in Women's Position in Icelandic Fishing Villages.* Unpublished Doctoral Thesis. New York, The Graduate Centre of the City University of New York.
Snævarr, Siguður, (1993): *Hagl'ysing Íslands.* Reykjavík.
Solberg, Anne, (1990): "Negotiating childhood: Changing Constructions of Age for Norwegian Children", pp. 118-137 in Prout and James (eds.) *Constructing and Reconstructing Childhood: Contemporary Issues in the Sociological Study of Childhood.* London.
Social Security in the Nordic Countries. Scope, expenditure and financing 1993. 1995 (2). Copenhagen, Nordic Social Statistical Committee.
Statistics of Iceland 1967. *Supplementary series, no 1. Primary education* 1920 – 1966. Reykjavík, Statistical Bureau of Iceland.
Statistics of Iceland II,82 1984. *Statistical Abstract of Iceland.* Reykjavík, Statistical Bureau of Iceland.
Statistics of Iceland III,5 1991. *Statistical Abstract of Iceland*. Reykjavík, Statistical Bureau of Iceland.
Statistique de l'Islande 1922. *Les écoles primaires en 1909 – 1914.* Reykjavík, Statistical Bureau of Iceland.
Stjórnartíðindi (Governmental bulletin) 1938, 1947, 1974.
Tíminn 21.7.1965.
Valdimarsdóttir, Þórunn, (1986): *Sveitin við sundin. Búskapur í Reykjavík 1870 – 1950.* Reykjavík.
Þjóðfélagsþróun 1880 – 1990. Ritgerðir. Reykjavík.

Anne Solberg

Seeing Children's Work

Introduction

The broad aim of this article is to throw light on contemporary Norwegian childhood. My entrance to this comprehensive issue is, however, concrete; it is based on empirical investigations of children's work during their school age. Initially, these studies, which were conducted in the second half of the 70s and throughout the 80s, aimed at getting research-based knowledge about issues that had largely been ignored by the social sciences. However, while investigating children's daily activities with the intention of filling gaps of knowledge, I discovered that the gaps widened, and that this widening was closely related to how I looked at what children were doing. For example, not before I set aside my conception that work did not belong to contemporary Norwegian childhood, which I had previously taken for granted, was I able to recognize the productive elements in several daily activities in which children took part. [1]

The present analysis reflects my line of thinking about children and childhood developed over a period of years. Starting from the beginning I explore the work life of Norwegians 10-12 years old, letting my own research history structure the account by representing the research questions and answers to them chronologically as they appeared. From here I move to fishing work carried out by children living in small-scale communities in Northern Norway to housework conducted by a nationwide sampling of the childhood population. My style of writing allows me a presence in large segments of the text. I appear as a guide, inviting my readers to follow me through the process of recognising children's activities as productive, and offer them the opportunity to look through my eyes 'outwards' at some parts of social reality, and 'inwards' at how I perceive this reality.

My Discovery of Children's Work

My sociological interest in children and childhood was aroused in the seventies, while I was engaged in a community study on the coast of Northern

Norway. Our focus was living conditions and welfare, and data were collected through participant observation in the local fish processing industry, and through interviews with one adult from every household (Midré and Solberg 1979). On one of the first evenings of my stay, while I observed the fishermen at work on the quay, I noticed something that made me curious: three or four boys, the youngest not more than nine or ten years of age, seemed to take part in the work.

Moving closer to them, I could see what they were engaged in. As the fishermen were cleaning the fish and cutting off the heads, the boys picked them up, threaded them on a stick and cut off the heads so that only the tongues were left. The boys would later, I was told, offer their products for sale to the local households. I learned that fried cod-tongues were considered a delicacy. For some time I kept the tongue-cutters on the fringes of my research interest, as a peculiarity, and continued to concentrate on what I perceived as the real work life, the work in which the adults took part. Gradually tongue-cutting became, however, my main research interest, and its study became the first step in a research interest in which I was to be engaged the next twenty years.

To me the cutting of cod tongues was an exotic phenomenon. I was brought up in the suburbs of Oslo, and, except on a few rare occasions, paid work was not a part of everyday life experiences of either myself or my peers. Neither did my sociological education connect work and childhood. What I had read about work in western industrialised societies, had no connection with children's lives. In the few studies made of children, no reference was made to work. My observations of children at work elicited associations to the olden days and distant skies – to me the familiar 'locations' of such phenomena. To the local people there was, however, nothing exotic about cutting cod-tongues. This and other kinds of work activities were, I learned later, part of children's everyday life. Some were introduced to fishing work even before they began to attend school. By the age of ten most children were experienced workers.

Even if work was taken as a matter of course in children's life by the local people, no one seemed indifferent to it. Rather, most people held a very positive view of work children. When I showed my interest in the matter, I got stories about children who had entered work life at an early age and earned large amounts of money. Endurance and industry were emphazised as important virtues, and early signs of these qualities were highly appreciated. The cutting of cod-tongues was mentioned with particular enthusiasm. Parents of eager tongue-cutters showed great pride in their offspring. The cutters themselves obviously enjoyed talking about their work.

My First Concern: Child Work As Meaningful Participation

From the very beginning I evaluated the cutting of cod tongues positively. In my first publication about the project, written while I was still doing fieldwork, I made this positive evaluation of children's work explicit (Solberg 1976). In the introduction to this paper, I emphasized that the phenomenon I was exploring had no connection with exploitation and social problems. On the contrary, I said that the proper term for these activities was 'meaningful participation'.

To convince my readers, I pictured child workers from the early industrialisation period as the opposite of the contemporary tongue-cutters. Against the depiction of pale and unhealthy miners, deprived of play and schooling, I presented a picture of the strong and healthy tongue-cutters, engaged in easy work, getting plenty of fresh air and enjoying what they were doing. I further emphasized that even if all tongue-cutters worked to get paid, none of them did so because of necessity. Rather, in many ways the tongue-cutters formed an economic elite among the children.[2]

The local children turned out to be involved in other kinds of fishing work as well. Quite a few reported that they were involved in work at the quay during the summer, mostly in cleaning (Norw.'bløgging') coal fish. However, according to the children themselves, the most central work activity next to tongue-cutting was peeling prawns. This work took place at the local fish processing industry, in a room that was specially equipped for this business with tables, chairs and a weighing machine. Peeling was done by hand and the workers were paid according to the weight of the ready peeled prawns.

Unlike the cutting of cod tongues, shelling of prawns was not done by minors only. Housewives formed the greater part of this work force, and schoolchildren helped them. Sometimes the children filled the entire prawn-peeling room by themselves. The work was less formally organized here than in the work making up the main part of the fish processing industry: the cutting of filets for freezing. Prawns were delivered only occasionally, and in rather small quantities. On these occasions people who had time to spare, and wanted to earn some money, would simply turn up at the fish processing industry. Housewives would ordinarily do so in the morning, while children of school age would join them after having finished their schoolwork.

Later I included a second fishing community in my study, and here I learned about another work activity – baiting long-line – in which local people from early school age to the age of retirement, formed the labour force. This work consisted of putting pieces of bait (mackerel or squid) on the hooks of a fishing tackle called a 'long-line'. Like peeling prawns, the baiting work took place in rooms specially equipped for this activity, it was done by hand and paid according to the amount of work completed by each worker. The work organisation was similarly informal; those who wanted to bait turned up at the baiting place and took part for a longer or shorter period.

A cod-tounge-cutter in action. (Samfoto, Oslo)

Observing these groups of young workers, and talking to local inhabitants, influenced my positive evaluation of the children's work. Besides, I attached a strong positive meaning to the position these children seemed to occupy in the communities. My observations differed distinctly from the prevailing sociological accounts of children's societal position at that time (f.i. Liljestrøm 1979). While contemporary childhood was generally characterized by segregation from adulthood, and particularly by no participation in work, being a child on the coast of Northern Norway seemed to imply integration into the central aspects of community life. Besides getting an informal education for future work in the fisheries, these work children possessed, in my evaluation, a particular welfare dimension in their lives that children in contemporary society lacked. They were allowed entry into activities with a high degree of significance.

My concern about child work as meaningful participation was particularly enforced by two Norwegian educators' contribution to the contemporary debate about children's position as non-participators (Linge & Wille 1981). By taking the daycare setting as their point of departure, they suggested that to compensate for the lack of 'real' participation in children's everyday life, the educational programme should be reorganized to include children in the running of the daycare centres. Their educational recommendations contained two main principles. On one hand, the staff should offer children 'real' and useful tasks, like setting the table, picking up the phone and bringing out the household refuse. Inventing tasks to make the children feel they shared in the running of the daycare household, would not, according to the educators, have the same positive implications for children's upbringing and quality of life. On the other hand, the educational programme contained a warning about not giving the children too much responsibility. The tasks should be properly adjusted to the children's level of development.

Relating my analysis of children's work to this educational programme, I found that the first recommendation was definitely fulfilled. Participation in the fishing industry was certainly not invented to make the children feel useful. Rather, the activities went on as part of the broader local business of which the significance was obvious to everyone. The tongue-cutters and prawn-peelers, in the first community, all contributed to the local production of food to be consumed within or outside of the local community. However, while these children were useful, the young baiters in the second community played an even more significant role in the local work life. On my first visit here I was told that if the children did not take part, the long-line fishing could not be carried out the way it was.

Baiting was obviously 'real' participation. But, it was work that was properly adjusted to a child's level of development, when, for example, a boy of ten years of age was pushed to bait one or possibly two tubs every afternoon? I found this question difficult to answer, and gradually lost interest in trying to do so. The decisions as to how often to sail out fishing were made by the fishermen based on weather conditions and catch prospects. Their choices were decisive for the work demand put on the baiters – adults as well as children. At a certain time a specific number of long-lines were to be finished. Within these frames, it was a matter of course to make no particular exceptions because of young age. This absence of age-graded considerations strengthened the picture of children as integrated. I could hardly consider the fact that from time to time children did not appreciate this integration, and preferred to do something else, as an indicator of maladjustment.

However, it seemed unproductive to address a kind of universal standard of proper involvement according to age, which was implied by a developmental perspective, when what was considered 'proper' obviously differed. Clearly, my own surprise when I discovered children involved in fishing work illustrated this point. When I arrived at the fishing community, work of this kind did not belong to childhood. Little by little, however, I realized that my way of perceiving the agents and activities surrounding me was about to change.

The material conditions for children's work participation were obvious in the fishing communities in Northern Norway. Simple tasks to be done by hand were available, and the work hours were flexible. Simultaneously, letting the children perform these work activities obviously presupposed that these tasks were considered appropriate for children. In reaching this 'circle' it seemed highly significant to understand why work occupied such a central position in the lives of children. Further, it seemed obvious to me that concepts of childhood and what was considered 'proper' activities in children's lives could hardly be grasped directly. Exploring particularly the local children's work life, its material conditions and its concrete shapes, seemed a fruitful point of entry to the more abstract question of the construction of childhood. Besides, the acquisition of this knowledge seemed important and interesting in its own right.

My Next Concern: Child Work As Work

During my fieldwork among cod tongue-cutters and prawn-peelers, their peripheral position became obvious to me. Even if the children made useful contributions to the production of goods, nevertheless, this work did make up but small 'niches' on the fringes of the local economy. By including a second fishing community, in which children seemed to form a more central part of the local work life, I could pursue my interest in child work as work. This second community shared central characteristics with the first one. Both were islands off the coast of Northern Norway, and the size of the population was the same – about 50 households. The particular part of the population in which I was most interested, those between the age of ten and thirteen, numbered up to 20 in both localities. Most of the families earned their living from the fisheries, as fishermen or workers at the local fishing industries. At both locations most of the fishermen fished 'from home' and took their catches to the local fish processing industry.

However, one element, which was easily recognized, differed between the two localities; while the fishermen in the first community used nets, the other group fished with long-lines. This difference in fishing technology seemed quite decisive for the children's position on the local labour market. Many people were needed to prepare the long-line for fishing, and children of school age formed a significant part of the work force. In comparison, nets required no similar work effort to be prepared for use, and the fishermen did not, even in any other ways, depend on schoolchildren to keep their fishing going. While there was an extensive supply of work for children in the 'long-line community', in the 'net community' there was shortage of work. Only a minority of the child population was offered as much work as they wanted. They were all boys.

To me this 'experiment like' reserch setup allowed me to compare two similar communities in which different fishing tools were in use, and formed a fruitful point of departure for exploring relations between technology, work organisation and the position of children. Gradually, however, I realized there was no simple connection between the work tool in use and the children's involvement. It was necessary to include other matters to understand how children's work life was shaped. In both communities I recognized a general 'open-mindedness' towards involving children in work connected with the fisheries. But how did 'the cultural' and 'the material' aspects combine into what I observed as very different work positions for children?

Line-Fishing and the Children's Position
One obvious way of explaining why children enter work roles in the line-fishing community, is that 'all hands are needed'. One might argue that if the adult population is already heavily involved in work, and there are important remaining tasks to be done, children, who are close at hand, will be included, if the general attitude to do so is positive. However, a closer look at the work organisation of baiting shows that this argumentation is too simple, it seems to imply a concept of the youngest workers as a 'reserve', or, at best, equal to other categories of workers. In my view children occupied a much more central position. They were not only included because many hands were needed, and their hands were as usable as those of others, they were actually preferred as a work force because their special qualities 'fitted' the tasks to be done so well. The children and the adults work in line with them had hands that were particularly suited for the special task of baiting long-lines.

Flexibility was the most important quality of the work force involved in baiting. To be fresh, the bait should be cut and attached to the line just before the shooting of the line.[3] Therefore, the baiters must be ready to start their work as soon as possible once the decision to go out is taken by the fishermen, and they must keep work until a sufficient number of long-lines are completed. During the periods when the fishermen simply waited for weather and stream conditions to improve, the baiters should have alternative activities to attend to. The fishermen's closest family members – their wives, parents and children – all possessed this flexible quality.

Family members were also in demand because of their feelings of commitment to the fishermen. They were expected to 'stretch' and to be pushed further than non-relatives or distant relatives in adjusting themselves to the demands of the fisheries. This adaptation was not only in one direction, however. Work was organized to 'fit' the number of workers available. This was done physically by giving the shortest of the workers small crates to stand upon to get the right height for baiting. The work hours were flexible – just as the amount of work to be done. The baiters were free to take breaks while work, and there was food available at the work place to be consumed at the wish of the workers. This particular 'coupling' between people and jobs made the baiting of long-lines appear as a segment in the local labour market.[4]

No training was needed before their participation, since this was acquired while work. The local children were all introduced to the work gradually, most of them by being brought by their mothers to be looked after, and little by little by watching and given some assistance. Sons and daughters of fishermen formed, from about the age of eight or nine, a significant part of the labour force of baiters. However, the number of baited long-lines made by a 10-year-old could not be 'deduced' from his or her kinship position. Even if close relations to long-line fishermen increased a child's possibility of getting an informal education in baiting, and would later imply strong expectations to take part in the work, the child's actual work contribution was a matter to be negotiated.[5]

Net-Fishing and the Children's Position
Just like in baiting work, both prawn peeling and cod tongue-cutting were closely connected with fishing. To provide a high quality product, peeling is to be completed as soon as possible after the prawns are delivered by the trawlers. Since the work is done by hand and is time consuming, many hands are required. Like in baiting, flexibility was a central asset of the work force involved in prawn-peeling. Housewives and schoolchildren, with time to spare but not ready for full employment, made up the group of workers. Also, just like in baiting, the housewives formed the morning team workers, while the children joined them in the afternoon when school was over.

Their introduction to this work happened in a similar way. Children would accompany their mothers or grandmothers, and they would weigh in their first prawns with the 'senior' peelers and get some amount from them. When they could make at least one kilo during the afternoon, they would get their own prawns weighed – and get their salary directly from the supervisor. At this level of experience, as were my informants aged 10-12 years, they would prefer to be in the company of shellers of their own age.

However, while the similarities in work organisation of baiting and peeling were obvious, work seemed to hold a different meaning in the lives of the two groups of children. First, this was, as previously pointed out, connected to the supply of work. The demand for a labour force was rather moderate in peeling. The economical output was therefore moderate. This production was, second, peripheral in the local economy. And third: peeling of prawns was considered women's work. While children in the line-fishing community of both sexes worked as baiters, boys and girls in the net-fishing community did different kinds of work: Girls peeled prawns and boys cut cod tongues. This division of labour between the two genders was to a large extent accepted as a matter of course by the children and, by that, maintained by them.

I noticed a distinct difference in the way they talked about their work. The girls emphasized the value of having 'something to do' and stressed the importance of the social relations of work. On the other hand, the boys, in particular the big cutters among them, talked about their work with enthusiasm. They showed great pride in their own work capacity and endurance, and pointed to the high financial outcome as 'proof' of their virtues.

The big tongue-cutters never considered shelling prawns. They would rather be out of work, they told me, than they would take a seat among women and girls in the prawn-shelling room at the local fish processing industry. One tiny 11-year-old explained this reluctance with reference to the male anatomy, "Our hands are too big for shelling prawns." The girls did not reject tongue-cutting with the same force. Some of them questioned the boys' monopoly in tongue-cutting, and a couple of girls had made attempts to gain access. They wanted to have a share in the economic output from cutting, which was much better than that obtained from peeling. These attempts, which will be discussed later, were not successful. Looking at the work conditions of the tongue-cutters may give some background for understanding this.

The tongue-cutters depended on the fishermen. Large quantities of fish brought ashore meant many cod heads from which to cut tongues, and no deliveries meant no supply of raw material. The choice of net was a prerequisite for cutting tongues. With this method of catching, contrary to the line-fishing, the head was not damaged. The quay, on which the boys where cutting tongues, was also the place where the fish was delivered, cleaned and weighed by the fishermen. Thus, the possibilities for territorial conflicts were present. And since fish delivery was a central part of the local work system, and tongue-cutters operated on its periphery, they were careful not to get in the fishermen's way.[6] Those who had already gained entrance enforced the restriction of cutters. More cutters in action meant competition for the supplies of cod heads. While the young baiters and peelers ordinarily welcomed co-workers and in particular peers, the cutters who were 'in' expressed no interest in being social.

Tongue-cutters were introduced to the work differently than baiters and peelers. While the others were accompanied to work by mothers or grandmothers, and little by little became involved in the production, the cutters had to fetch their own work equipment, and find themselves a position at the quay. Besides, these children could not collect their salary from an employer. The tongues had to be sold, before any earnings were gained. Those who found good marketing possibilities for their products would also be eager cutters. Nobody wanted to make efforts to cut for their own family's freezer only. Cutters of cod tongues could be seen as self-employed; the single cutter had to manage on his own to a far greater extent than the two other categories of workers, which have been discussed.

Yet, the cutters did not operate independently of the other agents on the quay, and what particularly separated the big cutters from the modest ones was just their social connections. The big cutters were all sons of central men in the fish processing industry and masters of the fishing boats. This kinship relationship was of central significance both to get access to the raw material and to get marketing possibilities. Two brothers were far ahead of the other cutters in this respect. Their father, the owner of one of the local fishing industries, arranged the tongue sale by taking them to a fish shop on his regular business trips to the nearby town. Relieved of the time-consuming burden of selling the tongues, they concentrated all their energy on cutting.

Clearly, girls would have to enter a 'male' world to take up tongue-cutting. The cutter recruits had to compete, often fiercely, for their place of work, and to push themselves in to conduct the work activity. The work did not permit socializing, neither while cutting nor selling. Besides, the territory in which the cutting took place was dominated by men. The quay was mainly a place for male encounters. Females passed through only on their way to and from the local ferry.

Two girls, both sisters of big cutters, explained the varieties of obstacles an outsider to this world was confronted with, when they told me their experiences in their attempts to cut. In the first place they did not possess the necessary work equipment; a knife and a 'pik'[7] – and they did not know how to obtain these tools. Boys just 'had' knives, while they did not. 'Piks' are specially made, and the girls did not know how. One of them had once asked her father to help her, but he was busy. Turning to her teacher in woodwork did not bring any results either. Still eager to cut, the girls managed to borrow the tools from their

Boy cutting cod tounges. (Samfoto, Oslo)

brothers a couple of times. Approaching the pile of cod heads at the quay, they faced an additional obstacle: comments and teasing about their business from the people already work on the quay, the boys and the men. Besides all this, they disliked the sight and smell of blood and fish entrails. After cutting a few tongues, they agreed to withdraw. In their view, all these efforts were not worth the money.

In the net-fishing community, children's work was organized in a way that confirmed and strengthened traditional adult gender roles. Recognising that this gender-based division of labour among children as similar to that of the adults, it might be argued that the work pattern is automatically transferred from one generation to the next. My point of departure has, however, been another. I have emphasized how some elements of technology and work organisation were decisive in the different work position of boys and girls. This line of arguing opens the possibility that under certain conditions a traditional work pattern is strengthened, while under other circumstances it weakens the traditional pattern. More fish deliveries, and a different organisation of work at the quay might open room for more tongue-cutters, and possibly also female ones. Extending the prawn-peeling season and increasing the economic output might attract more boys.

However, even if I put a strong emphasis on material conditions, this does not imply that I see children's work pattern as solely decided by these conditions. The children act within these frames and question, to some extent, the gender based division of labour. For example, a couple of the boys who did not succeed in getting access to cutting tried actively to change the dominant way of perceiving peeling as the work of women and girls. They did so by rejecting the tongue-cutters insistence that this work was not 'fit' for male workers, and turned up at the work place and shared in the work. By that they took part in a verbal and nonverbal exchange or negotiation about what is girls and boys' work. In a similar way, the girls took part in exchanges about the boys' monopoly in tongue-cutting. To understand why the girls seem less motivated than the boys to gain access, it should be noted that their aim might be to gain different kinds of rewards. While the boys strongly emphazise the economic rewards from their work effort, the girls underline the social rewards. This different orientation is further strengthened through their work experience, so that boys become increasingly occupied with money – and the girls become increasingly involved with each other (Solberg 1982).

Does Child Work Belong to the Past Only?
My early accounts of children's work in the fishing communities were received with enthusiasm by my social science colleagues doing child research. They were delighted, as I had been myself, to be informed about a childhood with

strong elements of exotic activities. Even if they were unacquainted with the content of what I told them – about the cutting of cod-tongues, peeling of prawns and baiting of long-lines – they seemed to recognize an underlying theme in what I said, which merged into the basic sociological story of the major transition in children's societal position – from integration to segregation. Within this frame the strange childhood appeared familiar through a resemblance with the picture of children's position in previous times.

This frame of interpretation, gradually made explicit to me by my listeners' confirmation, disquieted me. My feelings were partly linked to the actual situation – the fact that my accounts seemed of little concern to contemporary childhood. Since this child work was located in a society conceived as 'in the past', the notion of a 'present-day' society, with no ties between work and childhood, remained unaltered by my analysis. Simultaneously, I felt my analysis contributed to a reinforcement of the contemporary childhood concept in which work was unfamiliar. When I pictured the participating child, the negation of this child – the nonparticipating child – almost drew itself.

It was my small-scale analysis that set me on the track of questioning the past-present interpretive frame of children's position. Exploring the work tasks in which children were involved, revealed that there was no simple and direct connection between the level of technology and the integration of children. The technology certainly was simple in these forms of production, and technical inventions, like peeling and baiting machines, would make most of the hands superfluous. However, the fact that such innovations were not used, should not be seen as 'old-fashioned'. That the line-fishermen and the management of the fish processing industry did not use the available technology to 'modernise' the work organisation, for example by speeding up the production and 'normalizing' work hours, should not be seen as a 'throwback' from the past, but instead as a strategic adjustment to – and utilisation of – the available resources.

With prawn peeling, the fish processing industry chose to produce manually peeled prawns as a high-quality product, which was in demand by a small category of consumers. Their access to a flexible workforce in great numbers, which did not demand a high financial output, was an important element in this choice to exploit this 'niche' in the market. Similarly, the availability of baiters was an important element in the line-fishermen's choice to have their lines baited by hand – and in their reluctance to use a baiting machine that was available in the market, which in the fishermen's opinion did not compare in quality to the baiting done by hand. The local fishermen also emphasized the superior quality of fresh bait compared to frozen bait, which was used in the neighbouring fishing community. From this perspective, choosing to fish with frozen bait, was a necessity when access to a flexible workforce was limited. Consequently, 'modern' work conditions, which imply full-time employment within 'ordinary' work hours, was a way of organizing work to compensate for the lack of a flexible work force. Thus, a large and industrious family was seen as an important asset in choosing the optimal adaptation.[8]

The point that there is no simple and direct connection between the level of technology and children's position in the local labour market is also illustrated by the fact that technological innovation in fishing in some ways has expanded the work available for the childhood population. Larger boats and improved fishing tools have resulted in larger catches being brought ashore than in previous times. An increased capacity in the fish processing industries, due to cold storage facilities, has also enabled larger catches to be delivered. In the late seventies, during my fieldwork, the line-fishermen used more lines and the net-fishermen brought more cod ashore than ever before.[9] Accordingly, the demand for a workforce in baiting and tongue-cutting was greater than before. In the tongue-cutting business, 'modern' elements in its work organisation were particularly distinct for two brothers who went into partnership with their father – and thus extended their marketing territory beyond the local community.

By discovering children, mingled with adults, dealing with fish and fish products, I became aware of how sociology treated children. This was, I noticed, largely a matter of neglect. Apart from the substantive areas of sociological enquiry, such as gender roles, education and family life, children were almost totally absent from sociological texts (Ambert 1986). In particular, this was the case with mainstream sociology and its 'classics'. Within the strong sociological interest in work, there hardly seemed any place left for children. 'Work' and 'adulthood' seemed defined by each other. Correspondingly, 'childhood' seemed defined by 'play' and 'socialization'. Those who studied the old times and distant peoples seemed the only scholars connecting 'work' and 'childhood'.

The discovery of children work in the fishing community also made me reflect on the ambivalence within social science towards children's participation in activities seen as belonging to adulthood. Based on a common understanding in contemporary society, in which 'work' and 'childhood' are separated, the interpretation of this separation is partly positive (children are liberated from the burden of work that weighed down the children of the past), and partly negative (children suffer from being segregated from 'real' participation). Observing children doing work, which held some modern traits, aroused my sociological interest in the work itself, and, through this, in the concept of children and childhood in contemporary society.

A Bridge From the Exotic to the Ordinary

As I finished my analysis of children's fishing work and moved with my family from Northern Norway to a suburb of Oslo, where I had no expectations of finding work children, I was very soon surprised to discover that they did. The first work child I noticed rang on my doorbell to sell flowers. It was a boy of about 11 or 12 years old, and he reminded me of the boys in the fishing communities selling cod tongues. His height was about the same as theirs, and he was similar to them also in his way of approaching me. Enthusiastically, this flower seller convinced me – like the tongue-cutters had previously done – that his article was just what I needed that day.

Accepting his offer, I took the opportunity to ask some questions about his work, and from what he told me, the business in which he was engaged seemed to share some important resemblances with the tongue-cutting business. Just like the tongue-cutters, the flower-sellers were closely connected to a broader chain of work, mostly involving adults. Neither were regularly employed, but worked by some sort of arrangement with adults. How these adults arranged their work was decisive for the children's work. "If you want to sell flowers, you have to be around when the flower car arrives," they told me. "If the man in the car recognizes your face, or you come with someone else he knows, you will be allowed to sell."

The flower car returned to the same residential area for as long as the marketing possibilities were good. With poor results, a new sales area was picked out, and other children got the chance to work. I was informed that the block of flats, in which I lived myself, was suitable for sales work. The potential costumers were all gathered in a small area.

I Notice Producers Where I Previously Did Not Recognize Any

After becoming acquainted with the flower-selling business, I recognized many young sellers at my door, offering a variety of products, like 'snow balls', magazines and lottery tickets. In my neighbourhood I ran across other categories of workers as well, most of them of the same age as the flower sellers. I noticed children putting advertising leaflets in the letter boxes, and assisting somewhat older newspaper boys and girls in bringing out papers. In the local vegetable shop I noticed from time to time a rather young helper, putting the goods on the scales, receiving the money and giving the change, and I caught sight of some young self-employed collecting empty bottles.

Why had I not noticed all these workers surrounding me before? These activities were certainly not, as tongue-cutting and baiting, totally unknown to me. However, my stay in the fishing communities seemed to have focused my eyes to observe children rather differently than I had done before. While studying children's work in Northern-Norway, I felt it was necessary to pay close attention to the process of production, simply to learn what was going on. This focus on 'doing' implied a certain ignorance of the 'doer'. Looking in the same way, at the well-known activities in the suburb of Oslo, made them appear more 'work-like' than previously.

On one of my first visits to the local vegetable shop, this shift became explicit to me. Entering, I recognized a girl, of about 10 years of age, 'assisting' the shopkeeper. She was allowed to weigh the goods and also to receive payment and to give back change. It was obvious to me that she enjoyed what she was doing – looking seriously engaged in making the calculations correctly. From time to time her supervisor nodded to her, discretely but undoubtedly with appreciation. I had great pleasure observing them. The shopkeeper showed an admirable patience in guiding without interfering, and it seemed to be a very good experience to be allowed to pretend to be a shop assistant in this realistic manner. To praise both of them, I remarked with a smile to the shopkeeper that she was lucky to have such a clever helper.

After leaving, I realized that my attention on the child had prevented me from fully recognizing the products of her activities. Whether she enjoyed attending to the costumers or not, or whatever the reasons that the shopkeeper let her, the girl had still weighed the vegetables and given the costumers the change. She had assisted the shopkeeper. I felt no need to use quotation marks around the notion of work.

Broadening the Work Concept

Embedded in my discovery of the variety of productive activities performed by children was a broadening of my own concept of work. In the fishing community children's status as workers was obvious to me through the signs of equality they shared with the adult workers. The term 'work' was here similar to the economists' work concept (Wadel 1979; 1984). While recognizing door sale as work, my work concept was still narrow. Children were the last link in a chain of adult workers – employed as some sort of assistants to the adults. Even if these activities took place on fringes of what we speak of as 'the labour market', the connections with ordinary paid work were obvious.

In characterizing the selling of lottery tickets as 'work', I took a significant step, however, in expanding the work concept. Selling tickets covered a variety of contracts; both voluntary work contracts of some sort with charitable organisations, very similar to that of the flower sellers, and sales work as part of their obligations connected to their membership in leisure-time activities, like school brass bands or local sports clubs. My choice to label both categories as 'work' was partly connected with the fact that both activities involved money. The children's way of using the work contract also blurred the seemingly significant division between 'voluntary' and 'obligatory' sales activities. Some of those who *had* to sell welcomed this duty as an opportunity to make some money, and appreciated the chance to sell more than their share, if they were given one.

However, my main reason for including such duties as 'work' was the recognition that these tasks contributed to the running of the institutions imposing the activities. I realized that until now I had reserved this frame of interpretation to adults' involvement in their children's leisure time activities. I recalled my mother's complaints about having to produce lottery prizes for my school marching band during my own childhood. Colleagues and neighbours often emphasized their own efforts in connection with their children's participation in leisure-time activities. While some of these informants openly complained, others underlined the rewards to be gained from taking part. None the less, they all maintained and strengthened the picture of themselves as the producers.

I had seen the children's obligations in a different light. I had no difficulties recalling my own worries about selling lottery tickets. However, these memories circled solely around my feelings about duties. In the same way I had paid attention, mainly, to the likes and dislikes of the young sellers coming to my own front door. Now shifting my attention to the activity itself, their contribution to the financial support of their organisation became explicit to me.

In Northern Norway one could not avoid noticing work children, and people were highly conscious about the young ones' productive role. In Oslo, by contrast, children's work was more difficult to glimpse, and people hardly seemed to pay any attention to the productive outcome of the work activities of young people. Moreover, work, even if taken broadly, seemed to form but a minor part in most of my neighbouring children's daily lives. Simultaneously, I had experienced how children's work life expanded during my observations, and that the extent of this phenomenon evidently was closely connected to the way one looked at it. Were there still work tasks hidden to me? Could I have overlooked any work activities in which most children took part, and did so regularly? When posing this question specifically, the answer nearly followed by itself. There was definitely one institution in which practically all children were members, and they probably made some contributions to run it – their own family household!

Investigating Children's Work Life
By including the daily and ordinary activities of running the household, the children's work life expanded greatly, and I started reflecting on the possibility of turning this phenomenon into the object of a more systematic investigation.

This time I wanted to produce statistics, to get an empirical base from which I could draw conclusions about the Norwegian children's work life in general, on the labour market and outside, covering paid as well as unpaid activities.[10] A few studies supported my own previous findings that children's work outside the home was extensive in parts of the country with strong elements of primary industry (Frønes and Tiller 1976, Haukeland 1979, Siverts 1976). A central question in the statistical study was to find out if this kind of work mainly was confined to such areas.

The results showed that it was not. Although children living in municipalities in which agriculture or fishing formed part of the local economic basis reported a wider range of work activities than the others, children in other parts possessed work experience outside home as well. For example, children in all parts of Norway turned out to make contributions within their own neighbourhood. Running errands was the task category that was most frequently reported. Housework in other peoples' homes, childminding and outdoor work, like gardening and snow shovelling, formed part of the work life also of the 11-12 years old. From our statistics we could also read about the sort of work activities I had previously 'discovered' in my own neighbourhood. A significant part of the childhood population reported having been involved in door-to-door selling of lottery tickets and other items.

Our questionnaire also included a few questions about the children's contact with their parents' place of work. The results showed that farming and fishing were among the occupations where a large part of the children often visit the work place and frequently participate. However, in several 'modern' occupations – such as shopkeeping, cleaning work, care work, carpeting and transportation – did children turn out to be involved in this way as well.[11]

Workplaces where children mostly pay 'social visits' covered a wide range of occupations. Those with fathers in technical, medical, pedagogical or juridical work, clerical work and work in public administrations, and mothers in nursing and other care work, pedagogical work (teachers in particular), and in transport and communication – all showed this pattern. As previously mentioned, I had some problems persuading the social science audience to be receptive to the analysis of children's fishing work as a story of contemporary childhood. Their resistance to do so made me recognize the powerful influence of the basic sociological theme of the major transition in children's societal position – from their being integrated to being segregated from work life. Social scientists may be particularly difficult to convince to broaden their perspective, since their own experiences are in line with the dominant assumptions.

Studying Children's Housework as Work

As the results of the statistical analysis indicated, in several ways work outside the home was part of the daily lives of Norwegian children, and by that answered the question whether children's work was mainly confined to primary industrial areas with a 'no'- I became increasingly occupied with the work position of children at home. This interest was based, firstly, on the fact that these work activities related to the running of their own household – and housework in particular stood out as the most common and ordinary part of children's work life. Children in all parts of the country were familiar with most of the housework tasks specified in the questionnaire, and most of them turned out to take part regularly as well as frequently. On this background, I was struck by the lack of research-based knowledge – compared to the extensive documentation of these activities when performed by adults. A few available studies indicated that children's contribution to the daily running of the household was worth counting (Haukeland 1979,White and Brinkerhoff 1981, Walker and Woods 1976). The results were, however, ambiguous.

Secondly, my interest in housework related to my own reluctance to recognize housework as production, when it was performed by children. As accounted for above, my discovery of children's work life came about step by step, and at a late stage in this process I broadened the work concept to include housework – after I had taken the previous steps through cod tongue-cutting and selling of flowers. On reflection, I find this late 'discovery' worth noticing, because at the time I would not have hesitated, to categorize housework activities as work when performed by adults. Neither was I unacquainted with statistics, which showed that this work took up a significant part of (adult) peoples' everyday life.[12] Yet this knowledge was not sufficient to make me notice children as houseworkers. I shared the dominant view that those who mattered, regarding division of labour at home, were the adults. In this perspective,children appeared – if they were present at all – mainly as work objects or elements, which influenced how housework was conducted (Oakley 1974). Even if some ways of referring to children granted them a more active role, for example in the saying that young people 'help' at home, carry out their 'chores' or do their 'duties', the connotations of these terms guided my attention more to the qualities of the performer than to the results of the performance.

However, my decision to approach children's housework in the same way as I had approached their cutting of cod tongues in Northern Norway, and selling of flowers in the suburb of Oslo, proved difficult to maintain. Colleagues with an interest in my work enforced a feeling that in some ways it was 'inappropriate' or too 'narrow' – when studying children – to focus on the *doing* alone. They encouraged a greater attention to questions concerned with the meaning of taking part in such activities for *being* a child.[13]

At the beginning a sense of 'fairness' kept me back from broadening the perspective. Why should a measuring of the extent of children's housework be seen as too restricted, when this was not so with adults? Gradually, however, I recognized in my own approach a *technique* for ignoring differences in age and generation, which was helpful in setting my own prior assumptions about children and childhood aside. I shall close this article by giving some examples of how this technique presented a different view of the domestic division of labour.

All together, our findings made children visible as houseworkers. The young members of the family emerged as producers of goods and services because of their frequent participation and extensive use of time. This was even more distinct when we related our informants' housework to a similar production performed by adults, as recorded by the Central Bureau of Statistics. Placing together the proportion of children and adults, who had carried out various housework activities on a particular day, produced a picture of the two generations as occupying a surprisingly equal position (table 1).

Table 1: Housework at home. The percentage of children and adults doing housework in the course of a day

	Children	*Adults*
Preparing food	71	63
Washing-up	38	52
Cleaning	49	51

Source: Central Bureau of Statistics 1983, Time Budget Survey 1980-81 and Solberg and Vestby 1987.

The differences between the two generations increased when figures of time use were placed together (not shown). According to these results, adults invested more than twice as much time in making food and washing dishes than children. In cleaning work (which includes the time-consuming tidying up) the difference was smaller.[14]

Since it is a well-documented empirical fact that housework is not shared equally among the family members, I wanted to explore the work position of boys and girls, men and women to see if the traditional division of labour between men and women also applied for children. Initially this was exactly what struck me (cf. table 2).

Table 2: Housework at home. The percentage of women, men, girls and boys doing housework in the course of a day

	Women	Girls	Boys	Men
Preparing food	90	75	66	43
Washing up	78	45	30	30
Cleaning	82	53	46	27

Source: Central Bureau of Statistics 1983, Time Budget Survey 1980-81 and Solberg and Vestby 1987.

However, placing together the male and female parts of the two generations in the same tables, made me notice something other than the well-known differences between the genders. Framed by the distinctive differences between men and women, the gender distinctions among children 'shrank'. The figures point to the four categories of family members as forming a hierarchy with women at the top and men and children at the bottom. The women are pictured here as we are getting used to see them, as the main producers of goods and services at home. However, the men's position does not comply with the familiar picture of them – as their wives sole collaborators. They have joined a group of assistants in which they are not the only participants.

My analysis of children's housework started mainly with the purpose of filling gaps of knowledge. The results that indicated that children, and in particular the girls, might surpass the men, attracted my interest. Some results in the further analysis also supported this line of argument. It turned out to be a positive association – although weak – between mothers' occupational status, their time-use on work at home and the children's use of time for domestic work, as well as between family size and children's time-use (not shown). I found this tendency for children to adjust their work contribution to the amount of work needed to be done in the families worth noticing, even if it was not a strong one, since a similar adjustment was not found among men.

However, step by step my gap filling project broadened to include a project of suggesting alternative ways to look at children. To some extent my interest in exploring perspectives increased at the expense of the gap-filling project. This change had something to do with the way my message was received. My suggestion that girls *might* do more than their fathers, was taken quite literally, and much attention was directed to the position of men in the household. By that my argument that children belong to the domestic division of labour was absorbed into the well-known argument that men do not take their fair share of work at home. This put me on the track of recognizing that it would not be sufficient to persuade the social science community to include children among family members sharing the daily running of the household, but also to bring forward the argument that conventional ways of looking at the domestic division of labour need to be revised. My suggestion for one possible revision was to look at family members of both generations in the same way, as home workers.

Notes

1. This article draws heavily on the first part of my doctoral dissertation (Solberg 1994).
2. The point that work children may form a well-to-do part of the childhood population is supported by others, see for example Morrow 1992.
3. To shoot a line = to set the line in the sea.
4. The baiting sector can be said to function as a particular market (segment) for housewives, retired people, schoolchildren and people 'accidentally' passing by. Within such a part-market, as Kalleberg (1980) has shown for the cleaning trade, work conditions cannot be changed without undermining the pattern of recruitment.
5. The point that children take part in 'deciding' the outcome of concrete work processes as well as the broader and more abstract matter of what childhood is and should be, is further discussed elsewhere (Solberg 1990; 1994; 1996).
6. There seemed to be an established rule that no more than two cutters should be operating by each cleaning basin at a time. To compare, in baiting there were few restrictions as to the number of workers. These tasks were performed in territories used exclusively for this production, and they were equipped to give access to a large number of people.
7. A 'pik' (Norwegian) i.e. a metal bar with a head at the end on which the cod heads are 'treaded on' and then cut off, so only the tongues remain.
8. Two unmarried brothers, lacking the work support of wife and children, fished less intensively than the others; less frequently and with a smaller number of line-tubs. They also took part in the baiting themselves to assist the baiters who didn't have commitments to others and would turn up in their baiting-place. Another fisherman whose wife was 'not much of a baiter' chose for a period of time to fish from the neighbouring community, where frozen lines could be bought; an arrangement which implied a considerable travelling time, and increase in his own work hours.
9. After my fieldwork was completed, new restrictions in fishing quotas have significantly reduced the local work possibilities for people of all ages.
10. We turned to 800 11-12 years old for information with a questionnaire covering 80 specific work tasks, connected to two main areas: at home and outside home. For more details, see Solberg and Vestby, 1987; Solberg, 1994.
11. For example 55 per cent of children with a father in a farming occupation and 40 per cent of children with fishermen fathers reported contributing once a week or more. So did 50 per cent of the children of shopkeepers, 16 per cent of children of truck or lorry drivers and 18 per cent of children of craftsmen in the building trade, like painters and paperhangers. Turning to the mothers, three occupations stood out from the others in that about 50 per cent of the children took part in the work once a week or more: farmers, daycare mothers and cleaning workers. A total of 19 per cent of those with a mother as a shop assistant shared in her work just as often.
12. Data produced by the Norwegian Central Bureau of Statistics was central in this respect. The first Time Budget Survey, reporting the total use of time of a representative sample of the Norwegian (adult) population, had been conducted for the first time in the early seventies. Researchers informed by a feminist viewpoint made extensive use of this data base to demonstrate

that unpaid work at home was comprehensive, and that this work was unequally distributed among the genders (Lingsom 1975, Wærness 1975). Thus, the notion that modern households were empty of functions was seriously questioned.
13 This argument is further elaborated in Solberg 1996.
14 Our own data did not offer the possibility for making a comparison in a strict sense, since we lacked information about the amount of domestic work carried out by the parents of the children we interviewed. The comparison between the two data-sets is crude, and it is difficult to estimate the degree of uncertainty involved, particularly in relation to time-use. To give a more thorough and valid answer to the question whether the girls were the most central collaborators of their mothers, further empirical research was obviously necessary. However, applying the results from the two studies – on the proportion of adults and children respectively who had been involved in housework during a particular day – did, however, give us a picture of the work position of the two generations, which we consider as fairly valid.

References

Frønes, I. & Tiller, P. O., (1976): *Sosial endring og oppvekstmiljø*. Oslo: Institutt for sosial forskning. (Arbeidsrapport 23).

Haukeland, J. V., (1979): *Ung i fjelldal. En undersøkelse av sosial differensiering blant yngre tenåringer i et jordbrukssamfunn*. Oslo: Institutt for sosiologi, Universitetet i Oslo. Mag.avh.

James, A. and Prout, A., (eds) (1990): *Constructing and Reconstructing Childhood: Contemporary Issues in the Sociological Study of Childhood*. London.

Kalleberg, A. (1980): "Arbeidsmarked, jobbutforming og familiebinding." In Hanisch, et al. (eds.): *Marked for arbeid. Lønnsarbeider*. Oslo.

Liljeström, (1979): *Opvækst til hvad? Samspillet mellom voksne og børn i et samfund under forandring*. København.

Linge, P. and Wille, H.P,.(1981): *Barn i arbeid, lek og læring*. Oslo: Aschehoug.

Lingsom, S., (1975): *Tid nyttet til egenarbeid*. (Time Spent on Household Work and Family Care). SA 19. Oslo: Statistisk sentralbyrå.

Midré, G. og Solberg, A., (1979): "Economic development and social change in two different communities i North Norway." *Norsk geografisk tidsskrift*, 33:39-50.

Morrow, V. (1992): *A Sociological Study of the Economic Roles of Children, with Particular Reference to Birmingham and Cambridgeshire*." Cambridge: Newnham College. (Ph. D. Dissertation).

Siverts, K., (1979) "Barnearbeid på vestlandssmåbruk." *Tidsskrift for samfunnsforskning*, 20:509-522.

Solberg, A., (1976): "Gutte- og jentearbeid" i Bratrein m.fl. (red.) : *Drivandes kvinnfolk*. Oslo.

Solberg, A., (1982): "Guttene får lønn og jentene får hverandre." In Holter (red.): *Kvinner i fellesskap*. Oslo.

Solberg, A. and Vestby, G. M., (1987): *Barns arbeidsliv*. (The work Life of Children). Oslo: NIBR (NIBR.rapport 1987:3).

Solberg, A., (1994): "Negotiating Childhood: Changing Constructions of Age for Norwegian Children". *Constructing and Reconstructing Childhood: Contemporary*

Issues in the Sociological Study of Childhood. See James, A. and Prout, A. (eds.) (1990)

Solberg, A., (1996): «The Challenge in Child Research: From 'Being' to 'Doing'». In Brannen, Julia and Magaret O'Brien, (1996): Children in Families: Research and Policy, London.

Solberg, A., (1994): *Negotiating Childhood. Empirical Investigations and Textual Representations of Children's Work and Everyday Life.*Stockholm: Nordic Institute for Studies in Urban and Regional Planning, Dissertation 12.

Thrall, C. A. (1978): "Who Does What? Role Stereotypy, Children's Work and Continuity Between Generations in the Household Division of Labour". *Human Relations*, 31:249-265.

Wadel, C., (1979): "The Hidden Work of Everyday Life." In Wallman, S. (ed.) *Social Anthropology and Work*. London.

Walker, K. & Woods, M., (1976): *Time Use: A Measure of Household Production of Family Goods and Services*. Washington DC: Center for the Family of the American Home Economics Association.

White, L. & Brinkerhoff, D., (1981): "Children's Work in the Family: Its Significance and Meaning." *Journal of Marriage and Family*, 43:489-798.

Wærness, K., (1975): *Kvinners omsorgsarbeid i den ulønnede produksjon.* Arbeidsnotat nr. 80 fra Levekårsundersøkelsen.

This collection of essays is a result of the research project "The work of Nordic children 1850-1990". The project has for a period of three and a half years, been financially supported by The Joint Committee of the Nordic Research Councils for the Humanities.

Contributors

Ning de Coninck-Smith, Ph.D., associate professor, Center of Cultural Studies, Odense University, Denmark. She is the author of a series of articles on the social and cultural history of children. She is presently writing a book on urban childhood and education at the turn of the Century.

Óløf Garðarsdottir, Research assistant, Institute of History, University of Iceland. Her interests include family and generational history, migration and children's works in Iceland. Her most recent article, written together with the late Gísli Águst Gunnlaugsson, is titled: *Transition into Widowhood: Life Course Perspective on the Household Position of Icelandic Widows at the Turn of the Century, Continuity and Change* 11(3) 1996.

Pirjo Markkola, Ph.D., assistant professor in Finnish History, University of Tampere, Department of History. Her Ph.D. thesis on the *Making of the Working-Class Home. The Question of Working-Class Families in Finland, 1870s through 1910s* was published in 1994.

Bengt Sandin, Ph.D., professor, Department of Child Studies, University of Linköping, Sweden. Bengt Sandin's scholarly interests cover social history and the history of childhood. He is currently the director of a research programme on the history of childhood during the 20th Century, entitled *The Century of the Child*.

Ellen Schrumpf, associate professor, Telemark College, Bø, Norway. Her interests include labour history and the history of children and women. She is about to finish a book on the history of industrial child labour in Norway at the end of the 19th Century (*Barnarbeid – plikt eller privilegium? Barnearbeid i to norske industrisamfund i perioden 1850 – 1910*). She is presently chairing the Norwegian Historical Association.

Mats Sjöberg, Ph. D. lecturer in history, Department of Teacher Education, University of Linköping, Sweden. His Ph.D. thesis on schooling and child labour in rural areas (*Att säkra framtidens skördar. Barndom, skola och arbete i agrar miljö. Bolstad pastorat 1860 – 1930*) was published in 1996.

Anne Solberg, Ph.D. and research manager at the Norwegian Institute for Urban and Regional Research. Her Ph.D. thesis, titled *Negotiating Childhood. Empirical Investigations and Textual Representations of Children's Work and Everyday Life* was published in 1994.